SUCCESS SECRETS
OF THE

ONLINE
MARKETING
SUPERSTARS

MITCH MEYERSON

Entrepreneur
PRESS®

Entrepreneur Press, Publisher
Cover Design: Andrew Welyczko
Production and Composition: Eliot House Productions

This publication is designed to provide accurate and authoritative information
in regard to the subject matter covered. It is sold with the understanding that
the publisher is not engaged in rendering legal, accounting or other professional
services. If legal advice or other expert assistance is required, the services of a
competent professional person should be sought.

Library of Congress Cataloging-in-Publication Data
Meyerson, Mitch.
    Success secrets of the online marketing superstars / by Mitch Meyerson.
        pages   cm
        ISBN-13: 978-1-59918-558-3 (paperback)
        ISBN-10: 1-59918-558-X (paperback)
        1. Internet marketing. 2. Internet advertising. I. Title.
    HF5415.1265.M47 2015
    658.8'72—dc23   2014039154

Printed in the United States of America

19 18 17 16   10 9 8 7 6 5 4 3 2 1

Contents

SECTION I
Strategy, Conversion, and Mindset

SECTION II
Traffic

SECTION III
Leveraging Apps

Acknowledgments

TO THE Superstars in this book for sharing their wisdom and insights into our changing digital world. Special thanks to Barb Rozgonyi for inspiring me to compile this edition of the Superstars series.

To Jillian McTigue and the team at Entrepreneur Press for supporting my work for the last decade. Karen Billipp and Charlotte Evans for their expert editing. To Craig Valentine, Laurie Ashner, Tina Cook, Michael Neuendorff, and our Certified Guerrilla Marketing and World Class Speaking Coaches. And finally to Steve Jobs—his ideas and innovations have inspired me for decades in my careers in business, writing, and music.

Introduction

IN 2005, the internet had already begun to profoundly change the world of business, yet for many online entrepreneurs the roadmap to success was unclear. In response, I complied the first edition of *Success Secrets of the Online Marketing Superstars*, a book that celebrated the ways in which the most successful marketers on the web had blazed trails, set records, and created benchmarks to make the internet overwhelmingly relevant to modern business practices and the business world.

In 2010, as social media began to explode and once again changed business as we know it, I developed a second book, *Success Secrets of the Social Media Marketing Superstars*. The wisdom of a new group of social web experts including Chris Brogan, Gary Vaynerchuk, Mari Smith, and Keith Ferrazzi illuminated this edition of the Superstars series, showing us how to navigate the emerging and changing social landscape.

Now, in 2015, the social internet has not only transformed the business world but the world at large, too. Once an interesting tool, the internet has done much to redefine the way in which we learn and the way in which we relate to one another as humans.

As essential as internet technology and social communications are to our businesses, though, they are still mysteries to many. And to make matters more confusing, influential sites like Facebook keep changing the rules of the road. The proliferation of mobile devices such as smartphones and tablets has also created a new style of consumption on the web that also must be taken in account.

So once again, with this new installment of the Superstar series, *Success Secrets of the Online Marketing Superstars*, we turn the spotlight on the constantly changing landscape that is online marketing, and the men, women, and technologies that continue to define and redefine it.

May the insights in this book help you reach your goals and help you create the life you truly desire.

—Mitch Meyerson
Scottsdale, Arizona

Get your free bonus content including audio
interviews, downloads, and more by visiting
www.MasteringOnlineMarketing.com

Strategy, Conversion, and Mindset

CHAPTER 1

The New Rainmaker
Why Building Your Own Digital Media Platform Is Smarter than "Marketing"

Brian Clark

BRIAN CLARK began publishing online in 1998, and by 1999 he had his first successful business built by what is now known as content marketing. Between 2001 and 2005, Brian went on to launch two additional businesses, which attained even greater success. In January 2006, he started a one-man blog called Copyblogger, which quickly evolved into an influential digital trade magazine for the online industry and became the catalyst for the multimillion-dollar software and training company he heads today as CEO. www.Copyblogger.com

In this Chapter, You'll Discover:

▶ How to create marketing that people actually want

▶ What a personal media brand is and why you want one

▶ How to give away what you're selling for fun and profit

▶ Why leadership is the key to lead generation

▶ How to maximize your marketing wealth with new media

▶ The reason you'll likely succeed (big), if you start now

Without a rainmaker, you're in trouble.

This was true for the Native Americans living on sun-bleached plains. When the life-giving rivers began to dry up from lack of rain, life became hard.

The plants withered, the animals weakened, and the tribe despaired.

It's also true for businesses trying to survive and thrive in any economy. The rainmaker is the one who brings in the clients and customers, the revenue, and the profits. It's the rainmaker who saves their own "tribe" from the withering despair—and dire consequences— of failure.

In all cultures, the rainmaker is a powerful person. Secure, respected, and paid in full.

Ultimately, *the one who makes it rain makes the rules.*

The traditional business rainmaker typically enjoyed some unfair advantage outside of standard channels; this is how *they* made it rain. The right family, the right Ivy League connections, the right country club membership. Privilege perpetuating more privilege.

The new rainmaker enjoys a different kind of unfair advantage, except in this case it's now available to anyone who understands—and, more importantly, acts on—how new business generation works today. This unfair advantage is now built on the principles of attracting and engaging an online audience, not the circumstances of your birth.

An Improbable Run at Entrepreneurial Success

In my past life, I was an attorney. I didn't much enjoy the practice of law, but looking back now, I realize that I learned two fundamental rules of smart business while doing my time in the big law firm environment.

In addition to realizing that the practice of law often had little to do with the actual law, I found out that success as an attorney often had little to do with technical proficiency. In other words, the best lawyers weren't necessarily the highest paid or most powerful attorneys.

The lawyers with their name in the firm title were the most powerful, because they had the clients. Other attorneys worked for them to handle these clients.

Another type of attorney had a different form of power, in the form of a great life. They came in late and left early, often heading to the golf course. These people also had an almost magical knack for bringing in new business, and maintained relationships while worker bees like me racked up the billable hours.

These were the *rainmakers*. And they made the rules that worked for the life they wanted to lead.

Call me naive, but this was a revelation to me. Especially since I absolutely hated the practice of law. I realized that what I had to do was learn how to bring in business, not grind out more hours, if I wanted to succeed.

The other foundational lesson I learned came from observing the firm's business clients. Contrary to stereotypes, I discovered that the key to smart business was not trying to screw the other side. It was giving them the best deal—the absolute highest value possible—while also achieving your own goals.

The idea of the rainmaker, combined with the understanding that you serve others to succeed, would form the basis of my improbable run as an internet entrepreneur.

The Rise of the New (Media) Rainmaker

Historically, the magical knack of making it rain was predetermined early on. For Native Americans, future rainmakers were chosen to become apprentices at a young age, after showing an innate gift for a relationship with the weather.

In business, future rainmakers were often chosen even earlier: by birth. Being born into the right family under the right circumstances opened up a lot of doors. You had an innate gift for a relationship with *money*, and those who had it.

Our friends the old-school rainmakers of generations past could never imagine in their wildest dreams that such a machine of communication, connection, and commerce could exist.

But it *does* exist, and it's turned "business as usual" on its head with the shift of power to the prospect, not the provider. It was in this new context that I learned the ropes.

In 1998, I took the leap. I quit my promising law firm position, and vowed to make a living on my own terms or starve trying. It took a bit to get going, but between 1999 and 2005 I started three successful businesses powered completely by online marketing and the internet.

I went from someone who was absolutely clueless about marketing to a scholar of advertising, direct marketing, and copywriting techniques dating back to the 1920s. The underlying fundamentals still applied (and they still do), but the context of the internet makes the application very different.

In January 2006, I started a blog called Copyblogger to share what I knew, which quickly evolved into an online magazine that became the centerpiece of the multimillion-dollar company I run today.

I didn't have a particular product or service to sell in the beginning, but it didn't matter. I knew that *building an audience* was the crucial thing, and that the audience would reveal what it needed.

I had found my rainmaker magic. And it was *media*, not traditional concepts of marketing.

Media, Not Marketing

If you've been following Copyblogger for any length of time, you know I've been teaching people online marketing for over eight years—specifically, something that is now known as content marketing.

Here's the main thing you need to understand about content: It's different from traditional marketing, but it accomplishes what marketing is supposed to do. It's those differences that cause so many people to struggle with content.

At this point, I've come to the conclusion that the terminology is part of the problem.

First of all, there's the word *content*. What a horrible term to characterize what are essentially creative works, whether articles, audio, movies, books, and music. It's all technically "content," like something that fills a bucket. Apparently, the Louvre in Paris is filled with "content" that just so happens to be surrounded by frames. Let's face it: It's a bad term we unfortunately have to work with.

But even worse, I think, is the word *marketing*, especially the way most people use it, which is as a euphemism for selling people crap they don't want.

Like I said, what we're talking about here does what ethical marketing is supposed to do, but it operates in a way where people actually seek it out, instead of trying to avoid it.

Once you tell traditional marketers it's "marketing," though, the traditional practices creep right back in, and customers start running away. And that's the problem.

Let me give you a few examples of why I now say media, not marketing.

Marvel

I was a Marvel kid growing up. Spider-Man, X-Men, Captain America: These were the characters that fueled my imagination. So when these same characters came back into my adult life through blockbuster films, I was thrilled—and even more thrilled that they were really well done.

But did you know Marvel was in the throes of complete failure 20 years ago? The iconic comic book publisher was bought and turned around, emerging out of bankruptcy in the late 1990s with a new plan.

The X-Men movie franchise began in 2000. But things really cracked wide open in 2002 with the first *Spider-Man* movie, which did a combined billion dollars in ticket and DVD sales.

Contrary to what you might think, Marvel only received a tiny fraction of that haul. They had neither the cash nor the expertise to produce a blockbuster film of that caliber, so they took their characters to the big studios. While they only received a small licensing fee, they also laid out zero cash and took zero risk related to the films.

So what was the strategy?

Marvel was in the business of merchandise to produce revenue: comic books, video games, T-shirts, toys, and scores of other consumer products—you name it. Marvel relied on partnering studios to create multibillion-dollar "commercials" for its characters.

These commercials are called *movies*.

Notice that these "commercials" were not in the form of advertisements that people wanted to avoid. To the contrary, people paid good money to watch the amazing stories that fueled Marvel's business model. *Because they were well worth watching.*

In 2009, Disney acquired Marvel for $4.2 billion.

Love It or List It

How about another example, one that doesn't involve iconic superheroes?

There's a cable reality show that my wife watches. It's called *Love It or List It*, and it's a Canadian production that airs in several places, including the home and garden channel, HGTV.

Each episode involves a home that is simply not working for the owners. Usually it's too small for a growing family, poorly configured, hopelessly outdated, or all of the above. The show's stars are Hilary Farr, a designer, and David Visentin, a real estate agent.

Hilary takes the budget the owners can manage and works up a plan to redesign the home so it will work again for the family (this is the "love it" outcome). David, on the other hand, looks for other homes that work as-is within the purchasing budget to convince the owners to sell and move (this being the "list it" scenario).

So Hilary and David are full-time TV stars, right? Uh, no . . . not on a niche reality show on basic cable. Both continue to be practicing professionals.

Let's take a closer look at David, who works alongside his father Nick Visentin as a Canadian Realtor for Country Living Realty in Barrie, Ontario. David actively sought out the role on *Love It or List It* by auditioning for it, and likely won the part not only because he knows his stuff, but also because he's not afraid to be himself.

Do you think David gets plenty of new business thanks to the show? You bet.

Do you think those new clients feel like they were marketed to, such as they might if they chose a Realtor based on—I don't know— the postcards that stuff the mailbox each month, or the glamour shot on a bus stop bench, or the cheesy magazine ad claiming to be the "Number One Realtor"?

You get my point. David *demonstrates* his expertise while reaching prospective customers via a media production that people actually enjoy watching.

Now, let's look at one more example, where the exact same dynamic is at play, but no television show or audition is required.

Gary V

Gary Vaynerchuk owns a wine shop along with his parents in New Jersey. To grow the business, Gary built an online platform called WineLibrary.com, which is an educational resource for wine buyers that naturally helps move product.

Vaynerchuk then took the next step with Wine Library TV, a self-produced video show starring just him, from a table in the corner of the office above the store. Gary turned traditional "wine talk" on its head, dispensing with elitism and opting for plain-spoken advice and even bombastic commentary on his wine recommendations.

Gary's DIY wine show grew to an audience of 100,000 people. More important, his wine *business* grew from $3 million to $45 million.

From each of these three examples, a media platform performed the role of what marketing is supposed to do, but rarely does anymore. And in each case, a rainmaker emerged.

There's something that Spider-Man, David Visentin, and Gary Vaynerchuk have in common, and it's *a personal media brand*. This is what works to generate a flood of business in the age of media, not marketing.

And yes, it will work for you as long as you're known for value, instead of something more dubious, or worse—nothing at all.

Why a Personal Media Brand Beats Marketing Every Time

Picture this.

A young lady from a well-known family pouts in dissatisfaction. Despite fantastic wealth, she feels she's not getting enough attention.

Suddenly, scandal emerges.

An illicit recording has leaked to the public. The sex tape presents our princess in several compromising positions. The corresponding scorn, ridicule, and—most important of all—attention of the world is the result.

But the young lady does not retreat in shame, oh no. To the contrary, she's suddenly everywhere, starring in reality television shows, appearing in films, and landing lucrative endorsement deals.

Now ask yourself: *Is he talking about Kim Kardashian here, or is it Paris Hilton?*

Next question: Do you actually care?

Welcome to the world of being famous for being famous—a term for someone who attains celebrity status for no real reason—instead of for talent, or leadership, or just maybe creating some value for the world.

This crowd generates their own fame by exploiting their existing privilege. And yes, they have an audience. But let's face it: Calling someone *famous for being famous* is an insult, and rightly so.

It's the separation of fame from greatness, from talent, from quality, and from value itself.

Hey, maybe it works for Kim and Paris. But unfortunately, there are plenty of people who think this is the path they should follow to promote their business online. Maybe not the sex tape part, but the misguided notion that all you have to do is become known via the internet.

In other words, they've got the media part down, but their efforts are not functioning as good marketing. They're *known for being known*, and that doesn't translate into economic success.

Let's talk about personal branding, a term I've never liked. It's all about presenting an image, not necessarily value. And in line with the example set by Kim and Paris, it promotes the idea that *being known for being known* is enough, and it's not.

Any fool can become *known*. And they often do.

After all, we all watch the online train wrecks pile up, and we get plenty of opportunities, right?

But do you want to do business with a train wreck? I don't, either.

You need to be known for something more. And that's why the new rainmaker develops a *personal media brand with a solid content foundation*. This is what beats simple personal branding and traditional concepts of marketing any day.

A New Rainmaker Is Known for Being a Valuable Resource

Rule number one for the new rainmaker:

> You must be a valuable information resource via your own media platform, with a key emphasis on providing value.

As a natural consequence of that, you'll also demonstrate the value of your paid solution.

What does that mean? First, you have to show that you understand your potential customer's problems and desires. And you have to begin to satisfy those problems or desires *before* you stick out your hand for payment.

Here's a great example:

A really nice Australian guy named Darren Rowse created an online resource called Digital Photography School, which provides an immense amount of free information. He makes his money selling ebooks on the very same topics.

Isn't he shooting himself in the foot by giving away his "product" for free? No, because people happily pay for a well-organized, comprehensive treatment of the topic they need help with, even after they've had a free "taste."

The quality of the free information is why Digital Photography School is so well-known and well-respected.

But it's more than that. You sell a lot more books (or any other product or service) when you can demonstrate value upfront. It's a sharp contrast to what everyone else is doing—claiming authority and value using ordinary "marketing" tactics.

Book-selling entrepreneurs since at least the 1960s have known that giving away the best part of a "how to" book leads to much higher sales. The internet just made it work better.

You sell more, not less; that's the goal, right?

Now imagine if you're selling something other than information, like a service.

Wouldn't demonstrating that you know what you're doing work better than claiming to be the number-one whatever?

A New Rainmaker Is Known for Being an Expert

It's absurdly obvious: There's more information on the internet than any of us will ever be able to consume, on just about any topic you might be interested in studying.

That sounds like a good thing, and it is.

But we also know how incredibly hard it can be to find *good* information and media on the topics we care about.

That's where the opportunity lies for the new rainmaker: The one who is willing to become an expert in her field, to generously demonstrate that expertise for all to see, and to execute it in an authentic way.

We want to do business with someone who knows what they're doing and talking about it. Just common sense, right?

The power of expertise, though, goes much deeper than that.

People have problems and desires, and they want solutions. They want you to be the person to help them with those problems and desires, so they can stop searching and begin the process.

When you use your media platform to *demonstrate* that your expertise can help, something very powerful happens.

It's just like David Visentin in our example from the show *Love It or List It*. Every episode allows David to demonstrate that he knows what he's doing and knows what he's talking about. And that opens the door to a powerful psychological mechanism in a very noncreepy, nonmarketing way.

That mechanism is called *authority*, and its effectiveness cannot be overstated. All you need to take away for now is this:

> A personal media brand makes you into a likable expert, and that sets the stage for the rain to fall. That's because media allows authority to be demonstrated and earned, rather than just claimed.

A New Rainmaker Is Known for Being Generous

Business success through generosity is much older than the internet. Giving first to get later is a timeless reciprocity strategy, which we'll talk about more later on.

The thing about generosity, though, is you have to give without expectation of getting in return—that's the definition of the word.

In my experience, I've always been rewarded for being generous, even though what comes back to me often ends up being pleasantly unexpected. That's also part of what makes generosity-powered business so interesting.

In fact, it's surprising how often the "return" hugely outweighs the original generosity. It truly never ceases to amaze me.

Back when I was giving away valuable information to sell legal and then real estate services, I made a killing, even though I was far from the most experienced or traditionally connected choice.

And maybe most astonishing of all was all the *resistance* I heard from those who did have more experience, when I suggested they try generosity, too.

Think about it. The legal and real estate professions require a license from the state and specialized training. But somehow there was this silly fear that if professionals gave away information, people wouldn't need them! Others just plain hated the idea of giving anything away to people who might not ultimately hire them.

This is what's known as scarcity mindset at its ugliest, and it's completely limiting.

Here's the thing: When you freely share your expertise, perspective, and experience, you're not giving anything away. *You still have it.* Rather than losing something, the sharing leads to more people knowing you and hiring you than would have otherwise.

Again, that's the goal, right?

A New Rainmaker Is Known for Being Authentic

Countless studies show that human beings instantly judge others based on two primary types of social perception: *competence* and *warmth*.

I talked about competence already in the context of expertise and authority. Simply put, you have to actually know what you're doing, so you can help your audience solve its problems.

I also touched on warmth with generosity, but it's more than that.

People want an authentic, relatable human being involved when they buy.

What does that mean?

According to the book *The Human Brand*, countless social psychology studies show that warmth is characterized by people who are:

- ► Helpful
- ► Honest
- ► Trustworthy
- ► Generous
- ► Fair
- ► Understanding

All of this is accomplished by an online media platform, which creates your personal media brand. And that last point—understanding (also known as empathy)—is the key.

Your prospects have problems and desires. You are a trustworthy resource, because you can show that you understand those problems and desires, and that you're here to help.

Is that marketing? Or is that something stronger that accomplishes what marketing is supposed to, except better, and does a whole lot more in the process?

Authority without warmth makes people envious and suspicious. But add in your relatable nature as an authentic human being, and the people you're looking to reach are magnetically attracted to you.

Know + Like + Trust = Belief

You've likely heard it said that selling just about anything comes down to you and your solution being known, liked, and trusted. And it's true, but what's really happening here?

We've seen that being known alone is not enough. But once you are, and you add in a couple more powerful ingredients, you're well beyond just being known for being known.

The first extra ingredient is liking. We simply prefer to do business with people and brands we *like*.

And then we get to *trust:* We have to trust the integrity of the provider as much as we trust that our problem will be solved.

At that point, the result is something magical; it's the special something that makes it rain, even for the Native American shaman: *Belief.*

Notice the language we use to talk about these behaviors.

We hear about product *evangelists*. We refer to people taking the actions we want online as *conversion*. It truly is a process of transformation . . . from a nonbeliever to a member of your audience.

I'm not going to tell you that it's easy, but it does boil down to a simple structure:

> Know + Like + Trust = Belief

Now you're ready to make it rain at will. And enjoy the freedom that comes with it.

CHAPTER 2

Youtility
Why Smart Online Marketing Is about Help, Not Hype

Jay Baer

JAY BAER, marketing keynote speaker, president of Convince & Convert, and *New York Times* bestselling author of *Youtility*. For more information, visit: www.JayBaer.com.

▲ ▲ ▲

Marketing today is harder than marketing yesterday. And tomorrow? Tomorrow, marketing will be even harder, because the competition will be even greater.

Consumers are being subjected to an invitation avalanche, with every company of every size, shape, and description asking people to like them, follow them, friend

In this Chapter You'll Discover:

▶ Why online marketing is more difficult than ever
▶ Why mobile is driving the useful marketing trend
▶ Why customers' needs are more information than ever
▶ Why being disproportionately honest is a key online marketing tactic
▶ Why relevancy is the most important marketing characteristic

them, click, share, and +1 them. This is in addition to the interruption marketing tactics that envelope us all like a communications straitjacket. At best, it wears thin. At worst, it does more harm than good to your company's reputation.

In addition to the enormous volume of competition for attention, who your business is competing against has changed as well. Think about Facebook, Twitter, Instagram, Pinterest, or your email inbox. Within those venues, you'll find communications from your friends and family members adjacent to messages from companies—maybe even your own business.

> Online marketing is now rooted in this simple truth: You are competing for attention against your own customers and against your own friends.

You are competing for attention in the same venues, using fundamentally the same approaches we all are using to connect with people we actually love! That is not an easy assignment for business, and this circumstance of consumers as competitors is unique to online marketing. Your friends are not buying magazine ads to make sure you know that they are eating dinner at a great restaurant. Your family isn't buying billboards to talk about summer vacation plans (I hope).

So what are you supposed to do? How are you supposed to succeed online when the amount of competition increases every day, and the nature of that competition is more personal than ever? You have two options.

1. *Be amazing.* Many consultants and advisors will tell you to be amazing; to do disproportionately fantastic things, and to shock and awe. The theory is that you can break through the clutter by being remarkable. The problem with this approach is that you will fail far more than you will succeed. It's marketing based on

trying to catch lightning in a bottle, and that's not a strategy; it's hope.

> *Telling someone to "be amazing" is like telling someone to "create a viral video." After all, there's no such thing as a viral video, just a video that becomes viral—and most do not.*

2. *Be useful.* The second way to succeed in today's massively competitive online marketing environment is to be truly and inherently useful. To focus your energy on creating marketing that people actually cherish, not marketing that people simply tolerate. Create information and education that is disproportionately useful, and attention, sales, and loyalty will follow, eventually. This is "Youtility," and more and more companies are using it in their online marketing.

> *Youtility is marketing so useful, people would pay for it if you asked them to do so.*

The Three Types of Youtility

There are hundreds of companies using resources to provide marketing of real value to customers and prospective customers. You'll find Youtility examples from all across the business spectrum, from large to small, global to local, B2B to B2C, software to retail, services to manufacturing. But not all Youtility is precisely the same. In fact, there are three distinct flavors of Youtility.

The first is self-serve information: giving people the opportunity to inform themselves how and when they wish, instead of being funneled through contact mechanisms of the company's choosing.

Hilton Suggests' Youtility on Twitter

Hilton Hotels has a Youtility program on Twitter called "Hilton Suggests." In 2012, @LTHouston wrote on Twitter, "Good places to eat near the Magnolia Hotel in Downtown Dallas for Saturday?"

@HiltonSuggests answered back, "@LTHouston, Wild Salsa on Main or Campisi's on Elm are awesome, both within walking distance of your hotel in Dallas, enjoy."

Useful and kind, right? But here's the difference-maker: The Magnolia Hotel in Dallas isn't a Hilton property. Hilton Hotels is going out of their way to provide real-time restaurant recommendations to a person who isn't a current customer. But someday, @LTHouston is going to be in a different city, he's going to need a hotel, and he's going to remember the help that @HiltonSuggests provided, and what hotel is he going to think of first?

You see, Hilton is playing the long game, which is what Youtility requires. You give away information and resources that are legitimately beneficial to customers and prospective customers and you trust that some percentage of those people will reward your business down the road. One of the big problems in online marketing is that all the attention paid to conversion rate and real-time marketing conspires to make us think solely of immediate success, often at the expense of long-term opportunities.

The Hilton Suggests program has proven so successful that the company has expanded it to include hundreds of cities, worldwide.

As Gary Vaynerchuk has said, the problem with marketers is that everyone wants to be a hunter, and nobody wants to be a farmer.

The second is radical transparency: providing incredibly forthright answers to nearly every question a customer could conceivably ask, before they think to ask it.

The third is real-time relevancy: being massively useful at particular moments in the life of the customer, and then fading into the background until the next opportunity to help arises.

Winning Customers with Self-Serve Information

Have you heard the phrase, "Your customers don't want to see the sausage being made"? You probably have, because that saying has been around for decades, and the reason it has persisted is that it has historically been true. But it's not true any longer. Today's consumers WANT to see the sausage being made. They WANT to know all the facts about what you do, how you do it, and for whom.

Google's landmark Zero Moment of Truth research provides mathematical evidence of the beginning of this shift in information consumption, finding that in 2010, Americans needed 5.3 sources of information before making a purchase; but in 2011, they needed 10.4 sources of information. Think about that: In ONE year, the amount of information we needed before parting with our money DOUBLED.

> *Today's consumers are kicking the informational tires like never before, secret shopping your business online, right under your nose.*

Why do we need so much more information? Are we just less certain about what to buy, and where? No. We need more information than ever as consumers, because we HAVE more information than ever. Always-on internet access via smartphones and tablets has accelerated our need for research by removing the barriers to that research. It's so easy to hyper-research everything today that if you make a bad purchase decision, maybe you were just lazy.

You must supply an increasing number of those 10.4 sources of information for your customers and prospective customers. How?

Maybe it's a comprehensive blog that functions as the ultimate FAQ. Maybe it's a series of videos. Maybe it's a regular system of ebooks and Slideshare presentations. Maybe it's a definitive podcast. Probably, it's some combination of all of these, and more.

This kind of self-serve information is what turns interest into action. Have you ever been on a website, and were interested in the company or product but purposefully did NOT fill out a contact us form, because you didn't want to be emailed or called by a salesperson? I'll bet that has happened to you. We used to talk to a real person as a first step. To get familiar with the company. To learn more. To create bonds. Not now. Now we talk to a real person as a last resort when we have a question so specific only a human being can answer it.

Self-serve information is even more important in B2B, where the transactional stakes are the highest. In 2012, Sirius Decisions research found that in B2B, 70 percent of the purchase decision has been made before the prospective customer ever contacts the company, meaning that whether or not people buy from you in B2B is based on self-serve information.

Self-Serve Help with Lowe's Fix in Six

Home improvement retailer Lowe's has a terrific self-serve information program called "Fix in Six." It's a series of six-second videos originally produced and distributed on Vine that provide helpful tips around the home, such as:

▸ How to use a Post-it™ note to catch dust when drilling holes
▸ How to use a magnet to hold your nails when hammering
▸ How to use masking tape to keep your pictures straight
▸ How to use an empty milk jug as a watering can

The Fix in Six videos proved so useful and popular that Lowe's decided to repackage and redeploy them in other ways, which is one of the secrets to efficient content marketing and Youtility.

Lowe's "atomized" the Fix in Six program and collected all of the videos on a Tumblr blog (lowesfixinsix.tumblr.com). They also created a Pinterest board that contains all of the Fix in Six tips. They routinely

> *"Atomize" your content. If you have a good idea, create several smaller versions of it in multiple formats. Don't reinvent the wheel; make copies of the wheel you already own.*

feature them on their Facebook page. And they even created a series of YouTube videos by taking the original six-second clips, and adding short opening and closing sequences. Ta-da! New, atomized Youtility.

> *Remember, the key to online success is to be a digital dandelion. Your website is the stalk, but all the other places people can access your self-serve information are the seeds.*

Building Trust with Radical Transparency

Fundamentally, many people don't trust business. In fact, the public relations firm Edelman releases an annual study on trust and finds that roughly half of Americans do not trust businesses. This aligns with a separate study from Nielsen that found that 47 percent of Americans trust advertising from companies.

This matters because trust is quite literally the most important ingredient in your success, online or offline. Without trust, you have no customers and you have no future.

Unfortunately, however, we often engage in online marketing activities that diminish trust. Squeeze pages that are too aggressive. Email that isn't opt-in. Stalker-ish retargeting ads. There are lots of

> *Trust is the prism through which all online marketing success must pass.*

McDonald's Canada Puts Radical Transparency to the Test

McDonald's Canada certainly isn't ashamed of their food. Their "Our Food, Your Questions" program invites any Canadian to ask any question whatsoever about McDonald's food on their special website. To ask a question participants must connect with either Twitter or Facebook, providing greater visibility and a ripple-in-the-pond viral effect, as questions appear on the inquisitors' social network. Within the first four months 16,000 questions were asked, at a rate of as many as 450 per day. In that period more than 10,000 questions were answered.

The program is only dedicated to McDonald's food, so questions about non-food topics are directed to other resources, and some questions are of course duplicates. But there's no dodging the tough questions, and that's the most amazing, radical transparency element of this project. McDonald's Canada is addressing head-on the rumors about food quality and safety that have dogged the brand seemingly forever.

As an example of the types of questions McDonald's is going out of its way to address, take this zinger from Jani S. in Nova Scotia: "When you say 100 percent beef, do you mean the whole cow: the organs, snout, brain, kidneys, etc. or just the plain beef we buy at the grocer?"

Whoa. Historically, companies would do whatever possible to put as much distance as possible between themselves and that line of inquiry. But the rules are changing. Here's McDonald's answer—comprehensive, factual, and not laden with artificial marketing hype: "Hi Jani. We wouldn't call it plain beef, but it sure is beef. We only use meat cut from the shoulder, chuck, brisket, rib eye, loin, and round. In fact, our beef supplier is Cargill, a name you might recognize. They're the biggest supplier of beef in Canada."

According to Joel Yashinsky, chief marketing officer for McDonald's Canada, the impact will be long-term trust. "We knew you're not going to get an immediate return on investment. But we believe that the return on investment

> ## McDonald's Canada, continued
>
> will be over the long-term, because it's going to grow our brand trust and brand health. What I like to call the 'love of the brand' is going to get much stronger, and in the end, we all firmly believe that the return is going to be greater than the investment . . . it's going to be such an important part of our culture moving forward."
>
> And it works. In pre- and post-consumer research conducted after the first phase of the program (before significant advertising dollars were expended to drive awareness of it), the "curious skeptic" segment of McDonald's prospective customer base gave the company 21 percent higher marks for "good quality ingredients," according to Yashinsky.

ways to chip away at trust, and other contributors in this book will help you avoid those mistakes. But there is also a way to gain trust with Youtility.

In an environment where every customer is a reporter, and three-fourths of the population is carrying the equivalent of a mobile television studio in the smartphone in their pocket, it's pretty difficult to hide the truth. The truth ALWAYS comes out. So what smart companies are doing is being massively proactive and transparent. They are providing Youtility that doesn't force prospective customers to wonder about the motives or details of the company; they just offer it up quickly and conveniently.

Does radical transparency actually work? Absolutely. Consider Domino's Pizza. This is an oversimplification, but Domino's positioning is essentially "Our pizza used to suck. But now, not so much!" Since they adopted that radically transparent approach, they've enjoyed nine consecutive quarters of increasing stock price.

Using Hyper-Relevancy to Create Incredibly Useful Youtility

There is no courtship, ramp up, or slow build with Youtility. You're either sufficiently useful at any given moment, and thus can connect with the customer, or you're not. It's real-time relationship building.

Like an endless game of informational hide and seek, Youtility consists of popping out from behind a tree to assist when necessary, then fading back into the woods waiting for the next opportunity.

The key is to create Youtility that serves as the best possible resource for people looking to solve a particular problem in a specific context.

> You are better off being massively useful in a very specific set of circumstances than being partially useful in a broader set of circumstances.

There are three ways to provide real-time relevancy with Youtility. The first is to be useful based on the customer's location. The second is to be useful based on the customer's situation. The last is to be useful based on seasonality or external factors.

In nearly every case, providing value via a mobile app or mobile-enabled content marketing program is the easiest path because when using a mobile device, customers and prospective customers are often sending a steady stream of information about what they might need. Tapping into a consumer's location and then providing geography-specific usefulness is the most common way companies can be helpful in a mobile context. Many of our most used applications—like Google Maps—rely on it.

Location-based usefulness may very well become the most common form of mobile usefulness, but it's not the only alternative. Companies and other organizations are also providing customers and prospective customers with information that's important in particular situations and scenarios.

One of my favorite (and most inherently useful) examples of this form of marketing is the Vanderbilt CoachSmart application. A collaboration out of Nashville, Tennessee, between the Vanderbilt

University Medical Center and the Monroe Carell Jr. Children's Hospital at Vanderbilt, the app is becoming a must-have for youth sports coaches across the country, as it provides an array of useful tools to keep players safe. Perhaps the most interesting is a lightning sensor. If lightning strikes nearby, the app sends an alert to the phone and tells coaches what to do next, recommending whether an outdoor practice should be immediately aborted.

The app also helps coaches prevent heat exhaustion, by providing real-time data on heat, humidity, and the heat index. A comprehensive collection of information for coaches is also included, such as hydration tips, injury prevention guidelines, and concussion symptoms. Coaches can even use the app as a contacts tool, notifying all players (or parents) from within CoachSmart. It's currently in use by hundreds of sports leagues across the country, as well as two National Football League teams.

The CoachSmart app was born from a legacy program where athletic trainers affiliated with Vanderbilt went to high school football practices in the Nashville area to let coaches know whether it was safe to practice based on the current heat index.

While CoachSmart was developed to serve the needs of coaches in Nashville, it's now being used by a much broader audience. The information it delivers is relevant almost regardless of location. The future of hyper-relevance may be taking applications like this to their logical extreme, using "anticipatory computing" to push information to participants before they even realize they need it.

Youtility Is the North Star for Online Marketing

There are so many options and alternatives in online marketing today. So many new tactics, techniques, and technologies. Which make sense for your business? Which should you deploy? Which should you ignore? It's a lot to consider, and it's not going to slow down any time soon, if ever.

What you need—and what we all need—is a north star; a guidepost that helps us make better decisions about our online marketing. I believe that north star is Youtility. When you're confused or frustrated or uncertain about what and how to deploy and optimize your online marketing program, just ask yourself this simple thing, and then reassess your options:

Is your marketing so useful that people would pay for it? Is your marketing a Youtility?

CHAPTER 3

Total Online Presence
The Seven Essential Stages

John Jantsch

In this Chapter, You'll Discover

► Content platform
► Organic SEO
► Email marketing
► Social media marketing
► Online advertising
► Mobile and location
► Analytics and conversion

JOHN JANTSCH is a marketing consultant, award-winning social media publisher and author of the best-selling books *Duct Tape Marketing, Duct Tape Selling, The Commitment Engine,* and *The Referral Engine.*

His blog was chosen as a *Forbes* favorite for marketing and small business, and his podcast, a top ten marketing show on iTunes, was called a "must listen" by *Fast Company* magazine. He can be reached at www.DuctTapeMarketing.com.

▲ ▲ ▲

There are many moving parts involved in marketing, and the online elements increase in importance with each passing day.

But marketing is a system, and to effectively operate this system you must assemble and integrate each of the important parts into something that looks like the whole.

Your online presence is your key to success no matter what your business sells; no matter if all of your transactions are done face-to-face; no matter if you don't yet see a way to get a return from your Facebook page; no matter if you've never bought an online ad. The key is to build a Total Online Presence™.

I believe the following model is the surest way to view your online marketing as a system.

I will outline the core components of a Total Online Presence in this chapter and give you a taste of the specific details that must be considered as you build your own presence.

Content Platform

So much of what happens online revolves around content. It's how you get found, why people pay attention, and how you start to exchange value. Without a content platform to build from, a great deal of effort in other stages will be wasted.

People today have come to expect to find information about any product, service, company, individual, cause, or challenge they face by simply turning to the search engine of their choice. So, if they're not finding content that you've produced, there's a pretty good chance you won't be worthy of their trust. Which brings us to the two most important categories when it comes to content strategy: **educating your customer and building trust.**

These must be delivered through the creation of very specific forms of content and not simply through sheer volume. Every business is now a publishing business, so you've got to start to think like one.

Building Trust

> ▸ *Blog*. This is the absolute starting point for your content strategy because it makes content production, syndication, and

sharing so easy. The search engines love blog content as well, and this is the place where you can organize a great deal of your editorial thinking. This can easily be expanded and adapted to become content for articles, workshops, and ebooks.

▶ *Social media*. You need to claim all the free opportunities to create social media profiles on sites like LinkedIn and Facebook, but also in *BusinessWeek, Entrepreneur,* and *Inc.* online magazine communities. Building rich profiles, and optimizing links, images, and videos that point back to your main site is an important part of the content-as-strategy play.

▶ *Reviews*. Ratings and reviews sites such as Yelp, MerchantCircle, and CitySearch have become mainstream user-generated content hubs. Throw in the fact that Google, Yahoo, and Bing all allow folks to rate and review businesses and you've got an increasingly important category of content that you must participate in.

▶ *Building trust*. Customer testimonials are a powerful form of content. Every business today should seek customer content in multiple forms: written, audio, and video. This content adds important trust-building endorsements and makes for great brand-building assets out there on Google and YouTube.

Content that Educates

▶ *The point-of-view white paper*. Every business should have a well-developed core story that's documented in the form of a white paper or ebook. This content must dive deeply into what makes your firm different, what your secret sauce is, how you approach customer service, and why you do what you do.

▶ *Seminars*. Presentations, workshops, and seminars (online and off) are great ways to provide education with the added punch of engagement. Turning your point-of-view white paper into a 45-minute, value-packed session is one of the most effective ways to generate, nurture, and convert leads.

▶ *FAQs*. There's no denying the value of information packaged in this format, but go beyond the questions that routinely get asked and include those that should get asked but don't, particularly the ones that help position you favorably against your competition.

▸ *Success stories*. Building rich examples of actual clients succeeding through the use of your product or service offerings is a tremendous way to help people learn from other individuals and businesses just like them. When prospects see themselves in a success story, they are more likely to put themselves in that boat.

Organic SEO

Generating leads by putting lots of valuable content in the places where people look for just such a thing is central to marketing success these days. There are four key factors that I believe help do this. So instead of trying to illustrate my point by using a technical diagram, let's think of the cupcake. I mean, who doesn't like a cupcake?

▸ *Content*. You can't exactly have a cupcake without, well, the cup. The paper wrapper that sometimes gets stuck and can be annoying is actually the foundation for the entire thing. Likewise, content is the underpinning of any attempt to score well in SEO—you need lots of it, in many flavors. Think of when you walk into a cupcake bakery; they don't just offer one or two flavors. There is variety. So apply that to your content.

▸ *Keywords*. Now, if all you did were serve up wrappers of content you wouldn't have a very tasty treat. We need to add the cake in your cupcake. We need to test out the flavor combinations that keep your customers coming back for more. Keywords, the actual stuff that prospects put into search engines to find a business like yours, are what give your SEO efforts tastiness and set the table for surfers and search engines.

▸ *Links*. Piling on the icing is a sure fire way to attract the search engine spiders. You can do so in the form of links pointing the way to your content. The best way to attract lots of links is by creating great keywords and rich content.

▸ *Social media.* You've got an awesome cupcake, now it's time to add the finishing touch. Lots of folks get the connection between social media and SEO, but they don't fully appreciate that social without content turns a scrumptious desert into a healthy snack. It's nice, but it won't satisfy the surfer's sweet tooth. In this case, one of the best reasons to even grow raspberries (participate in social) is to top off the cupcake and add a very attractive package to your overall content play.

While you're probably hungry and craving sugar by now, I hope that helps to simplify the important aspects of SEO.

One thing we know for sure is when people want to find a business, they go online and search for it. You, as the marketer, need to make this easy for them and become a master of online local marketing before your competitors do. This means you must be very, very focused on winning searches that are done with the intent of finding something local. This includes showing up in mobile browsers and on maps.

Action Steps to Build a Strong Local Search Presence

1. *Make your web pages scream local.* There are many ways to make your website pages localized. This is one of the underlying elements that tell the search engines that yours is indeed a local business.
2. *Claim and enhance your local search profiles.* The local search directories at Google, Yahoo!, and Bing want you to claim and build rich information for local profiles. This makes their job easier when people search for local businesses.
3. *Participate in the ratings and reviews game.* Lots of local business directories exist with the added feature of user ratings and reviews. If you're not paying attention to the major sites and monitoring what's being said, you may be losing business because of one poor review.
4. *Update your listings and citations.* Citations are mentions of your business and address that appear on other websites. These are

a key component of the ranking algorithms because they help assure your business is truly local.

5. *Own a social network topic group.* Start a local niche group and build a community of users around the local theme on social media sites such as Flickr, Facebook, LinkedIn, Meetup, or Biznik. If you can find an area of interest to others, you might be able to build a useful and vibrant local tool while greatly enhancing your own local presence.

Don't Bother with Social Media Until You Have Email Marketing Nailed

I think there's a hierarchy in the world of building a total web presence for your business, and mastering things like Facebook and Pinterest fall somewhere far behind getting your content strategy, SEO, and email marketing machine oiled and ready for prime time.

One thousand responsive email followers trumps 25,000 Twitter followers every day when it comes to actually promoting the things that make your money. Focus on building a list of email subscribers that want to hear from you, and social media will become a tool set to help you do more of that. So while this may sound shocking and hard to hear, ditch social media for now and focus on email marketing first.

First things first, you need to have a value-filled ebook that motivates people to hand over their email addresses. If you already have one ready, you are one step ahead of the game! But if not, get moving and come up with a plan to put together an educational ebook that can carve a path to your lead capture program.

Here are some helpful email marketing tips for a basic email capture plan:

▸ Choose an email service provider (ESP) such as Constant Contact, GetResponse, AWeber, MailChimp, or Infusionsoft.

▸ Use your ESP's form-building tools and place a lead capture form on every page of your website. (Don't ask for more than name and email at this point.)

▶ Create an email subscription landing page—a page that describes and promotes your ebook and lists all the benefits of why a viewer might give you their email address.

▶ Create a series of emails, delivered through your ESP's auto-responder function, that provides additional information on downloading the ebook.

▶ Consider using a pop-up form, such as Pippity for WordPress (if you have a WordPress blog) that can be programmed to bring focus to your offer in smart ways.

▶ Many ESPs have a "tell a friend" function that allows readers to easily email your offer to friends—use it!

Promote your free ebook in social networks on a regular basis.

Social Media Marketing

Here are five ways to view your social media activity as a layer of your entire system:

1. *Move to email.* Email is still the most effective form of marketing and relationship building. It is a tremendous tool for building the kind of long-term relationship that allows you to convert sales. While many have concluded that the same thing cannot be said for social media relationships, you can and should view your connections in these networks as a way to gain more email relationships.

2. *Find your referral champs.* By appending your customer data with social media data, either by way of a service, API, or CRM add-on, you can often discover your more active and potentially influential customers and prospects. This information can hide in your standard customer profile because the way people act offline and the way they participate online is often dramatically different. A customer that buys very little from you currently may turn out to be your greatest potential referral champion, but may go unnoticed and therefore ungroomed without this layer of data.

3. *Understand your customers.* You need to dig deep and really find out what makes your customers tick on all levels. That means

knowing what their interests and hobbies are, what restaurants they love, their favorite music and TV shows, and how much they love coaching their son's Little League games. You might guess where this is headed: What do people on social media love to do? Talk about what they had for lunch and give reviews of movies like they were a critic. So it just might be important after all to really know your customer.

4. *Improve your SEO.* Great content isn't great until somebody reads it, shares it, and links to it. It's almost like the popular kids in high school, but that's just the reality of inbound marketing today. It's not enough to produce lots of content; you've got to get people talking about it and bringing attention to it.

5. *Build PR muscle.* One of my favorite uses of the social media layer is the ability to draw closer to the journalists that cover your industry or community. Today's journalist relies on social media as a lifeline to real-time information and as a tool for collecting resources; it also makes them much more available through direct communication. By targeting key journalists and using the social layer to build a relationship as a resource, you can quickly enhance your overall chances of media coverage.

Online Advertising

Online advertising is quickly becoming the main advertising platform for all businesses. Competition is getting fierce as the online marketplace begins to get overcrowded with ads. It's easy for small businesses to get lost in the crowd. If your ads aren't getting seen by your target audience, then you are basically throwing money away.

Whether you use Google AdWords, Facebook Ads, content marketing, or a combination of everything, you need to make sure you are using them to your best advantage. This will get your business seen and allow you to spend less in the process. So it's a win-win in my book.

Let's look at a handful of tips to help you get more from your online ads.

Use Google AdWords Features

One of the most beneficial features is **ad site links**. These let you add a few additional links to your website at the bottom of your ad. These links can say anything, such as "Free Trial," "Pricing," "Locations," etc. And the great thing about these features is that most of them are free. This will also help your click-through rates.

Define Your "Negative" Keywords

Negative keywords are those that you do not want your ads to appear for. For instance, if you do not offer free trials, free software, or free samples, then the last thing you want is for people to click on your ad in search of something free. That will just cost you money for zero return.

Look through your current analytics detail to help find negative keywords and spend some time using the free Google Keyword Tool or the **free Negative Keyword Tool from WordStream**.

Be Clear about Your Facebook Ad Targets

The more targeted your ads, the more effective they are going to be. When you are creating your Facebook ads, you get to choose your targeting options. Precise interest categories are broken down even further to help you capture a smaller, but more specific audience. These categories come from Facebook profiles and activities.

Attach Images to Your Facebook Calls to Action

As the saying goes, a picture is worth a thousand words, so keep this in mind and know that images draw the most attention. Take full advantage of the call to action and bring more attention to it by adding an image. Images of people tend to draw the most attention rather than just a logo.

Consider Retargeting

Retargeting, or what Google calls remarketing, is a feature that lets you reach people who have previously visited your site, and show them relevant ads when they visit other sites on a particular ad network or in the case of Google, the Google Display Network.

Aim for quality over quantity in your advertisements and avoid being a pushy salesperson no matter what method of online advertising you choose.

Mobile and Location

It's time to get real with ourselves and accept that we as a society are completely reliant on our phones and tablets. Since that's the case, we need to make sure that our websites look great and are optimized for mobile content.

Having a mobile-friendly site is not the only step you can take to integrate mobility into your business. Let's look at how mobile trends are affecting businesses and what else you can do to stay on top of each.

Mobile Shopping

Many consumers use their mobile devices to look between competitors for the best price before buying, either in person at the store or from the full website.

Mobile Search

Location is a key factor of mobile search, making more locally oriented content a must for your site. Use your major keywords in your titles and content, add appropriate tags, and use keyword-rich anchor text for your internal links.

Look to these services for mobile advertising options: **Google Mobile Ads, MSN Mobile** and **YP (www.yellowpages.com)**. Some advertisers are also starting to experience success using **Twitter ads for mobile.**

With mobile integration, you can reach out to all potential customers through emails, local search, and social media as well as mobile messaging. Get started on implementing more mobile actions into your typical marketing efforts and watch the impact.

Analytics and Conversion

Luckily, there are plenty of tools out there that can turn all of that collected information about your website visitors into an easy-to-understand report that gives you much-needed insight into their behavior. When you are armed with this knowledge, you get to see how effective your website is and what changes you need to make in order to make it even better.

Let's overview the top ten tools that you can use to gain more understanding about your website traffic.

1. *Google Analytics* is one of the best free tools that any website owner can use to track and analyze data about web traffic.
2. *Spring Metrics* has taken the analytics tool and made it simpler. You don't have to be a professional data-miner to get the answers to your questions.
3. *Woopra* is another tool that offers real-time analytics tracking, while Google Analytics can take hours to update. It is a desktop application that feeds you live visitor stats, including where they live, what pages they are on now, where they've been on your site and their web browser.
4. *Clicky* also offers a free service if you have only one website, and a Pro account for a monthly fee. You get real-time analytics, including Spy View, which lets you observe what current visitors are doing on your site.
5. *Mint* is an analytics tool that is self-hosted and costs $30 per website. You get the benefit of real-time stats, which you don't get with the free Google Analytics. You can track site visitors, where they are coming from, and what pages they are viewing.
6. *Chartbeat* lets users get the most from their data with instant information. They keep constant watch on your visitors and what they are doing on your website.
7. *KISSmetrics* is another analytics tool that allows clients to track the movements of individual visitors throughout their websites. You can see how behaviors change over time, identify patterns, and see the most typical and recent referrers, among other stats.

8. *UserTesting* is a unique way to gather information about site users. You are paying for a group of participants of your choosing to perform a set of tasks on your site. The user and his activity will be recorded on video.

9. *Crazy Egg* uses the power of heat map technology to give you a visual picture of what site visitors are doing on your web pages. It shows you where people are moving their mouse on the page and where they click.

10. *Mouseflow* is somewhat of a combination of UserTesting and Crazy Egg. You can see video of users interacting with your website, including every mouse click and movement, scrolling, and keystrokes. You also get to view heat maps from different time periods so that you can see the effect of changes that you make on your page.

My goal of this chapter was to help you realize how vital your online presence is to your ultimate success. I hope all of this offers ways to expand your thinking and begin viewing your online work as a manageable system. Good luck!

CHAPTER 4

Creating Your Social Media Strategy

Kim Garst

KIM GARST is the award-winning, internationally recognized founder and CEO of Boom! Social, a leading social media marketing firm headquartered in Tampa, Florida. Kim built her company around helping business owners harness the power of social media as a major component of their overall marketing plans. A master strategist, Kim's advice and counsel is sought by everybody from solo entrepreneurs to major corporations alike. For more information, visit: www.KimGarst.com.

In this Chapter, You'll Discover

▶ Why social media?

▶ What is a social media strategy and why do you need one?

▶ How Zappos is using a social media strategy to CRUSH the competition

▶ Key points to consider before building a social media strategy

▶ Building a social media strategy

▶ Analytics, monitoring, and reporting

▶ Plan adjustments

41

couple of years, social media has matured from a
little practical business application into a recognized
iver. With increased competition in the space and
media sites, tools, ranking algorithms, and advertising
appearing almost daily, it is more important than ever
ision, build, and follow a sound social media strategy that
iently targets, reaches, engages, and eventually converts your
get audience into community members, brand apostles, and
customers.

Why Social Media?

Many business owners assume they have a solid grasp of the uses and
benefits of social media for their business. They understand that their
target market is using social media, and that they need to interact with
customers by providing valuable content and engaging in meaningful
dialogue. However, many business owners don't fully understand how
to harness the power of social media to help them meet their specific
business goals.

There are a number of very real benefits to using social media for
business, including:

- ▸ Reputation monitoring and management
- ▸ Branding
- ▸ Building customer loyalty
- ▸ SEO benefits
- ▸ Website referral traffic

Why social media? **Because it's highly likely that your target
market is spending a good deal of time there**. In fact, recent
research indicates that 73 percent of all internet users are now actively
using social media. Think about it: Approximately 7 out of 10 members
of your target market are on social media. This means if you're relying
on outdated methods of marketing to reach this market, you're likely
to be sorely disappointed with the results.

So how do you use social media in a strategic way in order to reach
this market and achieve your marketing goals? It will be helpful here

to look at what exactly a social media strategy is and why you need one for your business.

What Is a Social Media Strategy?

A basic social media strategy will be a clear articulation of your goals in using social media, and practical applications of these goals. It will typically include:

- ▶ An overview of the sites you will be using (Facebook, Twitter, etc.)
- ▶ A content generation plan
- ▶ A growth or promotion plan
- ▶ A conversion strategy (i.e., once we get people to our site, how will we turn them into paying customers?)

We'll cover each of these in detail later in this chapter.

Why Do You Need a Social Media Strategy?

Using social media for business without a strategy is kind of like getting in a car and driving without a clear destination in mind. How will you know when you've arrived?

A social media strategy is simply a tactical plan for how a business will use social media to achieve its business goals, how social fits into its overall marketing plan, and how they will know when they've "arrived"; in other words, how they will measure the effectiveness of their strategy.

Without a strategy in place, you risk spending a whole lot of time and money on social media without reaping all of the potential rewards. A well-planned social media strategy gives you a roadmap to follow and keeps you focused on the specific outcomes of your efforts.

How Does Social Media Marketing Fit within a Company's Overall Marketing Plan?

The good news is that, in some ways, social media marketing is simply using new tools and strategies to accomplish the same objectives. For instance, some of your high-level marketing goals or objectives may be to increase brand awareness or improve customer satisfaction. You can then drill down and pinpoint *specific* goals that will help you achieve your overall goals.

Some examples of specific goals may be:

▶ To increase page views by 10 percent this quarter
▶ To generate ten new leads this month
▶ To grow market share by 5 percent this year
▶ To increase your website conversion rate to 5 percent

A social media marketing strategy then looks at how you can use social media to achieve these objectives. In other words, social media works best when it's part of a bigger package. It doesn't replace your current marketing strategy, but is rather one component of the bigger picture. It represents an important opportunity to meet your business goals through new and more engaging channels.

How Zappos Is Using a Social Media Strategy to Crush the Competition

Online retailer Zappos.com has made its mark not only by having the best selection of shoes, but through excelling at customer service and thereby creating reams of passionate brand advocates. They obviously have a clear understanding of what their customers are looking for and how they can use social media to help achieve these goals.

Their social media efforts are implemented in a consistent manner across platforms, and are congruent with their goal of being a leader in customer service. Answering questions and concerns promptly on Facebook, using Twitter to show the human side of their employees, and strategically promoting content across platforms are just a few of the elements of their social media strategy.

Another key aspect of their strategy is encouraging customers to share their recent orders on social media. Customers who are excited about a recent purchase are often happy to share the good news with friends, so having a "Share your order on Facebook, Twitter, and Pinterest" call to action helped to increase social shares. Zappos took things a step further, however, and decided to revisit this portion of their strategy. By simply changing the wording to "Love your order? Share it!," social sharing increased by 7 percent.

This is a great example of how a solid social media strategy can help businesses achieve their overall marketing goals; and it's also a good reminder of how revisiting and adjusting the strategy as needed can have a big impact on outcomes.

Key Points to Consider Before Building a Social Media Strategy

Before you jump in and begin creating your strategy, it's imperative that you take a careful look at the many factors that will influence, affect, and limit your plan. Failing to consider these factors may influence not only the effectiveness of your strategy, but have the potential to completely undermine it.

Following are five foundational factors to consider prior to creating your social media strategy.

Budgeting

While social media is often touted as a low-cost alternative to expensive, traditional marketing methods, don't be fooled into thinking it's free. There are many potential costs that may be overlooked at the outset, so it's important to build these into your strategy.

Some costs that should be considered include:

- ▸ Content creation costs (if you won't be doing this yourself). This may include hiring a writer for your blog or social media updates.
- ▸ Graphic design costs for your blog or social media images
- ▸ Social media consulting costs
- ▸ The cost of hiring a social media manager, if needed
- ▸ The cost of video, slideshow, or podcast creation
- ▸ Opportunity costs

Keep in mind that these costs will vary depending on whether you're doing social in-house or outsourcing. If you're doing social in-house, be sure to include the cost of training, salary, and benefits.

Education

Before you create your strategy, it's important to take a step back and quantify the education, skills, and competencies of yourself and your staff when it comes to social media.

Do you know what you need to know? What are your potential blind spots when it comes to social media? Are you and/or your staff trained and educated in social media best practices?

If you've identified lapses in your social media knowledge, how can you remedy this? What training or education do you need to get up to par? Could an intern be useful as part of your social media team?

Allocation of Work

Simply put, why build what you can't support? Prior to setting a strategy in place, it's important that you know whether or not you have the resources and personnel to implement it.

Without a clearly defined person or team who will be responsible for day-to-day social media efforts, the plan you've worked so hard on is unlikely to work. Some important questions you will need to answer include:

▸ Who will respond to questions and concerns on social media?
▸ Who is ultimately responsible for your overall social media efforts?
▸ Who will monitor social media conversations taking place about your brand?
▸ Can you spare the resources that will be needed?
▸ Is your staff or team on board with and supportive of your social media strategy?

If you'll be the one to manage and implement your entire strategy, you can of course skip this step. However, if you have one or more staff members who will be responsible in any capacity for your social media, ensure you have clear guidelines and expectations in place for how the work will be allocated and where responsibility will lie.

Ideal Client Analysis

A key factor in creating an effective social media strategy is having a solid understanding of who your ideal client is. Without this basic knowledge, it will be difficult, if not impossible, to find and connect with them on social media.

In preparation for your strategy, be sure to identify:

- ▶ Who is your ideal client?
- ▶ What demographic are you going after?
- ▶ On which social networking sites are they most likely to be active?
- ▶ What are their interests, needs, and pain points?
- ▶ How do they want to interact with me on social media?

If you've never taken the time to formally identify your ideal customer or client, there's no better time than now! This is a foundational part of any marketing plan, not just for your social media strategy.

Competition

Finally, it's important to understand what your competitors are doing on social media. Through some simple competitive analysis, you will be able to find out what your competitors are doing well on social media (and what you can replicate), as well as where they are falling short (and what you can do better).

Armed with this knowledge, you have the ability to, at the least, even the playing field. At best, you can differentiate yourself by exceeding your customers' expectations and by setting yourself apart from your competitors.

Building a Social Media Strategy

Now that you've covered the foundational factors that will influence your strategy, it's time to dive in and start creating your social media marketing plan.

Basic Plan Components

A picture really is worth a thousand words. The diagram in Figure 4.1 on page 48 is a graphical representation of my actual social media platform, along with the key sites I use and how everything feeds, is

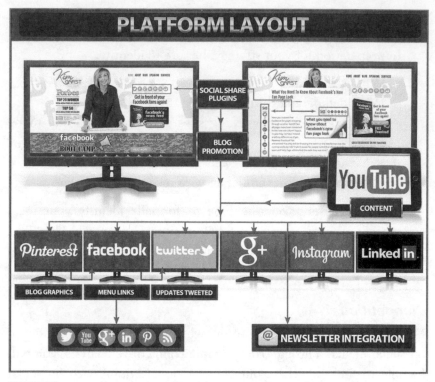

FIGURE 4.1

related to, or interacts with everything else. Do not be intimidated. We will just take this piece by piece and it will all make perfect sense.

Social Media Site Selection

With so many social networks, and new ones emerging nearly every week, it's important that you determine which ones will work best for your business and niche. I encourage you to select a few sites where you will focus most of your efforts so you don't spread yourself too thin.

To determine which sites you'll use, do some research on the demographics of each of the sites to see which ones your target demographic is using. For instance, if your ideal client is a 30-something, college-educated female, you will likely want to be on Pinterest. If you're looking to connect with Millennials, Instagram will likely need to be a big part of your social strategy.

Turning a Collection of Social Media Sites into a Platform

Using various social media sites as insular groups will be effective to some extent, however, having a clear plan for how you're going to use these various networks *together* is what will bring you optimal results. If you think of your various social profiles as part of a single platform, you'll be able to leverage your online presence in ways that simply aren't possible in any other way.

Each of the channels you use will have a specific purpose and part in your overall plan and will work together as one platform. This will ensure that your efforts are as streamlined as possible and that redundancies are avoided.

Content Generation Plan

Once you've established which social networks you'll be utilizing as part of your plan, it's time to lay out a plan for what types of content you'll be creating. The specific questions you'll need to ask include:

- ► What specific types of content will we produce to help us meet our goals?
- ► How often will we create new content?
- ► What percentage of our content will be curated as opposed to created?
- ► Will we create different types of content for different segments of our audience?
- ► Who will be responsible for creating content?

The more specific you can be at this stage, the better. Don't forget to articulate exactly who will be responsible for each aspect of your content generation.

Content Promotion Plan–Organic and Paid

Once you have an understanding of what types of content you'll be creating, it's time to consider how you'll be promoting it. This may involve "free" methods such as simply posting to your social media accounts, or it may involve paid promotion via social ads. In either case, it's important to lay out a specific plan for how to get your content in front of your target market.

Conversion Strategy

The final piece of the puzzle will be figuring out how to move your social media audience into your online marketing funnel. If your social media content keeps people interested and engaged, but they never end up at your website, you'll never see most of the potential monetary benefits or achieve the ROI you're hoping for.

Some questions you may want to consider include:

▶ What page(s) on our site will we send our social media traffic to?
▶ How will we capture the emails of these visitors once on our site?
▶ And finally, how will we turn these leads into sales?

Analytics, Monitoring, and Reporting

A critical component of your social media strategy, but one that business owners often neglect, is gauging whether your efforts are achieving the results you're hoping and planning for. This will necessitate coming up with objective methods of monitoring and reporting the growth and effectiveness of your social media accounts.

Each network has its own on-site analytics tool you can use, however, if you want to delve a little deeper into your analytics or measure and track cross-platform performance, there are some great third-party tools you can use. Some of my favorites include Hootsuite, Simply Measured, Klout, and of course, Google Analytics.

The specific metrics you'll want to track vary between networks, so it would be helpful now to take a look at which analytics you'll need to pay attention to for each of the big three networks.

Facebook

Facebook Insights is a great starting point for monitoring your important Facebook metrics. Using Insights as well as some of the third-party tools I mentioned above, you'll want to pay attention to:

▶ Overall page likes
▶ Net page likes (growth and decline)
▶ Organic and paid reach

- ▸ Overall engagement levels
- ▸ Engagement levels broken down into likes, comments, and shares
- ▸ Per-post engagement levels
- ▸ Quality and quantity of leads generated
- ▸ Website referral traffic from Facebook

Twitter

Metrics you'll want to monitor carefully on Twitter include:

- ▸ Follower count and growth/decline
- ▸ Number of retweets
- ▸ Number of mentions
- ▸ Quality and quantity of leads generated
- ▸ Website referral traffic from Twitter

Google+

- ▸ Number of circles you're in
- ▸ Total circle followers
- ▸ Followers of your business page
- ▸ Google author stats
- ▸ PageRank of your Google+ page
- ▸ Post engagement: total shares, comments and +1's your posts have received
- ▸ Quality and quantity of leads generated
- ▸ Website referral traffic from Google

When you have decided which metrics you'll be monitoring, it's important that you plan how often you'll evaluate the results. Set up regular appointments to sit down with your social media staff or consultants to evaluate what's working and what's not.

How to Make Decisions Based on Your Results

While it's critical to have a clear understanding of your social media results, it's equally important to know how these findings will impact your business decisions. Part of your social media strategy will be figuring out what actions you'll take based on your discoveries.

For instance, seeing that your total number of Facebook fans is in decline is one thing, but what actions will you take to counteract this? Or seeing that your Klout score is going up can feel good, but how will your business and content marketing decisions be impacted by this knowledge?

Keep in mind that your results should be helping you gauge whether you're meeting both your high-level goals and your specific goals. For instance, if your business goal is to improve customer satisfaction, you will want to find a way to measure positive sentiment of your brand. One way to specifically measure this could be to monitor and keep track of brand mentions cross-platform.

Some decisions that may become necessary as a result of your analytics monitoring may include:

▶ Creating different formats of content that your audience will prefer

▶ Promoting content more or less frequently

▶ Segmenting social media followers to ensure a better quality of referral traffic to your site

▶ Spending more time and money on the networks that are performing well

▶ Learning how to create content that increases engagement

Plan Adjustments

Chances are good that despite your best efforts, there will come a time when you'll need to make some adjustments to your social media strategy. If you reach a point where it becomes clear that what you're doing just isn't working, it's time to make some changes.

It's important to know both *when* to revisit your strategy and *what changes* need to be made to get things working properly. Adjusting your plan shouldn't be seen as a sign of weakness, but should be celebrated as a sign of a company that is flexible enough to keep up with emerging trends and discoveries.

As mentioned earlier, set aside specific times when you will sit down to evaluate how your strategy is working and whether any changes need to be made. Ensure that anyone who is involved with your social media efforts are included in these meetings to give input and to make sure everyone is on the same page.

Conclusion

Now more than ever, businesses need to be intentional about how they're using social media, and actively pursue strategies that help them reach their business goals. This is what will set them apart from companies that use social media on the fly. Having a strong plan in place will ensure you're allocating your valuable resources—your time, money, and staff—in ways that are helping you achieve the best possible return on your investment.

CHAPTER 5

The No-Baloney Essentials of Content Marketing That Work

Sonia Simone

SONIA SIMONE was a founding partner of Copyblogger Media when it formed in 2010, and serves as the company's chief marketing officer and publisher of the Copyblogger blog. She has a long background in traditional marketing, both with startups and in more established corporate environments. She's also a longtime veteran of social media (she first got online in 1989), and as the content marketing revolution is evolving, she's finding that her once "weird" ideas are becoming mainstream. For information, visit: www.copyblogger.com/author/sonia.

In this Chapter, You'll Discover

► Why you must produce content that creates an emotional connection with your audience

► What to do if your business is "boring"

► How to structure content to pave the way to a sale

► The three most important types of marketing content and how they work together

► The "dying" content medium that's an essential component of your marketing program

A Baloney-Free Approach to Content Marketing

For all the buzz around content marketing, we have to face facts: It confuses an awful lot of people.

Some marketers think of it as "really good advertising," the kind of remarkable ads that Coca-Cola or Apple has been producing for decades.

Some think that "content marketing" means you can't ever sell anything. (Why any business agrees to this is beyond me, but I've heard highly paid consultants spouting this as gospel.)

Some think it's new. (It isn't.)

Some think it's only applicable to the internet. (It isn't, but the web is an unsurpassed delivery mechanism for content.)

Content marketing is the most interesting elephant in marketing these days, and we have no shortage of blind men explaining to us how it works.

Maybe you'll benefit from the definition I use. It's practical, simple, and focused.

> *Content marketing is the strategic creation of text, imagery, audio, or video that delivers a relevant, interesting message to a customer or prospect, while at the same time paving the way for a sale.*

Content marketing doesn't necessarily need to be complicated or difficult, but it *does* require that certain elements be firing on all cylinders to make it work. Let's talk about what those elements are.

All Communication Is Marketing

Let's start with one of my core principles: Everything your business communicates is a form of marketing.

Of course, your advertising, blog, and public relations are marketing.

But the way your employees talk with customers is also marketing. And because of that, the way you communicate with your employees becomes marketing.

The way you treat your suppliers is marketing, as is the integrity of your supply chain.

Everything you say and do communicates something. And all of that comes together to form a complex and subtle message; one that can either attract and sway potential customers, or repel and anger them.

Every forum post and Facebook remark. Every gripe an employee makes to a family member. Every move that someone driving a company truck makes in traffic.

This can be pretty overwhelming. But it's also kind of exhilarating.

So when we set that into the context of your content marketing, we start to see that it's about more than a blog post or a piece of native advertising. It's about a nuanced, layered message that's created and refined over time.

If everything you say and do is marketing (both positive marketing, which builds your company, and negative marketing, which tears it down), content marketing is a way to build more assets in the Positive category. It's a way to produce what people want (interesting, useful content) instead of producing what they shun (intrusive, arrogant, or clumsy advertising).

It also *shows* (rather than tells) potential customers that you're the right choice to solve their problems.

Let's talk about some of the ways we can recognize content marketing that's on the right track.

Good Content Moves the Audience

We might as well tackle the hard one first.

Good content is inherently worth reading, listening to, or watching. It delivers an enjoyable experience for the audience.

It's entertaining. It might make the audience laugh, or cry, or stand up in righteous outrage, but it must *move* them in some meaningful way.

That's why the old-fashioned "keyword stuffed" verbiage that was optimized for SEO does not qualify as effective content marketing. (You should know that it no longer qualifies as effective SEO, either.)

Quality content must be a pleasure to consume. The smart content marketer thinks in terms of an audience, rather than "prospects" or "leads."

> *The audience does not owe you their attention.*
> *It is your job as a content marketer to*
> *deserve their attention.*

One of the greatest challenges for companies is fighting an internal attitude of entitlement that any and all information about your product or service will fascinate your audience.

Your CEO may believe that the founding story of the company is riveting. Your brand manager may believe that getting the right Pantone value for your blog header is more important than telling a story the audience cares about.

It takes courage and commitment to produce content that meets the audience's needs first, rather than satisfying egos within the company. But without that commitment, you're dead in the water.

What to Do If Your Business Is Boring

Businesses often come back with, "Our industry just isn't interesting, it's impossible to write about in an interesting way."

I'm sorry to be the one to deliver the bad news, but this is laziness.

I think we can safely assume that 100 percent of your potential customers are human beings. (Even if they happen to be organized into these large, irrational groupings called *companies*.)

Human beings enjoy stories. They have a sense of humor. (It might be different from your sense of humor, but they do have one.) They worry. They get excited. They get angry.

If your product is technical, find an engineer who also loves to write (they're out there) to create your content. Engineering humor is a beautiful, if rarely understood, thing.

If you have a consumer-oriented service business like plumbing or air conditioning, find a writer who also does stand-up comedy, and ask her to study what's driving your customers crazy about your competition. A good writer will be able to work up a funny, engaging ten-minute monologue without much trouble on what most of those other guys do badly—and that's great content.

When you're looking for content creators, you need people who are artists first. Artists devote themselves to moving other human beings. If you can't deliver that, none of the rest of it can work. But every topic, however "boring," can find it. Some just take more work than others.

The Power of Metaphors and Analogies

Sometimes, the answer is to link your topic with something more interesting, in the form of a metaphor, example, or analogy.

For example, this is an introduction to a post I wrote about the phenomenon of digital sharecropping:

> *We have a great bookstore in my town—the kind of place you picture in your mind when you think of a great independent bookshop.*
>
> *It's perfect for browsing, with lots of comfy chairs to relax in. The books are displayed enticingly. There's a little coffee shop so you can relax with an espresso. They get your favorite writers to come in for readings, so there's always a sense of event and excitement.*
>
> *They do everything right, and they've always had plenty of customers.*
>
> *But they still closed their doors last year.*
>
> *No, not for the reasons you might think. It wasn't Amazon that killed them, or the proliferation of free content on the web, or the crappy economy.*
>
> *They closed the store because they were leasing their big, comfortable building . . . and when that lease ran out, their landlord tripled the rent.*

Literally overnight, their business model quit working. Revenues simply wouldn't exceed costs. A decision made by another party, one they had no control over, took a wonderful business and destroyed it.

And that's precisely what you risk every day you make your business completely dependent on another company.

This intro uses traditional storytelling techniques (conflict, detail, dramatic tension) to bring the reader in, then segues into the primary topic. Metaphor, analogy, and storytelling are potent weapons in your war on boring content.

Great Content Is Structured

Throughout this chapter, you're going to see me talk about writers. You need writers even if your content is primarily video or audio. That's because even what looks like "freeform" content needs a solid, well-crafted structure if it's going to work well.

Your charismatic CEO may want to fire up his iPhone and record a rambling 20-minute conversation that he calls "content."

And if your charismatic CEO has the communication skills of a Richard Branson, it might work. A few people have a strong innate sense for the structure of effective communication.

The rest of us mortals are going to need at least a loose script.

Not every script is verbatim; some companies can create compelling content with an outline. But you need to be sure that all of your content is structured to solve a customer problem in an engaging way. And that isn't likely to happen if you just wing it.

Effective content is structured with:

- ▸ A headline that instantly commands audience attention
- ▸ An introductory few sentences that pull the audience in, making it tough to turn away
- ▸ Useful information that solves a problem the audience genuinely cares about
- ▸ A single, focused point or "moral" to communicate
- ▸ Stories, metaphors, or examples to teach that point

▶ A call to action at the conclusion that rouses the audience to take the next step

> *Remember that old, politically incorrect Mad Men-era advice about how long your content should be: Like a skirt, it needs to be short enough to maintain attention, and long enough to cover the subject.*

If you don't get likes and shares, if Google suddenly hates you, or if your traffic tends to bounce like a Super Ball, you have to take a hard look at the possibility your content just isn't as good as it needs to be.

And how can you tell if your content is worth consuming? Content is worth consuming if people consume it.

You don't decide. The audience decides.

That means you watch what gets the most traffic, the most links, the most social shares, and the most comments. Keep trying new and creative approaches, and observe the results carefully. Do more of what works, and less of what doesn't work.

You either create content worth reading (or watching, or listening to, if you're doing multimedia) or you don't. Anyone who tells you otherwise is slowing you down and will lead you to failure.

A Note on Working with Writers

The larger your organization, the trickier it will be for you to work with talented writers. Like many types of creatives, they tend to march to their own drummer, and don't always fit comfortably within "big-organization" structures and culture.

It can also be difficult to find someone who excels at both the *art* of moving the audience and the *craft* of working within a solid marketing framework.

We maintain a list of certified content writers at Copyblogger. com, if you're looking for a qualified content professional. We also publish lots of highly talented guest writers, many who are available to work with clients.

And if you have a smart "artist" on your team who needs some help with the marketing side of things, we have free materials to help bring them up to speed. The site features free ebooks on writing better headlines, how to structure content, SEO copywriting, and other crucial content marketing topics.

Craft Your Cornerstone

In order to create a content marketing platform (as opposed to just publishing a bunch of stuff you find interesting), you need to understand your cornerstone.

The cornerstone of your platform comes from what interests and engages your audience.

To begin crafting your cornerstone, you need to know what kinds of important customer problems your business is designed to solve. If you're familiar with copywriting, these are the benefits of doing business with you.

> ▸ The **features** of your product or service are *what it does* and *what goes into it*. The dimensions, horsepower, ingredients, and so forth.
> ▸ The **benefits** are *what the product or service does for the customer*; what they get out of the experience.

Your company exists to make customers happier, more confident, healthier, better connected with their family, more successful, wiser, less anxious, or some other wonderful benefit. All effective marketing communication needs to come around to the benefits, and not just the features, of the product.

For a brand-new content marketing program, start with 10 or more posts that really encapsulate your company's fundamental beliefs and values about your topic. (These can be text, audio, video, or a mix of formats. The right format is the one that your audience prefers.)

Think about what you would want every single reader of your site to know about. And focus on educational content that solves a few simple prospect problems relating to your business.

If you've been creating content for a while but your site lacks focus, look through your most popular material and pull your best individual efforts into a series of well-focused content landing pages.

A content landing page is simply a page on your site that aggregates your best material on a particular topic. Write a great intro that pulls the audience in, and end with a call to action to connect more strongly with your business. (Very often, this means subscribing to a permission-based email list.)

These solidly useful pages are a great place to focus your SEO copywriting efforts, because audiences love them and they naturally tend to attract links and social sharing.

Your "cornerstone" content will help you start to build strong relationships with the people who can eventually become your customers. It does this by educating them on how to begin to solve the problems that matter to them.

(At Copyblogger we focus on what we call the "Benefits of Knowledge": everything your audience will be able to do, become, or attain as a result of what your content has taught them.)

Attraction Content Builds a Wider Audience

Now you've got to find readers for that content, which means you'll create content that's specifically designed to attract and widen your audience.

Attraction content is typically where you'll put most of your daily effect in your content marketing program. It's the regular blog posts, the YouTube videos, the podcasts.

Because this content is all about getting the attention of an audience that isn't familiar with you yet, you'll need to bring your best headline-writing skills into play. Content that attracts attention also tends to have a strong, well-defined point of view: This is no place for wimpy, wishy-washy messages.

While your cornerstone content tends to lean a little more in the direction of usefulness and education, your attraction content will lean more toward entertainment and fun. You still want to be useful, but you *must* be entertaining, or at least interesting.

A little controversy can be good for attracting new readers, as long as you don't fall into the trap of seeking attention for its own sake. (Yes, there is such a thing as negative publicity. No one wants to do business with a train wreck.)

This is where you'll probably do the most experimentation. Try new formats, alternate long-form with short-form, and try out different venues. Take some risks.

Above all: Don't be boring.

Send Your Audience to Focused Action Pages

Cornerstone content educates your audience, teaches them what they need to know in order to do business with you. Attraction content builds a wider audience for your cornerstone.

The final step is action content: focused landing pages that take your traffic and translate it into the action you desire. That action might be signing up for your email list, or registering to vote, or buying a product, or visiting a brick-and-mortar location.

Every business or organization must define these actions, based on your organizational goals.

Each landing page focuses on one and only one desired action. Remove sidebars and other distractions—this isn't the place for them. And make sure that every link on the landing page goes to that one well-defined action.

Landing pages call for a more experienced professional, persuasive copywriter, so this is a good place to bring someone in if you don't have a resource in-house who has strong landing/sales page experience.

Take the Relationship Further with this "Dying" Content Medium

One of the most useful calls to action for your content is to sign up for a permission-based (also called "opt-in") email list. This allows you to keep delivering additional useful content, and to nurture the relationship with the prospect or lead until she is ready to buy.

"Permission-based" means that you will *entice* your prospect to join your email list, rather than buying lists of email addresses. The painful truth is, you simply cannot buy your audience's attention. Sending email to addresses that you've bought, rather than earned, will gain you little more than spam complaints.

You earn the right to that attention by creating interesting attraction content and leading the audience from there to your useful, problem-solving cornerstone content. At that point, you've shown that you can deliver useful, interesting, relevant information that the prospect would like to see more of.

A few social media "gurus" dismiss email as ineffective, because it's so often used poorly.

Your useful, interesting, relevant content does not stop with your email list. The bulk of your email messages need to continue to earn prospect attention and loyalty. Yes, you will send offers to your email list, but most of your messages will focus on delivering value with content.

Most larger businesses don't earn permission to email, and most of them deliver virtually no value in their email content—only offers to make a purchase. If your commitment to high-quality content ends when the prospect has been added to an email list, 95 percent of your work has been wasted.

Email has shown itself in study after study to be the most cost-effective final mile to the sale. Give it the attention it deserves. Shortchanging your email content is like giving up a marathon at mile 25.

Hope to See You Again!

For much more information than I can possibly share in a single chapter, I invite you to swing by the Copyblogger blog. It's devoted to keeping you up to date on content marketing strategies, techniques, news, and inspiration. We publish five days a week, and you can find us at www.copyblogger.com.

Hope to see you there!

CHAPTER 6

Website Conversion
Turning Strangers into Customers

Mitch Meyerson

MITCH MEYERSON is an entrepreneur, speaker, trainer, and author of 11 books, including *Mastering Online Marketing*. He has also co-created four online programs, including The Guerrilla Marketing Coach Certification Program and The World Class Speaking Coach Certification Program. For more information visit www. MasteringOnlineMarketing.com.

▲ ▲ ▲

In this Chapter, You'll Discover

▶ What website optimization is and why is it so important

▶ Why people choose one business over another

▶ Five key steps to increase conversions on your website

▶ Why marketing and selling is a process much like dating

▶ How you can improve what you measure

Not long ago, I received an email from the Small Business Development Center in the Virgin Islands. It went something like this:

*Good Day Mitch, I found your book and explored your website.
So let me get to the point . . . Can we fly you to St. Thomas and St.
Croix to be our keynote speaker and trainer for the week?*

During a subsequent phone conversation with one of the principal organizers at the business center, I knew right away that I didn't need to sell myself to close the deal. Someone at the Small Business Development Center in the Virgin Islands had researched my products and services on my website. What they saw had even sealed the deal! All I had to do was say yes and book my flights.

▲ ▲ ▲

The story I have just shared is a perfect illustration of the power of the internet and a website that does its job. With the information in this chapter, I will help you optimize your website so you can enjoy results like these (although, unfortunately, I can't guarantee you'll get a trip to the Virgin Islands from any of what I am about to share, but you never know).

Before we begin, let me also first say something about the title of this chapter. As you can see, it has the word *conversion* featured quite prominently. But I don't really like this word. I never have. For one thing, it is very impersonal. It also seems to define people as objects to convert. I don't think such a perspective is at all helpful.

I use it, however, to illustrate that online marketing is a process of conversion—a process of turning a complete stranger into a warm prospect, then into a paying customer, and finally into a raving fan. And that is exactly what we are about to discuss in this chapter.

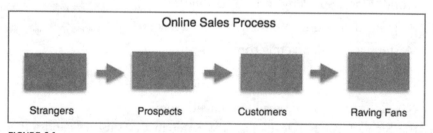

FIGURE 6.1

Optimize Your Site Before Generating Traffic

Over the past 15 years, I have consulted with many businesses as they have prepared to go online. Time and time again, their first question is this: *How do I get more traffic?*

It is a logical question and, yes, we all want traffic but consider this:

If you send traffic to your website before it is ready, your new visitors may experience some of these difficulties:

- ▶ Navigation that is confusing and frustrates your visitors
- ▶ Broken links and sub-par graphics that destroy confidence
- ▶ Copy, audio, or video content is bland, boring, or just unfocused
- ▶ No clear sense of what you want them to do—no call to action for them to follow

If any of these things happen on your website, your hard-won visitors probably won't join your mailing list and they will hesitate to purchase your products or services. Worst of all, your visitors won't think twice about avoiding your site (and your brand) in the future.

Such is the reality of the online world. First impressions count and you have one chance to make them. That means you need to do it right and you need to do it fast. If you don't, there's every chance that your competitors will.

> *First impressions count and you have only one chance to make them.*

Now that we have held up the caution sign, let's discuss some of the ways you can optimize your website to make sure your prospects and customers feel *interested, engaged, and compelled to take action.*

What Do You Want Your Visitors to Do?

To have a profitable online business, you need to get your customer to do five crucial things when they visit your site:

- ▶ Read, listen to, or view your content.

▶ Share your content with others.

▶ Opt in to your mailing list.

▶ Learn more about your products and/or services.

▶ Feel comfortable purchasing from you.

For any of these to happen, you need to help your visitors *know, like, and trust you*. And to do this in a competitive online marketplace, you must help your customers feel *confident* in you and your company.

Five Confidence-Building Tips

The good news is that confidence can be built and strategies for it abound. The most important ones are outlined for you below.

1. Give Your Website a Professional Look and Easy Navigation

This may seem obvious (it really should *be* obvious), but so many people forget this golden rule. Consider how many times you have visited a site and left it in less than 10 seconds simply because of the way it looked.

While there are many ways to cut costs on the internet, my suggestions is to spend a few extra dollars on a quality website or graphic designer. Your conversion rates will increase dramatically if you have a well-crafted website. Visitors will assess you and your business as confident, competent, experienced, and authentic. And they will apply the same estimation to your products and services.

Remember to keep your navigation simple and ensure your visitors understand exactly what to do and where to find any information they might need.

To assess the navigation of your website, ask yourself whether you have the following:

▶ A clear call to action (we will discuss this in more detail later)

▶ Clear navigation links that lead to relevant and useful content

▶ An easily located opt-in box with an enticing free offer

▶ A clear path to your products and services as well as your "about" page

> "Make it simple. Make it memorable. Make it
> inviting to look at. Make it fun to read."
> —Leo Burnett

Once you have created or updated your website so that it instills confidence, it's time to let visitors experience what you offer.

2. Let Visitors Sample Your Cookies

Have you ever walked into a shopping center and passed a cookie shop? Have you noticed that cookie shops love to give away free samples? If you are like most people, you grab a sample when you see it—especially if it's a free cookie. If it's a really good cookie, too, you turn around and head back over to the store like Cookie Monster himself, right? "Me want more cookie!" This is the power of a great free sample!

Remember my story about the email from the Virgin Islands? When the director of *Small Business Week* in St. Thomas visited my site at MasteringOnlineMarketing.com, looking for a speaker, essentially she "ate the cookies on my site." My cookies (free samples) included the following:

1. A well-crafted video of me on stage on a six-city speaking tour for *Entrepreneur* magazine (building confidence in my speaking ability and credibility)
2. Three free downloadable audios of me training students on important online marketing topics (showing my skills in online marketing education)
3. Dozens of well-written how-to articles on marketing as well as content from my books (further building trust and confidence)
4. She was also able to opt in to my mini course and receive my enewsletter (giving her automated content over time)

In effect, she *knew me before she ever spoke with me.* This is the beauty of the internet, and this is exactly what you want to do with your website as well.

Here are some questions to ponder.

- ▸ How can you add more valuable free content to your site?
- ▸ Can you transfer your written content to other media like audio and video?
- ▸ Can you chunk down articles to smaller bite-size bits to share on social media?

The more visitors can experience you through various forms of media on your website, the quicker they will know, like, and trust you. The quicker they will want to do business with you, too. Your content needs to be well crafted, valuable, and relevant to your target audience.

3. Build More Confidence through Testimonials and Social Proof

Social proof is much more effective than tooting your own horn when it comes to promoting buyer activity. It helps, in other words, to have evidence of satisfied customers. And this can be easier than you think.

Ask some of your satisfied customers to write a short testimonial for your website. Assuming they are happy with what they bought from you, most customers will do this quite gladly. Ask your customers to be specific about what they valued and ask them to show results. A picture adds the personal touch as well (see Figure 6.2).

In the past few years, many businesses have also included audio and video testimonials. These can work, too, but make sure they are well presented.

I'm so glad that I enrolled for the Guerrilla Marketing Coach Certification class. I was amazed to look at my books and realize that my business has grown 300% in the 12 weeks that we have met! "

Don Lawler, Certified Guerrilla Marketing Coach

FIGURE 6.2

4. Sell the Result

Never underestimate how much people care about their own problems first, last, and always. In fact, for the moment, set aside any notion that people care about how great your company is.

People want to know how your product and services will *solve their problem* and they want to know why your solution is better than what everyone else offers.

What this means is that you must clearly define the benefits of your products and services for your target audience. What result do your audience members want to obtain?

To do this, put yourself in your prospects' shoes. Imagine what it is that they are trying to do. Why do they want what you have? How are they going to use it and why is it the best solution for their problems?

If you listen to your customers, you'll know the answer to these questions and more.

> People want to know how your product and services will solve their problem and they want to know why your solution is better than what everyone else offers.

People purchase things for one of two reasons. Either they want to increase pleasure (e.g., glowing health, freedom, popularity) or they want to decrease pain (e.g., stress, financial problems, poor health). It's remarkably simple when you think about it.

So when communicating with your customers, emphasize the most compelling benefits (or results) of your products and services. Then make sure you deliver on your promises.

Take a few minutes to list the most unique and desirable benefits about your products and services. Use Figure 6.3 on page 74 as a guide. Tune in to their favorite radio station: WIIFM—What's in it for me?

Turning Features into Benefits

Features	Benefits (Results)
Driver airbags	Feeling of safety and security
Ergonomic chair	Relieves lower back pain
Drill bit	Creates holes to help you complete your project
Travel agency	Feel more relaxed, get re-energized, rekindle romance, have fun
Online coaching	Save money on travel, learn from comfort of your home or office, avoid airport hassle

FIGURE 6.3

Answer these questions:

▸ What are the top three to five results my customers really want to achieve?
▸ How are my offerings different from my competitors?

If you spent time and really drilled deep on this exercise, you have essential copy that you can use for all of your marketing (web copy, videos, elevator pitch, webinars, and more).

5. Give a Clear Call to Action

One of the biggest online marketing mistakes is not having a specific "call to action" or "next step" for a website visitor.

Once your target customer has made it to your website and sampled your cookies, make sure they know what you want them to do next. Give clear and specific directions. Be very specific about what is in it for them, but here are some sample actions you might want to encourage your customers to take:

- *Register for your webinar* that will teach them what they need to know.
- *Sign up for your Five-Part Mini Course* that shares secrets to make their life easier.
- *Call your office to set up a consultation* that will get them the service they need.
- *Press a "Buy" button to purchase your course* that makes learning a new skill easy and fun.

Another good call to action is information sharing. Make sure that you place social media "share" buttons at strategic points on your website. Encourage your customers to share information when they find something particularly interesting on your site. Some common sharing opportunities are:

- Pin this
- Tweet this
- Share this video
- Comment below

And while Facebook, LinkedIn, Twitter, Pinterest, and the like are all very helpful social media platforms, don't overpromote them on your site at the expense of having visitors sign up for your own list.

Email is a much more intimate and direct way of communicating. Email messages are also much more likely to reach their intended targets. They are more likely to actually engage those targets, too, in a way that will help you and your company.

Selling on the Web Is a Process Much Like Dating

Most every business online has the goal of making sales. But selling over the internet is not only about having a great product or service. It is also about building trust, confidence, and a human bond. Selling is really part of a larger process.

Proposing marriage on a first date? It sounds pretty ridiculous. But asking your online visitors to buy on their first visit can be as counterproductive—and businesses do it all the time.

> *Converting a web visitor to a paying customer is a lot like dating. No one in their right mind would propose marriage on a first date, yet that is exactly what most websites do by asking for the sale before first developing a relationship.*

Consider this:

- ▶ 37 percent of interested prospects take 0-3 months to become customers.
- ▶ 28 percent of interested prospects take 3-6 months to become customers.
- ▶ 18 percent of interested prospects take 6-12 months to become customers.
- ▶ 17 percent of interested prospects take more than one year to become customers.

In other words (looking at the statistics above), you have to devote some time to the conversion process. You also have to be patient. Unless you have truly exceptional copy and a killer product or service—something people absolutely cannot do without—you will need to do some work to turn your customers into buyers.

Yes, some sales page sites can actually make a sale the first time around. Such pages, though, tend to belong to established companies (think big name brands). They tend to have really exceptional copy or videos to build confidence before they make such a bold pitch. They also have a reassuring sales sequence, including these three elements: a dedicated sales page, a reassuring checkout page, and safe and secure transactions.

A Dedicated Sales Page

A sales page on your website is a **direct-response communication.** It is your opportunity for a goal-oriented conversation with the intended

FIGURE 6.4

end-users of your products or services. Ideally, it should contain a clear and direct offer and an invitation to take one or more specific actions.

Like your sales copy, your graphics should also contain a strong call to action, as demonstrated in Figure 6.4. This can be achieved using devices such as noticeable "purchase" buttons (e.g., "Buy Now" or "Order Now") placed strategically throughout the site.

A Reassuring Checkout Page

Industry experts estimate that a large number of online shoppers abandon a shopping cart before their purchase is completed. To avoid this happening, make sure your order page is consistent. Make sure it is branded with your logo and other identifying elements. It should present wording and graphics to reaffirm purchases, make clear what should be done next, and, above all, reassure your customers.

Evidence That You Offer an Easy, Safe, and Secure Transaction

People are more likely to hand over their money when they perceive the risk as minimal. It's best to reassure potential customers with robust guarantees, a solid privacy policy, and secure payment procedures.

A good way to improve your sales pages is to visit your competitors and see what they are doing. You will notice that over the past few years, web pages have become simpler and often integrate videos to accommodate their visitors' shorter attention span. See what elements of their sales process you want to model and add it to yours. And keep in mind that the web is always changing. Having a strong and effective web presence means always adapting, growing, and improving.

Measuring Your Progress

No matter how well you set up your site and create your strategy, there's always room for improvement. There are lots of measurement metrics you can analyze (many can be found with a simple Google search), but for the purpose of this chapter, let's keep it simple. You should be asking (and answering) several key questions to begin with:

▶ How many visitors come to my website? From where? How long do they stay?
▶ How many of my emails are opened? Is my subject line engaging enough?
▶ How many visitors opt in to my email list? Is my offer relevant and exciting?
▶ How many people click on the buy buttons? Where did they hear about us?
▶ What is my visitor value?

Why do you need to know these numbers and answer the questions above? Simply put, *you can't improve what you don't measure.*

Even if you are getting some sales, unless you are tracking how many visitors come to your site, how many people visit your page, and how long visitors look at your page, you won't know much about why people are buying from you. You also won't know much about the effectiveness of your sales copy and the other elements outlined in this chapter that are important to your website's quality.

Remember that headlines, bullet points, and other elements of website design and content are easy to change. And if your copy is a little off, if you haven't quite got your benefits outlined properly, if you haven't got the most eye-catching headlines set up to engage your customers, a few tweaks can affect your conversion rates quite dramatically.

If you don't keep track of your visitors, though, you'll never know what you should keep doing and what you should stop doing to build better relationships via your website.

Second, you think about how your *strategic partners* will use your sales. Most of the time, they will use your sales figures to help them decide whether or not they are willing to promote your products and services. If you have a good conversion rate, you can easily persuade strategic partners that you have a product or service that people want. Indeed, a good conversion rate shows you have just that.

Third, to know what you can reasonably spend on a *pay-per-click campaign*, you need to know how much one visitor is worth, and you risk losing your shirt if you don't get this information right!

The formula for calculating your average visitor value is as follows:

Price of the Product x Number of Sales / Number of Visitors = Average Visitor Value

The following is a straightforward example of how it might look for you. Let's assume the following is true:

▶ You offer only one product for sale
▶ Each sells for $97
▶ On average, you sell two products for every 100 visitors (2 percent conversion rate)

Therefore, your average visitor value is $1.94.
Here's why:

$$(\$97 \times 2) = \$194 / (100) = \$1.94$$

Clearly, you need to know this before you invest in pay-per-click campaigns, or you could end up spending more per click than you earn.

To Wrap Things Up

To end this chapter, I would like to put my coaching hat on and ask you some more questions.

Your Website

1. What is the purpose of your website?
2. What exactly do you want visitors to do when they arrive there?
3. Do you have a way of capturing their contact information? What could be a strong incentive for them doing that?
4. Given the content in this chapter what can you do to increase your conversions?

Now, use the scoring sheet in Figure 6.5 to score your website on a scale of 1 to 10 (10 meaning very strong) and then ask yourself what can be improved. There is also a column to get objective feedback from a partner. As I already suggested, you should make a point of visiting your

8 Keys To Optimizing Your Website	Your Score 1-10	Partner 1-10
1. Professional Look (layout/graphics/loading)		
2. Easy and Effective Navigation		
3. Build Confidence Through Testimonials		
4. Sell The Result (Relevant Benefits)		
5. Have A Clear Call To Action		
6. Social Media Integration		
7. SEO Keywords (title/headers/copy)		
8. Multimedia: Audio and Video		

FIGURE 6.5 **Eight Keys to Optimizing Your Website** (excerpted from the Guerrilla Marketing Coach Certification Program [Gmarketingcoach.com])

competitors' websites as you are working on yours. Make notes on what your competitors are doing better than you, and use your competitors' efforts as models (be influenced but never plagiarize).

To make sure you see what your audience does, too:

- ▶ Always check your website on two to three browsers.
- ▶ View your sites on smartphones and tablets. Make your sites mobile responsive as more people will be viewing sites from these devices in the future.

If you dig deep into the questions in this chapter and consider the points discussed here, you should know how well you are engaging your visitors (or how likely you are to engage them) on your website. You should also have some ideas on how you can improve your site to improve conversions.

At the end of the day, conversions are actually pretty simple. Simple isn't always easy. You are competing with a wealth of other online businesses that go around bombarding your prospects with offers and marketing messages. You have to be intentional, savvy, and very meticulous with every decision you make for your website. You have to be very deliberate about how you develop your headlines, copy, graphics, videos, and social media connections.

The more thought you put into these elements, though, the more persistently you monitor your site metrics, the more likely you are to see a positive conversion rate and compelling sales numbers. Who knows, you might even get invited to share your expertise overseas. You never know.

CHAPTER 7

The Shift to Visual Social Media

How to Create Visual Content that People Love to Share

Donna Moritz

DONNA MORITZ is the founder of Socially Sorted and winner of the Best Business Blog in Australia 2014. She helps businesses, bloggers, and entrepreneurs use visual social media and content strategy to get more reach, referrals, and results in their business. Donna is a contributor to Entrepreneur online, Social Media Examiner, and Social Fresh and has been featured in *Forbes*, NBC, and Yahoo!. Her infographics have been published on some of the world's top websites and her creative approach to marketing earned her a listing in Australia's Top 100 Cool Company Awards in 2013 by Anthill Online.

▲ ▲ ▲

It was the 2013 Super Bowl and the lights went out at the Superdome. The game stopped. The San Francisco 49ers, Baltimore Ravens, and all of their fans were left in the dark. Attention around the world turned to social media, and in particular, Twitter. In just a few minutes, the team at Oreo— guided by their savvy agency, 360i—designed and tweeted an image for fans arriving at Twitter. It consisted of a single, lonely Oreo cookie on a darkened background, and the simple words "You can still dunk in the dark."

The Oreo Blackout Tweet went down in history as one of the most talked about pieces of content on the internet. "Power out? No problem" it said. Brands that had invested $3.8 million in a 30-second advertising spot looked on as a single image, perfectly conceived, was retweeted more than 10,000 times in just the first hour alone. Many of the 10,000 retweets went out before the lights came back on in the stadium. Those same brands looking on, no doubt cringed as the image went on to make headlines around the world in over 100 countries. Just one tweet, impeccably timed, earned Oreo 525 million impressions around the world without paying for one single media dollar.

Of course you may have heard this story, but it is one that bears repeating. Here I am, still talking about it two years later. Why? Because the Oreo Blackout Tweet was the perfect storm of visual content perfection—it was original, optimized, relevant, snackable, and timely. It was perfectly shareable.

With just one image, on a platform known for rapid-fire text conversations of 140 characters, Oreo showcased a new way of communicating. They highlighted the shift toward visual content and visual communication. Terms like *visual social media* are no longer a new trend but rather part of our vocabulary, especially when platforms like Twitter get results like this with a single image. As I write this chapter, nearly every social platform has become image-centric. Welcome to the *visual web*.

Why Visual Content Is So Powerful

Why do images attract us? It's simple. As humans, we are hard-wired to connect emotionally with images from the moment we are born. Early peoples didn't write. They drew pictures on cave walls. It's in our DNA. And as consumers, we are drawn to visual content. We process it faster than any other medium. Faster than text. Faster than video. Faster than audio. In fact, a recent MIT study showed that it takes just 13 milliseconds for the human eye to process an image—almost eight times faster than previously thought.

Given how rapidly we process images, it's not surprising that on social platforms, consumers are craving visual content that helps them to rapidly filter out the noise. They are engaging with images that attract their attention, entertain and provide value, while skipping over content that doesn't. Do you want people to notice and emotionally connect with your content, and to take action on it? Then you need to be creating quality visual content, especially images.

The Shift to Visual Social Media—How and Why It Happened

How did we go from communicating in words to speaking in pictures on sites like Pinterest and Instagram? The "Visual Shift" has happened progressively. Websites went from static to dynamic in the mid-to-late '90s as **blogging** became hugely popular with its longer, text-based articles. From there we discovered the status update on Facebook and Twitter. Our conversations got shorter by **microblogging**. All platforms (including blogs) started to become more visual, and images were showcased everywhere.

The shift from *tell* to *show* continued with the advent of visually rich sites like Tumblr and its fast-moving visual newsfeed, while YouTube delivered engaging video. We were **multimedia microblogging** and loving any medium that allowed the rapid, visual transfer of information in entertaining formats.

It was inevitable that we would reach a point where we are communicating in pictures on platforms like Instagram and Pinterest, where no words are necessary, and a picture really is worth a thousand words. These image-based social platforms have grown at exceptional rates. Pictures may tell a powerful story, but the numbers do, too:

- ▶ Pinterest became the second largest driver of traffic from all social networks in late 2013.
- ▶ Six billion hours of YouTube videos are viewed monthly. (There are only seven billion people in the entire world!)
- ▶ Instagram had gained 200 million users by early 2014, and continues to grow exponentially now that it is owned by and integrated with Facebook.
- ▶ Facebook reports over 350 million photos uploaded daily, while 400 million images are shared daily via Snapchat (more than Facebook and Instagram combined).

The power of visuals is not just restricted to image-centric platforms like Pinterest and Instagram. Even networks like LinkedIn and Twitter are evolving to showcase visual content. LinkedIn acquired SlideShare, and its Professional Portfolio allows you to showcase images, videos, infographics, and presentations on your profile, and Twitter shows images by default on the newsfeed.

> *Every social platform is becoming more image-centric.*

What should brands and marketers expect when they start to use more visual content? The possibilities speak for themselves:

- ▶ Tweets with images uploaded to Twitter are nearly twice as likely to be retweeted.
- ▶ Photos on Facebook generate 53 percent more likes and 104 percent more comments than the average post.
- ▶ Instagram has up to ten times greater user engagement than other platforms like Facebook and Twitter.

As consumers continue to find new ways to cope with the onslaught of information online, communicating with them visually makes sense. Creating original, optimized visual content should be a priority if you want to reach more people with your message and drive traffic to websites, products, and services.

The Visual Content Continuum

There's a big difference between posting just any image up on social media, and posting an image that *grabs attention* and gets results.

Reach will put eyeballs on your content, but unless you grab the attention of those eyeballs, your image (and message) will just pass on by—no matter what social platform you are on.

Figure 7.1 on page 88 shows a simple continuum that starts by attracting attention with your visual content and finishes with advocacy for your brand. Each part of the continuum can be applied to all types of visual content, including images, photos, short videos, gifs, infographics, and slide presentations.

The Three Stages of the Visual Content Continuum

1. *Eyeballs on your visual content*—having people "see" your content is worth nothing unless your content catches the *attention* of the person who sees it.
2. *Engagement with your visual content*—images must entice someone to take *action* in some way, whether it be to like, comment, share, retweet, +1, click-through to your website, products and services, or become a customer.
3. *Evangelism of your brand message.* If fans are passionate about your brand's message, they will be inspired to share your visual content. When fans evangelize your message, they show true *advocacy* for your business.

As in the famous Oreo example, there are many elements that combine to make an image shareable. Each element plays a part on this continuum. Evangelism of your brand is what every business should aspire to when creating and sharing visual content. You can

FIGURE 7.1

have success at any point along this continuum, but true viral sharing and brand advocacy is where real reach, referrals, and results happen.

The Five Essential Elements of a Shareable Image

Images are more likely to gain attention, entice your community to take action and inspire brand advocacy if they accomplish one or more of these five goals: originality, timeliness, relevance, "snackability," and drives traffic.

1. It's Original

Have you ever noticed how we will gloss over an image that we have seen previously online, but stop dead at a new graphic or photo like it's a piece of hot gossip? We love things that are new, shiny, or different, and we love to share. It's the basis of storytelling and we've been doing this for thousands of years.

You may have heard of the statistic about Pinterest, where 80 percent of content is shared content or "repins." If you look at other social networks, such as Facebook, the ratio of original to shared content is similar. People love to share new content, especially new visual content. How can you get *your* content in the 20 percent being shared by 80 percent of us? The answer is to create original images that either help or inspire your target audience.

Here are some examples of original images that prove to be highly shareable across social networks:

- *How-to images.* How-to images explain a procedure. Think of any sequence or step-by-step process that you could teach your community in image format, using diagrams, photographs, screenshots, or images. Embed these images into a blog post where they are easily shared to social platforms.

- *Quotes.* Quotes are one of the most shared pieces of visual content across social media—in any industry. Consistently posting a mix of daily quotes from people in your industry, or motivational and humorous quotes, can result in shares and engagement.

- *Tips.* What simple tips can you give to your community that will solve their problems? What are their frequently asked questions? Put the answers into a snackable image (adding text overlays) to teach what you know!

- *Checklists.* Our society is so busy and overwhelmed that we covet the quick fix, easy option, and cheat sheet. Checklists take the information we can't be bothered to find, and package it up! Create visual checklists, and your audience will snap them up and share across sites like Facebook, Google+, and Pinterest.

- *Be consistent.* The best visual content is not necessarily the image or video with the best design, typeface, or high-end editing. It's the content that is posted consistently. Successful businesses not only *create* but *curate* content for others to share—we all value quality content creators in our industry. Be the brand that produces attention-grabbing original visual content on a consistent basis. Other businesses will seek you out because *you* deliver *quality visual content* on a consistent basis that helps *their* audience.

In 2013 our client Know Your Midwife (a group of private midwives) produced a range of engaging visual tips and quotes about natural pregnancy, birth, and parenting. For a small business, these images would attract 20-100 shares on Facebook, sometimes more. Other midwives, birthing, and parenting businesses shared the images to their own Facebook page on a regular basis. Know Your Midwife had become a reliable, consistent source of great visual content. In fact, some businesses would come to their page (rather than rely on the newsfeed) to access the images. That's the power of being a visual content creator!

> Be consistent. Start by posting one image at the same time, every day on the same platform.

2. *It's Timely*

The story of the Oreo Blackout Tweet demonstrates the power of acting swiftly to post visual content in response to an event, breaking news, or celebration. Posting in real time engages fans emotionally "in the moment" of an event, inspiring them to share and take action.

Tourism Australia had faith that the world would NOT end in 2012 despite claims about the Mayan calendar. So they planned ahead and prepared their content. On the morning we all woke up alive and kicking in Australia, they posted a simple status update saying "Yes, we're alive," on Facebook, attracting hundreds of thousands of shares and likes. They followed it up with an image celebrating our survival and the words "No Worries Mate."

Both posts spread throughout the world on social channels, website, and traditional media, establishing Tourism Australia as the world's biggest destination page on Facebook. Without spending a cent, Australia gained a phenomenal amount of earned media, showcasing the country as being alive and well . . . and the perfect place for a holiday.

What if you don't have a big marketing team? The good news is that anyone can create images and post them in real time, because the tools are so user-friendly. The image in Figure 7.2 was created for Know Your Midwife to celebrate International Midwives' Day.

FIGURE 7.2

Produced using the tool PicMonkey, it was shared over 1,400 times on Facebook in a 24 hour period—from Australia to Europe and then the United States.

Why was this image shareable? It's bright to catch attention, and the quote is original and highly emotive. While I am supportive of adding a website URL or logo branding on images containing tips/ideas owned by your business, an image released to celebrate an event will often get more shares when branding is removed or minimized. *People like to share content as if it is theirs.* There are businesses out there craving new content. Give it to them. The success of visual content is less about graphic design and more about catching attention and publishing quickly so others can share.

3. It's Relevant

It's important that your visual content is tailored for the platform you are using. As Gary Vaynerchuk says, *"If we want to talk to people while they consume their entertainment, we have to actually be their entertainment."* Your images should merge seamlessly into the newsfeed experience like the content people are coming for:

- ▸ *On Facebook.* Post images that entertain and inspire your target audience while they are there to share with their friends. Don't just talk about your business, but tell a story. Inspiring quotes or funny photos do well on this platform. People want to know about people on Facebook—they are there to be entertained, not to buy.
- ▸ *On Pinterest.* Post images that are high-quality and provide "eye candy" to the user—content and products that they'll want to save and return to. People come for the social shopping experience and to dream about what is possible on Pinterest.
- ▸ *On Instagram.* Instagram is about moments in time, a backstage pass, a sneak peek into the people behind the business, not the business itself. Take your community with you using the mobile camera in your pocket. Don't be afraid to use Instagram video either—15 seconds of video is effective for entertaining time-poor people. Play with it and get creative!

Remember to think about optimizing the size, description and link on your image to make your content relevant. Image sizes vary as platforms change their dimensions—experiment with what works for you.

- ▸ On Facebook and Instagram, square-shaped images will do well.
- ▸ On Pinterest, portrait-size images (2:3 aspect ratio) get shared the most (also posting well to Facebook and Google+).
- ▸ On Twitter, landscape-size images work well (approximately 2:1 aspect ratio) and this image proportion can also work for sharing from your blog to Facebook as a linked image.

4. It's Snackable

Use small, easily processed images that provide a quick visual snapshot or preview to a larger article or infographic. When shared, snackable images stand alone to provide content. They help fans to make a quick decision about whether to engage with your brand or click through for more. Create small graphs, quotes, tips, or an image containing a small section of content from a bigger blog post or article. Snackable images are best embedded on your blog and shared from there.

5. It Drives Traffic

Once you have a person's attention, what makes them want to engage with your content? An image should provide an invitation to click—it teases and dangles the carrot with a promise of more content that is worth their time. If *you* don't know where you want fans to go, how will *they*?

- ▸ Get clear on what you want fans to do and where you want them to end up when they engage with your visual content: Engagement? Drive traffic to your website? Subscribe to your list?
- ▸ The image should speak for itself. Add back text for context or provide further information in the description.
- ▸ Add a clickable link in the description where possible.
- ▸ Aim for one main *call to action* per image.

> ▸ Always drive traffic back to your blog or website.
> ▸ Include a header image on blog posts so they can be easily pinned to Pinterest.

Tools and Strategies for Creating Images

Never before have we had access to such user-friendly, intuitive, creative tools for creating visual content. You don't need to be a designer, you don't need a lot of time, and you don't need to be creative—when you use great tools.

A complete list of tools and mobile apps for creating images "on the go" are beyond the scope of this chapter. Go online at http://sociallysorted.com.au/secrets/ for an extensive, current list of tools, plus images/references mentioned here.

Here are five essential tools for creating original visual content:

1. *Canva* (www.canva.com) is an online platform for creating designs for web and print, including a huge selection of social media and blog templates and a stock library of over a million images.
2. *PicMonkey* (www.picmonkey.com) is an image and photo-editing tool that allows you to create great images as well.
3. *Snagit* (www.snagit.com) is a tool that allows you to capture what's on your screen—images, short video—plus effects to enhance the images. Great for creating "how-to" images and step-by-step content.
4. *Over* (www.madewithover.com) is a fabulous mobile app that allows you to add text overlays to images/photographs on the go.
5. *WordSwag* (www.wordswag.co) is an app that creates beautiful design-quality custom images and typography with your words—in just minutes.

> Don't just create one image—save time by batching 10 to 20 images at once.

Bonus Tip: A Secret Weapon for Creating Original Images

I have a secret weapon for you, called "batching." You might already be using batching to create content for your blog posts, Facebook page or video account (see below). Batching involves creating more than one piece of similar content at one time:

▶ Create template backgrounds in Canva or PicMonkey. Use the template to overlay text, quotes, or tips.

▶ Collect icons, logos, or illustrations in .png format so that you can overlay them on images or photos.

Inspire Your Brand Advocates

According to Curalate, up to 85 percent of images shared to Pinterest are shared from websites by users. "This is not about developing a Pinterest strategy, or an Instagram strategy, or a Snapchat Strategy," said their CEO, Apu Gupta. "This is about learning to communicate in a new way, and understanding that on visual networks, conversations are overwhelmingly initiated by the consumer, not the brand."

Your community has the power to share more visual content from your website than you! Have a Pinterest strategy, but more importantly, have a strategy for optimizing your website to include at least one high-quality, 2:3 aspect ratio image on every page. Check what is currently being shared from your site to Pinterest—go to www. pinterest.com/source/yourwebsite.com (where you enter your website where it says "your website.com"). So, if your website is travelsecrets. com you would enter www.pinterest.com/source/travelsecrets.com.

Finding out what your community loves and shares can be very enlightening. Start thinking not in terms of what traffic is coming to your site but what those people are taking away from your site to share with the world.

How can you put your fans in the driver's seat so they can better create and share visual content about your brand?

> ▸ Build platforms they can easily contribute to and invite them to contribute and share. Tourism Australia did this by handing over the content for their Facebook and Instagram accounts to their fans in 2011. Now more than 1,000 fan photos are shared daily using the hashtag #seeaustralia.
> ▸ Help fans share when they are "in the moment." Pro Dive Cairns does this by encouraging real-time sharing on board their three-day diving tours. Their secret weapon? Wifi on every boat. Divers are encouraged to share their images and video between dives and at night.

Anyone with a smartphone is a potential content creator for your brand. Listen to your community and follow up on what lights them up—they may just want to share it with you, their friends, and the rest of the world.

Are you ready to create awesome, shareable images that help or inspire your community? Think about your marketing from a visual perspective, and in terms of visual content, and you will start to take your social media marketing to another level—one that creates emotional connections with your community, drives traffic, and achieves more reach, referrals, and results for your business.

Traffic

CHAPTER 8

How to Use Short-Form Microcontent to Amplify Your Visibility on the Web

Denise Wakeman

In this Chapter, You'll Discover

▶ The definition of microcontent and why it's important for your content marketing strategy

▶ The best type of microcontent to create for your business

▶ How to use microcontent to send traffic to your site

▶ A sample microcontent distribution plan you can adapt for your business

DENISE WAKEMAN is an online business strategist, founder of The Blog Squad and cofounder of The Future of Ink. Denise is the host of the popular Hangout show *Adventures in Visibility*, focused on helping authors and online entrepreneurs to optimize, leverage, and strategically use social marketing tools to gain visibility, build credibility, and make more money selling their products and services. Denise is passionate about travel and how it can inspire you to think bigger and go for what's possible in your business and life. For more information, visit www.DeniseWakeman.com.

Before diving into the what and how of microcontent, let's take a look at some mind-boggling statistics that are shaping the way we use and consume rich media. In their book *The Power of Visual Storytelling*, authors Ekaterina Walter and Jessica Gioglio, report that:

▶ Studies have shown that the average modern adult attention span is somewhere between 2.8 and 8 seconds.

▶ Our brains process pictures 60,000 times faster than text. When you share a picture, your fans decide in a split second whether they want to see more.

▶ People upload about 250 million photographs to Facebook every day, and Twitter has become more visual, showing photos and videos right in your feed.

▶ The growth of other image-rich sites like Pinterest has been stratospheric, and apps such as Instagram, Vine, and even Snapchat aren't just for teenagers—savvy marketers are using them, too.

▶ According to research from social media analytics app Buffer, tweets with images receive 150 percent more retweets and 89 percent more favorites.

▶ Posts that include an album or picture receive 120 to 180 percent more engagement from fans than text-based posts.

▶ On Instagram, users post 40 million photos per day with upward of 8,500 likes and 1,000 comments per second.

▶ There are three billion views on YouTube daily.

▶ Viewers spend 100 percent more time on pages with videos.

What Is Microcontent and Why It's Important to Your Content Marketing Strategy

Is your audience (clients, customers, readers) feeling overwhelmed by the amount of content and information being delivered to them day in and day out? I hear this cry of frustration daily, yet as a savvy online entrepreneur, you know content is the backbone of your business.

Without a steady stream of blog posts, articles, free reports, and videos, your prospective clients will have trouble finding your business on the web. The content you create is essential for telling your story and getting found by your ideal clients so they can get to know you and how you can serve them. It's no longer enough to publish a blog post and expect readers to find you. While you will get some organic traffic from the search engines, to get more of **the right traffic**, you've got to promote your posts as well. So what do you do?

> *It's no longer enough to publish a blog post and expect readers to find you.*

While your long-form content is critical to your success, don't overlook the microcontent (tweets, short videos, and images, for example) that grabs your readers' attention and compels them to follow your links back to the in-depth articles revealing your expertise and how you serve.

Microcontent isn't a new concept. Blogger Anil Dash wrote about it in 2002:

> *Today, microcontent is being used as a more general term indicating content that conveys one primary idea or concept, is accessible through a single definitive URL or permalink, and is appropriately written and formatted for presentation in email clients, web browsers, or on handheld devices as needed. A day's weather forecast, the arrival and departure times for an airplane flight, an abstract from a long publication, or a single instant message can all be examples of microcontent.*

Things have changed dramatically since Anil Dash defined microcontent in 2002. That was before Facebook, Twitter, Google+, Pinterest, and Instagram—all platforms specializing in easy microcontent creation today.

Here's my take on microcontent:

The opposite of long-form content like blog posts, white papers, and reports, microcontent is the status updates, text images, Vine videos, Instagram photos, infographics, cartoons, e-cards, GIFs, and slide decks that act as shorthand for your content and grab attention. Microcontent acts as effective lead generators, driving traffic back to your site (when done with a strategic plan in mind). Microcontent is easy to create and takes less time than writing an article.

In a 2013 interview on *The Future of Ink* blog, Gary Vaynerchuk, author of *Crush It!* and *The Thank You Economy*, talked about "the stream economy."

> *[Y]ou've got to tell your story to the customer* where the customer actually is. *And to me where the customer actually is . . . is head-down, in their mobile device using their thumb to scroll their Facebook feed, their Instagram feed, their Twitter feed, their Tumblr feed, their Pinterest feed and so I call that streaming . . .*
>
> *[P]eople need to use* the stream economy to drive awareness to the blog . . . . *Blogging is now long form. You know, blogging used to be short form, right? But it's not anymore. Blogging is now long form so you need to figure out how to take the best . . . you know how when you read a magazine article and they always have two or three quotes featured? . . .*
>
> *You've got to figure out what are those two or three quotes, how do you turn them into a picture, a video, something that captivates somebody on Pinterest or Instagram or Facebook and they click that and it drives them to the article."*

Twitter, for example, has been referred to as a microblogging platform since it was launched in March 2006. Creating a 140 character snapshot of your blog post can create curiosity that encourages clicks back to the original post, as Vaynerchuk suggests.

Small and large companies alike can benefit from incorporating microcontent into their content marketing strategy. Short information bursts that are fast and easy to read address our short attention spans.

- ▸ It makes you a better writer because you are forced to communicate information in a short blurb.
- ▸ Microinformation is easily shared, casting a wider net for your voice to carry.

    ▶ Microcontent can drive traffic to your desired online destinations.

Think about your own behavior as you consume information on the web. How often do you share links to articles you read? Tweet blog posts you like? Post pictures from an industry conference or event? You're already creating microcontent; the next step is being strategic about what you're creating and how you distribute it on the web for the widest reach.

Before you jump into a microcontent creation frenzy, take some time to figure out the best type of content for your business. Let's start with a list of the types of short form content you can create.

- Photos
- Graphs and drawings
- Photos created by your clients and customers (user-generated content)
- Photo collages
- Images with text, captions, quotes, and stats
- Postcards and e-cards
- Word images
- Memes
- Cartoons
- GIFs
- Infographics
- Videos
- Presentations
- Text-only updates (tweets, status updates)
- Comments on blogs and link posts

Creating a mix of microcontent adds interest and variety to your social networks and blog. Knowing your audience is equally, if not more, important. Before you craft your content plan, start by polling your customers, newsletter subscribers, and blog readers to find out their preferences. Do they like image quotes? Do they prefer Twitter to get their information from you? On what social networks do they spend most of their time? If it's Pinterest, for example, then you'll want to add images to your content plan.

Knowing what your audience responds to best will help you develop a plan for creating content that tells your story and activates action by your fans.

If your business is visual by nature, there shouldn't be a question about whether or not you use the power of social networks to connect with your audience. Florists, art galleries, designers of all kinds, food bloggers, travel-related businesses, retailers, veterinarians, all lend themselves to visual storytelling. Photos and videos showcasing products and how to use them will do well on Pinterest, Instagram, and YouTube. And you can never go wrong with pictures of dogs and cats! "Caturday" is a popular topic on Facebook and Google+ on Saturdays with hundreds of photos, videos, and GIFs posted every week. How can you use an image of a cat to convey a message about your business?

What if you don't have a highly visual business? No problem. Statistics, how-tos, tips, and quotes can all be used in text images, infographics, slide decks, and text-only status updates. Text images work well on Facebook, Google+, Pinterest, and Instagram as well.

Here's what Joan Stewart, also known as The Publicity Hound, discovered when she started using text images on Pinterest for her "nonvisual" business (for the complete article, see http://thefutureofink. com/how-to-use-pinterest-for-authors):

> *"By using PowerPoint to create dozens of simple JPEGs featuring short "how to" tips . . . My board,* **50 Tips for Free Publicity***, has consistently ranked number one on Google search (unpaid) for the phrase "free publicity" for several months. It even outranks my website that features more than 2,000 pages of content!"*

Are you starting to see possibilities for your business?

Use Microcontent to Send Traffic to Your Blog

Your blog posts, articles, and ebooks take time and care to create. The next step after publication is to promote your content, and that's when you turn to microcontent to spark curiosity and drive traffic. Knowing that social networks are great for sending traffic back to your home base (your blog), here are some ways you can use microcontent to invite your fans and followers back "home."

- ▶ Post an image and link from your blog post as a Facebook status update (yes, this is very common; don't forget to do it).
- ▶ Create an image with a pithy quote from your article; post the image on Pinterest, Twitter, Facebook, and Instagram.
- ▶ Use the PushQuote plugin on your WordPress blog to create a tweetable quote embedded in the post.
- ▶ Use Vine to create a six-second video about the main theme of your article.
- ▶ Use the subheads in your blog post as tweets with a call to action and link to learn more.
- ▶ Include pre-written tweets for your readers to easily share with click to tweet.

Five Ways to Use Text Images to Promote Your Content

One of the simplest types of microcontent to create is a text image. Articles with images get 94 percent more total views, so, at a minimum, I recommend creating one text image for promoting your blog around the social networks.

Whether you call them "text images" or "text pictures" or "image quotes," using images with text is a content marketing trend that's not going away anytime soon.

Many bloggers use text images to promote their content, particularly blog posts. No doubt you've noticed the trend. If you want your blog post to be noticed, it's essential to include at least one image that can be pinned and shared on social networks. The easier you make it for your readers to share, the more likely they will do it.

There are two steps: create a quote image from your post and share the quote image.

There are two types of images generally associated with promoting blog posts:

1. The title of the blog post with an eye-popping image

2. A quote from the content of the blog post

You can easily create quote/text images on sites like PicMonkey.
com and Canva.com—two of my favorites—then save them to your
computer to use on your social networks. Many image creation sites
also have an option to share directly to social sites.

> *If you use an online site to create images,*
> *always save the image files in case you want*
> *to use them again.*

Following are some optimal sizes to keep in mind when creating
images for your blog posts and posting directly on social platforms (as
of April 2014):

- ▶ Facebook—1200 x 1200 pixels (will be resized appropriately)
- ▶ Twitter—440 x 220 (according to Twitter's site, there is no specific image size requirement; they will be automatically scaled)
  for best in-stream preview

FIGURE 8.1 Use PicMonkey to create a text image for your blog post.

- ▸ Pinterest—735 pixels wide x any length (perfect for infographics)
- ▸ Google+—506 x 300 (minimum) for shared images
- ▸ Instagram—612 x 612

Each social network favors different image dimensions. While you may be able to get away with creating one graphic image for all sites, the savvy online marketer will create multiple images designed specifically for each platform. There are also multiple options for every site so your best bet is to do a search on "ideal size for images on [social site]" to find up-to-date information.

Where to Share Your Images

My suggestions probably won't come as a surprise based on what I've outlined above. There are five primary sites where you can use your images to promote your content. Caveat: Every blog post may not be appropriate to share on every platform. You've got to know your audience.

> Make sure your image has a call to action and a URL for people to follow so they can get back to your post. Create a redirect link (use a plugin like Pretty Link) or use a link shortener like Bitly (bitly.com) or Google's URL shortener at https://goo.gl.

Google+

Like the other social networks, gorgeous, large images get a lot of attention on Google+. There are a couple of ways you can present your text images: Upload your image, and in the description of your update, include the link to your blog post; or share the link to your blog post, and your large image (minimum 506 pixels wide) will be displayed automatically along with the title of your post and a preview of the content (pulled from your post's meta description).

Facebook Business Page

If you have a Facebook page for your business, you probably do this already, right? Again, you can upload an image and include a call to action and URL in the status update description, or simply post the link and let Facebook pull in the image that's in your blog post.

Pinterest

It's well known that Pinterest can drive a lot of traffic to your blog posts, so don't neglect this social network. Pin your image to the appropriate topic board and make sure you include the URL in the description and source field. If you have several boards a post would work on, repin it to a new board the next day so it shows up in your followers' stream again.

Instagram

Do you promote your content on Instagram? Instagram is one of the most popular photo sharing apps. Most people don't use it strategically and neglect to share their blog content on the site, so you have an opportunity to stand out. Use a pithy quote from your content vs. the title of your blog post. Instagrammers love quotes. Then add the URL to the description. The link won't be clickable, but at least your followers can find your content if the quote resonates with them. Use the #quote hashtag to attract new followers.

When you share an image on Instagram, you have the option to also share it to your Facebook profile and Twitter. You get three posts with one upload.

Twitter

You can upload your image directly through your Twitter account or through Twitter's mobile apps and third-party management tools like Hootsuite. Be sure to include a few words about the image and use @mentions and hashtags, plus a shortened link that directs your followers back to the original content.

Tools for Creating Microcontent

There are hundreds of online tools and smartphone apps you can use to create microcontent. Apps for creating images and quotes are the most prevalent.

For those of us who are design challenged, I strongly recommend PicMonkey and Canva for creating beautiful, well-designed graphics. Both have free and fee options with templates you can customize, many fonts to choose from, and editing and customization tools. Try them both and decide which you like best.

Share As Image (https://shareasimage.com) is an online app and Chrome extension that makes it easy to create text images in a matter of minutes. Highlight content—a tip or a quote—from a blog post or

FIGURE 8.2 Create word clouds from your blog posts to tell the story.

article, click on the Share As Image button on your bookmark bar, and it's automatically pasted onto a colorful background. Choose an image, pattern, or filter, add an attribution or call to action, and click "Save and Share." It takes about one minute.

Wordle and Tagxedo are fun online image creators. You create word cloud images by typing or pasting a link to an article into an online form. Choose your colors, format, and go. An image is generated with all the dominant words in random patterns or a shape of your choice.

Plugins

There are hundreds of plugins you can install to customize the functionality of your blog. Two I recommend for creating sharable tweets are PushQuote and Clicktotweet. Each allows you to create and embed a pre-crafted tweet in your post that your readers can then share to their Twitter stream.

Short-Form Video

Vine and Instagram both offer a way to create super short videos, 6 seconds and 15 seconds respectively, on your smartphone. While it sounds challenging, there is a lot you can say and show in a few seconds. Share glimpses of your events, snap a quick video of your book or product along with a call to action and a URL, and create a short demo or how-to for a product. You're only limited by your imagination.

Animoto is an online video tool you can use to create videos with photos and short videos. Tell your story through images, include a soundtrack—either your own recording or choose a royalty-free piece of music—and click a button to render the video. Again, this is a terrific way to showcase events and products with a call to action at the end.

Create a Microcontent Plan

Your content deserves to be found and read. First, determine the fastest, easiest type of microcontent for you to create. Review the list

A Sample Microcontent Distribution Plan

You can adapt this for your business. What to create:

- ▸ 1 blog post

- ▸ 3 nuggets from the post, 100-120 characters

- ▸ 1 image at least 570 pixels wide with title of post and blog URL

- ▸ 1 image with a quote from the post

- ▸ 1 slide deck with primary bullet points from the blog article and call to action to read the full article on your site

- ▸ Record audio version of post

Day 0—Publish blog post; include at least one large image and a pull quote or embedded tweet in the post

Day 0—Tweet title and link to blog post; pin image on the appropriate Pinterest board; post the title and link as a LinkedIn status update; post a link with contextual introduction on Google+; tweet the pull quote or embedded tweet two to three hours after the initial tweet

Day 1—Post the title and link on your Facebook page; tweet nugget #1 from the blog post; create a text image from a quote in the post and share it on Instagram

Day 2—Share blog post in appropriate LinkedIn Groups; share post from Facebook page to your Facebook profile (if appropriate for your audience); tweet nugget #2 from the blog post; share Google+ post to appropriate communities you are part of (if allowed)

Day 3—Tweet nugget #3; pin quote image on Pinterest

Day 4—Post slide deck on SlideShare.net and share deck to Twitter, Facebook page, LinkedIn, and Google+

Day 5—Post audio version on SoundCloud and share on your social networks earlier in the chapter and pick three to five types of content that you know you can create consistently and will help you tell your story.

Make sure the sites you choose to share your microcontent are where your audience spends time (remember, do a poll asking them!). As soon as you hit publish on your blog post, create and share your microcontent. If you wait, it may not get done.

Create a checklist you can use to promote your blog articles with microcontent. Then it becomes second nature for you or an assistant to distribute the bread crumbs that lead fans, followers, and prospects back to your door.

You can see that what I've laid out is just the beginning. With so many microcontent options, you can craft the perfect distribution plan for your content and your audience. Creating multiple touch points with a variety of media extends the life of your content and will help your significant content get found, consumed, and acted upon by your ideal customer. At the outset, you may have to experiment a bit on each social platform to find the right mix of media and content. Ask your audience for feedback on a regular basis, make notes on the results you get, and then when you find a mix that works . . . repeat!

CHAPTER 9

Perfecting PR
How to Quickly Attract Attention, Clicks, and Customers

Barbara Rozgonyi

BARBARA ROZGONYI is the creator of WiredPRWorks.com, a training and resource destination for online marketers who need to know how to attract attention, build business, and connect with clients using social media marketing, with an emphasis on PR. An international social media consultant and speaker, Barbara is the founder of CoryWest Media, LLC and Social Media Club's Chicago chapter. Connect with Barbara at BarbaraRozgonyi.com.

In this Chapter, You'll Discover

▶ How to choose the right PR path for you

▶ Five steps to a powerful PR strategy

▶ Twenty-six-point Press Release Success Checklist

▶ Seven ways to integrate PR into social media

▲ ▲ ▲

The results you get from consistently focusing on PR (personality + reputation) can dramatically increase your visibility and reach, almost overnight.

While you can engage a PR company to manage your personality and reputation, you don't have to. In this chapter, you'll learn about simple, powerful PR strategies designed to help you quickly attract more attention, clicks, and customers with the power of free publicity.

Discover why PR is the most underrated, yet most effective, strategy you can use to position your business as an industry leader quickly, economically, and successfully.

> Today, everybody who wants to stand out
> needs to be a thought leader. PR is the
> easiest way to get there.

Two PR Paths: How to Choose the Right One for You

Whether you want to reach journalists who'll write your story for you or you want to bypass them and go directly to your clients or consumers, here's how to choose the right PR path for you.

For almost 100 years, the only way to get your name in the news was to write a press release, send it to a media outlet and cross your fingers that your story would be newsworthy. That's not the case anymore.

Today, you have two ways to get your name into the news: You can rely on a reporter or you can become your own media center that publishes news and connects with influencers.

Which way is the right way? Don't be surprised if you want to follow both paths.

Reaching journalists with press releases is getting harder and harder. As media outlets merge and reduce the number of reporters, the opportunity to connect with a reporter personally is challenging—but not impossible.

In fact, having a close relationship with a reporter is your best chance of getting your story covered. How do you do that?

Correspond with them. Email or comment on their blog when you agree, or even disagree, on their coverage.

Calling a reporter, especially when they're on deadline, isn't always welcome. They'd rather read than talk—unless they're interviewing you.

Did you get an interview? Send a thank you note when they write a favorable story. The personal approach works at the local level and even with larger media outlets that have blogs.

Comment a few times on a reporter's blog, and you may become one of their favorite sources. Another way to reach reporters is via Helpareporter.com (HARO).

You can also reach journalists by distributing your release via an online distribution service like PRNewswire, Vocus, and MarketWired.

Keep in mind your story will be one of thousands that cross their desk each week. That's why you'll want to release at least one news item every few weeks. Use the same distribution channels or mix them up to see which service gives you the best results. Don't expect journalists to contact you right away with your first online release.

The advantage of having a journalist cover your story is twofold: Their story is an objective, implied endorsement that reaches the media outlet's market, and there is no cost to you for the coverage. A story in *The Wall Street Journal* saves tens of thousands in ad dollars, but more importantly gives you priceless credibility that ad dollars can never buy.

Targeting your clients or consumers is much easier: All you do is prepare the story and release it online via a distribution service that automatically sends out your story where your clients can find you. For example, many services allow you to optimize your release with keywords and even guarantee that you'll show up on page one of Google News and Yahoo! News.

While seeing your story rank 5/92,000 news results can be very exciting, the effect wears off quickly. Yes, your story will show up in search engine results, but most likely you won't be on page one.

Paid distributions sites often include access to statistical reports that show you search terms, downloads, placements, and even the geographic location of the readers. When you release your news through a paid distribution service that releases your news to search engines, websites, and journalists, you'll reach the best of both worlds: journalists and consumers.

Five Steps to Powerful PR

Thanks to online distribution services, you can transform a simple press release into an always-on, stand-alone social media-enabled news site with global access. That's a lot to say about a project that usually encompasses 400 words or less—especially when it's one you can do yourself.

> *"Publicity, publicity, publicity is the greatest moral factor and force in our public life."*
> —American publisher Joseph Pulitzer

Here's how we position our clients as newsworthy subject matter experts. It's a simple system that works.

1. Select Keyword Search Terms

How do people find you and your business online? Do they search by location, industry, product, customer, needs, communities? Test out your sample keywords on Google News and Yahoo! News. What comes up when you type in your term? Does it look like you belong here? Set up a Google Alert for emails that tell you when and where your terms appear so you can track newsmakers and jump in with a news release of your own that tells your take on hot topics.

2. Write a Compelling Story in 400 Words or Less

Answer who, what, when, where, why, and how in your introductory paragraph. Then write three short paragraphs that each elaborate on one point or quote one person. Keep in mind that a single story can often be redirected to multiple audiences; focus on one topic at a time. Most online news distribution services allow you to upload images and videos to help you tell your story in words and pictures.

3. Come Up with a Catchy Headline

You gotta grab 'em to get 'em to read or click on your headline. Here's the formula that works for us: under 60 characters, include the top search term, mention a number, and be intriguing. This one, "50 Pizzas Rolled Into 1 Pie," got a call from a major metro magazine within 15 minutes of sending the e-release. Sending to local media contacts? Include your town in the email subject line.

4. Call to Action

A call to action tells your reader what to do next: Call for more information, request a free report, show up to an event, or get a discount. Put your call to action at the end of your first paragraph, and your contact information at the end of the release. What's your special offer?

5. Distribute to a Variety of Outlets

- ▶ *Personal networks:* alma mater, social clubs, house of worship
- ▶ *Professional networks:* chamber of commerce, trade associations
- ▶ *Social networks:* link to your release on LinkedIn, Twitter, Facebook, and your blog.
- ▶ *Local media:* make a list of the media outlets you'd like to be featured in—newspapers, magazines, radio, and TV. Email the reporter and introduce yourself. Let them know what you like about what they cover and how you can help them.
- ▶ *Online distribution:* Your options range from free to $500 and up; the more you invest, the more you get in terms of statistics and reach.

Socializing PR: Ramping Up Visibility and Connectivity

If you're looking for ways to raise visibility, generate traffic, grow business, and build an online community, connect PR with social

26-Point PR Success Checklist

Use this checklist to outline a template you can use over and over again.

❑ Who is the story about? Hint: your clients or your market first, then you.

❑ What is the issue or problem that needs to be solved? Make a list of how you save the world, stop pain, cut costs, or add value.

❑ When is there an event, an anniversary, a national observance? Tie into something bigger than you.

❑ Where is the story taking place? If locally, let your local reporters know you're an expert; industry-wide, contribute to association publications; social networks, comment and link on your blog and networks; nationally, release your story via an online distribution service.

❑ Why does this story matter—to reporters, consumers, the public? You have to be able to explain your answer to this question. If you can't, your story isn't newsworthy.

❑ How will you call for action? You need a call to action to measure results and inspire movement. Offer a free white paper, a complimentary analysis, or subscription to an information source.

❑ Headline—Between 60 and 80 characters. Get this right and you'll dramatically increase results, especially if the remaining points are included.

❑ Keywords—Choose a few top search terms you want to own; search Google News to see what's making news now.

❑ Subhead—One to three sentences that summarize the story and end with a call to action and a link to your site.

❑ Body copy—About 400 words in five paragraphs.

❑ Links—One for every 100 words; try to vary the links; include an affiliate link.

❑ Contact Information—phone and email.

❑ Image(s)—Flattering photographs only.

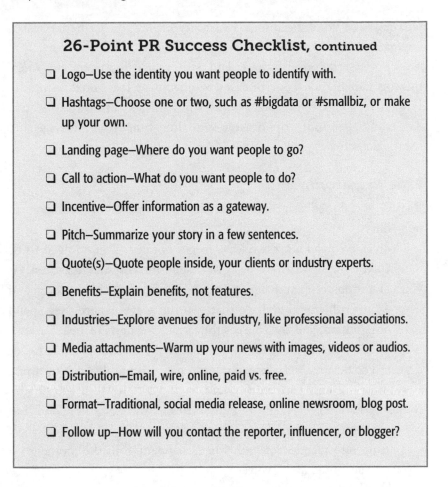

26-Point PR Success Checklist, continued

❑ Logo—Use the identity you want people to identify with.

❑ Hashtags—Choose one or two, such as #bigdata or #smallbiz, or make up your own.

❑ Landing page—Where do you want people to go?

❑ Call to action—What do you want people to do?

❑ Incentive—Offer information as a gateway.

❑ Pitch—Summarize your story in a few sentences.

❑ Quote(s)—Quote people inside, your clients or industry experts.

❑ Benefits—Explain benefits, not features.

❑ Industries—Explore avenues for industry, like professional associations.

❑ Media attachments—Warm up your news with images, videos or audios.

❑ Distribution—Email, wire, online, paid vs. free.

❑ Format—Traditional, social media release, online newsroom, blog post.

❑ Follow up—How will you contact the reporter, influencer, or blogger?

media. To get started conducting an effective public relations campaign to reach reporters and the masses, here's how to leverage social media.

1. Set Campaign Goals

Traditional PR campaign goals often include placements in target publications along with the total number of media impressions. Search and social media news campaigns allow you to be more creative and effective.

For example, do you want to reach out to bloggers, grow your community on Twitter, build a LinkedIn group, start a Google+ community, generate more site traffic, attract more YouTube channel viewers, raise your social media visibility profile, or get better search engine rankings?

You can do all of these and still reach reporters on social networks. Schedule your releases to go out at least once a month. Higher frequency positions you as a newsmaker and one to watch. And you'll get more opportunities to fine-tune your message and measure results.

2. Be Newsworthy

Because social media sites are searchable, every action or comment can be public.

You don't need a press release to get noticed. You do need to be newsworthy on a consistent basis to sustain interest and attention. As you're crafting your campaign, think about who you want to reach and why, what problems they have that you can solve, where they spend their time online, and the sources they go to for news or help.

For story ideas, focus on topics that relate to the specific area of expertise or business service you want to grow or highlight. Now think about why and how your stories need to be told. How can you tie into trends or national events? Look at stories in the news now and find connections to what you do.

To tie into trends, research what's happening in the moment on Google, Facebook, and Twitter.

And check out Cision's list of trade industry publications, and their editorial calendars by subject, here http://us.cision.com/edcals/edcals.asp.

3. Target Media

Who do you want to tell your story? Do you already have a media list that includes newspaper, trade publication, magazine, radio, and TV reporters? Great. Now, find the reporters and their media outlets on social networks.

To expand your coverage, include bloggers and community sites in your niche. To find them, search for *[niche term] + blog*, *[niche term] + community*, and *[niche term] + forum*.

If you have more than one area of expertise, for example young couples and entrepreneurs, segment your media list by contacts that cover each niche. To find reporters, check out Muck Rack (you can try it free for 30 days) and sign up for HARO, to reply to reporters' queries.

4. Make Connections

Check out each reporter, media outlet, blogger, and community to make sure that their audience would be interested in covering your stories. Look for reporters who write stories that match your topics.

For example, business reporters cover different stories than lifestyle reporters. To connect on social networks, send a personal introduction request with a mention of the reporter's work and let them know you are a resource in the area of your chosen expertise.

If you have more than one area of expertise, match your message to the media. Targeting bloggers? Check out GroupHigh (sign up for a free trial at grouphigh.com). Comment on their posts and find out who's who in their community. Get to know each media contact personally. It's better to have a small intimate group than a large email list with no relationships.

5. Craft Search and Social Releases

A search and social media release differs from a traditional press release in these important ways:

- ▶ Keyword search terms help readers find your news faster.
- ▶ Images and video add dimension to the story.
- ▶ Key points break up the content and underscore main ideas.
- ▶ Built-in sharing options allow news to spread easily and quickly online.

To transform a traditional press release with search and social elements, add key search terms, summarize the news in the first paragraph with a call to action, add in links, include images and video, and route distribution through share-enabled channels.

6. Distribute to Share

Now that your social media release is ready to go, you can get the word out in a variety of ways. Choose a free or paid distribution service to send your news to search engines, wire services, and industry-specific RSS feeds.

> "The only thing worse than being talked about
> is not being talked about."
> —Oscar Wilde

The leaders are Business Wire, Cision, MarketWired, Meltwater, PR Newswire, and PRWeb/Vocus. For free distribution, check out PRLog. The higher your investment, the more detailed the statistics and reports.

Although these companies offer distribution services, they also offer much more, including media lists, monitoring, and measurement. Each company is highly regarded. While their services may be more of an investment, it's worth looking into how their software applications can help you meet your marketing and PR goals.

Reach out to media contacts and send a tweet with a link to your release. Leverage your company's network connections by sharing the release and the link on your company's social profiles sites.

You can also post your news directly. For example, *The Chicago Tribune* accepts community news on their TribLocal.com site. When you post your news, your press release becomes an article that Google indexes.

When you invest in an online distribution service, your news release:

- ▸ Gets submitted to search engines-both regular and news;
- ▸ Allows for multimedia inclusions like video, images, and audio;
- ▸ Shares easily on social networking sites;
- ▸ Directs traffic to your site;
- ▸ Increases online exposure;

- Gives you free publicity;
- Connects you with influencers; and
- Positions you as a credible thought leader.

7. Measure Results

After your release is live, go back to your campaign goals and see how your results measure up. To see how your release performs on search engines, enter your key terms. Type the release headline in the search bar to see what sites picked it up. With social media, set up a search term, called a hashtag, to group results across channels. Activate a few tools you can use to monitor progress like Google Alerts, Talkwalker Alerts, SocialMention, and Topsy.

CHAPTER 10

SEO that Gets Results Today—and Tomorrow

Brian Dean

BRIAN DEAN wakes up every morning to accomplish one simple thing: help online marketers get more traffic, leads, and sales from search engines. Brian Dean largely accomplishes this goal by publishing insanely practical tips on his popular SEO blog, Backlinko.com.

▲ ▲ ▲

A few months ago I got an email from a fairly well-known blogging expert:

> "Webinar Tomorrow at 2 P.M.: How to Get More Traffic from Your Blog This Year"

In this Chapter, You'll Discover

▶ How to find keywords that your target customers use to find your products and services

▶ Simple-yet-effective on-page SEO strategies that you can leverage for more organic search engine traffic

▶ Content marketing techniques that generate links and social signals

▶ How to build high-quality backlinks without setting off a Google penalty tripwire

I thought to myself, "Why not? I could always use more traffic." I clicked the link and signed up.

The next afternoon, armed with a pen, notepad, and hot cup of coffee, I sat down at my desk. I opened up my laptop and logged into GoToWebinar. I was pumped to learn some ninja traffic secrets.

The webinar started off innocently enough. The host talked about personal branding, content design, and a few promotional strategies I hadn't heard about.

So far so good.

But his next slide almost made me spit out my coffee (which would have been a shame as it was Starbucks French Roast—my favorite).

The slide read:

Here's My SEO Strategy: **Forget SEO**

I could have typed a long tirade into the GoToWebinar chat box. But strong coffee puts me in a good mood. So I decided to shrug it off.

Fast forward to about two-weeks ago. I notice on Twitter that the webinar host now boasts a new site and brand.

Out of curiosity, I open up one of his older blog posts that was collecting dust in my Firefox bookmarks. This bookmark still pointed to the old site's URL.

I notice a huge banner at the top of the page:

"Site X Is Now Y. Click Here to Check It Out."

My nerdy SEO brain gets to work:

If he redirected that old URL to the new one with a 301 redirect, users and search engines would be quickly and easily sent to the new URL. A 301 redirect would also tell Google to count any links pointing to the old URL as pointing to the new URL.

Also, anyone who might consider linking to this old post would quickly change their mind. The content is still there . . . but the site's design looks outdated. Not to mention a big banner telling people that the site has moved.

Not only that but . . .

Why SEO Still Matters

I can understand why someone would be tempted to tell their followers to "Forget SEO."

Google's slew of recent updates—from Panda to Penguin to Hummingbird—have forced hundreds of site owners to trade in their Rolexes for Seikos.

That being said, ignoring SEO is still really, *really* bad advice.

> A Google outage in August of 2013 caused the web's traffic to *drop by 40 percent*.
>
> In other words, 40 percent of all the web's traffic starts with a Google search.
>
> Can you afford to ignore 40 percent of the internet's traffic?
>
> Read more at http://www.theregister. co.uk/2013/08/17/google_outage/

As you just saw, by forgetting SEO, that so called "traffic expert" was missing out on thousands upon thousands of visitors each and every month.

Some expert.

As I see it, you have three options when it comes to SEO:

1. You can bury your head in the sand and *hope* that Google rewards you with higher rankings.
2. You can manipulate the algorithm by blasting your site with black hat backlinks.
3. Or you can create an awesome site that's optimized for humans *and* search engines.

I think you can guess which one I'd recommend for you.

And in this chapter I'm going to show you *exactly* how to build a strong SEO foundation that will get you more search engine traffic in the short term, without having to worry about a Google slap down the road.

How to Find What Customers Search for (and Actually Care About)

Right now a potential customer is searching for something in Google.

If you know what this keyword is, you can optimize a page on your site around it and (ideally) rank number one. When that happens, your potential customer finds you, signs up for your newsletter and makes a purchase somewhere down the road.

If you don't, he or she finds another site (likely a competitor) and hands their cash to them.

Do I have your attention now?

Now that you see why choosing the right keywords is so darn important for your business, it's time to walk step-by-step through the keyword research process.

Step 1: Spy on Your Customers

Most people approach keyword research using this three-step "plan":

1. Open up the Google Keyword Planner (more on that later)
2. Enter a keyword that pops into their head
3. Pluck a keyword at random from the list

Needless to say, that doesn't usually pan out very well.

Here's what to do instead.

First, find where your audience hangs out online when they're not on your site (or on Google).

For example, let's say that you sell mail-order cakes and you've identified your target audience as foodies.

> *Keyword research is just market research for the 21st century.*

Where do foodies tend to congregate?

▸ Baking and cooking forums
▸ Pinterest
▸ Cake decorating blogs
▸ Mommy blogs
▸ Baking-related Facebook pages

Spend some time on these platforms and see what words and phrases people tend to use.

Pay special attention to any words they use that may not be directly related to what you sell.

For example, people interested in buying premium cakes may also be busy soccer moms or grandfathers looking for gifts to send to their grandson for his ninth birthday. The words they use online will tell you more about their wants, needs, and desires than any focus group.

Because you'll come across dozens (if not hundreds) of potential keywords, it helps to stay organized. I like to make a simple Excel spreadsheet to track any words that pop out. Words that crop up again and again are known as "seed keywords."

> Seed Keywords: Keywords that you enter in the Google Keyword Planner in order to discover new keyword ideas.

They're called seed keywords because they're the same words you'll use to find dozens of closely related variations in the Google Keyword Planner.

Which brings us to step two.

Step 2: Enter Your Seed Keywords in the Google Keyword Planner

If you notice people discussing "cake-of-the month clubs" on forums and social media, you better believe that this might be something people also type into a Google search field.

But how do you know for sure?

Thankfully, Google provides a free tool that allows you to see exactly how many people search for that keyword in a given month: The Google AdWords Keyword Planner (GKP).

To access it, head over to https://adwords.**google**.com/**KeywordPlanner**. If you don't have a Google AdWords account already, now's the time to set one up (you'll need it to use the GKP).

First, click on "Search for new keyword and ad group ideas."

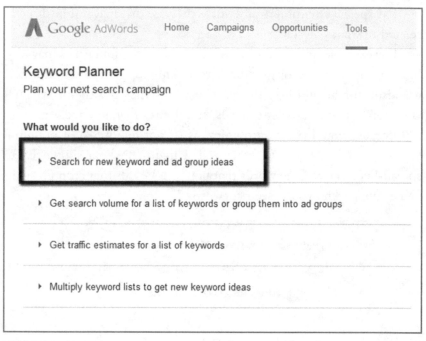

FIGURE 10.1

Next, enter one of the seed keywords in the field labeled "your product or service." See Figure 10.2.

Next, click on the "Get Ideas" button.

Finally, click on the "Keyword Ideas" tab. See Figure 10.3.

Now you'll see a list of keywords that Google considers closely related to your seed keyword.

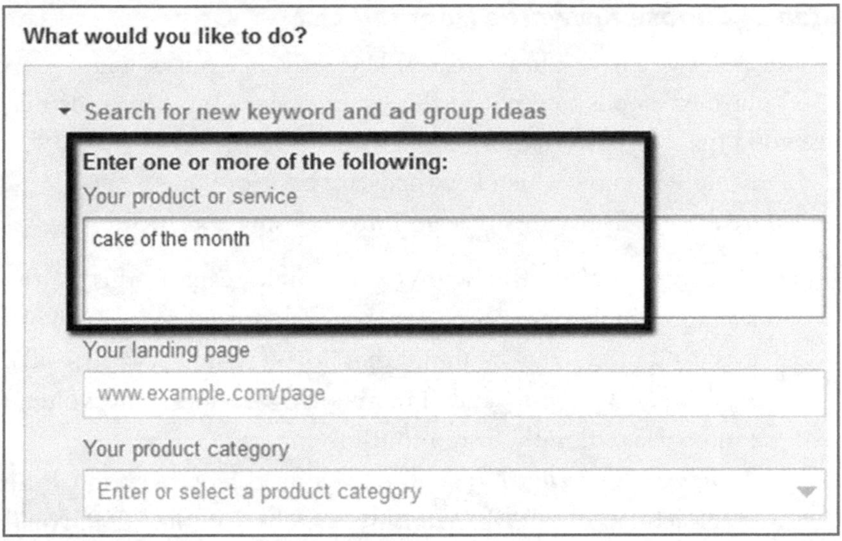

What would you like to do?
Search for new keyword and ad group ideas
Enter one or more of the following:
Your product or service
cake of the month
Your landing page
www.example.com/page
Your product category
Enter or select a product category

FIGURE 10.2

Your product or service
cake of the month
Ad group ideas
Keyword ideas
Ad group (by relevance)
Keywords
Avg. monthly searches
Cakes Online (33)
cakes online, order cak...
10,560
Cupcakes (27)
cupcake delivery, buy c...
93,640
Keywords like: Cake Sh...
personalised cakes, cel...
161,670

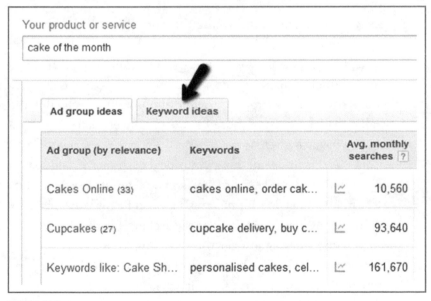

FIGURE 10.3

Step 3: Choose Keywords from the List

At this point you have a hearty list of keywords in front of you.

Your next step is to evaluate the list and pluck out keywords that are good fits for your business.

How do you know which keywords are best for you?

Here are the five factors that go into choosing a keyword:

1. *Average Monthly Searches.* As you might expect, this is the average number of people that search for a given keyword every month. Keep in mind that for certain keywords—like Halloween costumes and Thanksgiving recipes—the volume can vary significantly from month to month.

2. *Trending Popularity.* If you hover your cursor over the little graph icon next to "Avg. Monthly Searches" in the GKP, you'll see that keyword's popularity over the last year. If it's growing, that's a sign that investing in that keyword's rankings is a smart long-term investment.

3. *Suggested Bid.* This is the average amount that AdWords advertisers pay for a single click. Obviously, the higher the bid, the more likely someone searching for that keyword is in "buy mode." In general, keywords with a high suggested bid are very competitive to rank for in organic (non-paid) search. But the traffic that comes from those keywords convert better. So it's a bit of a balancing act.

4. *Market Fit.* Is this something your ideal customer would search for? Just because a keyword has stellar suggested bid and lots of search volume doesn't mean it's a good fit for your business. Think about how likely someone searching for that keyword is to turn into a customer over the short and long term.

5. *Competition in Google Organic Results.* Sizing up the competition in Google is more of an art than a science. There's no objective "difficulty meter" that will tell you exactly how many links you'll need to rank for a given keyword. But if you see the first page littered with heavyweights like NYTimes.com and Harvard.edu, you might be better off going after a different keyword.

> The "Difficulty" rating in the GKP measures
> how many people bid on that keyword in
> Google AdWords. It doesn't have anything
> to do with the difficulty of ranking in
> Google's organics search results.

Now it's time to optimize your pages around the keywords that you just found.

How to Optimize Your Site for Search Engine and Humans (Really)

In the early days of SEO, "on-page SEO" was synonymous with keyword stuffing, hidden text, and robotic sounding copy.

Like everything else in the SEO world, on-page SEO has undergone a renaissance. Today, the goal of on-page SEO is three-fold:

1. Strategically embed keywords into your pages so that Google can easily understand the topic of that page.
2. Create a site design and user experience that encourages people who find your site to stick to your site like superglue.
3. Awesome content that gets people to share your site on social media (and more importantly) link to it.

Now it's time to show how to create pages that are optimized for search without over-optimizing your site or turning readers off.

Step 1: One Page, One Keyword

If there's an on-page SEO mistake I see over and over again, it's trying to cram 10 keywords into a single page.

I come across *a lot* of small business websites that have title tags that look like this:

Boat Rental Miami | Florida Keys Boat Rental |
Charter Fishing Trips Florida | Scuba Diving Miami

And when I look at their meta keyword tag (which Google doesn't even use anymore), it's the same story:

Fishing miami, florida boating, boats, charter boats, boat rental . . .

You get the idea.

Think about it for a second:

How can your page—especially your homepage—be about renting boats in Miami, charter fishing in Florida *and* scuba diving?

Obviously, it can't. And because Google has no clue what your page is about, it doesn't rank it for anything.

What's the solution?

One page, one keyword.

Remember that Google wants to show users highly relevant results.

Which means they would much rather show someone searching for "Boat Rental Miami" an in-depth article about the best boat rental locations in Miami than a keyword-stuffed homepage "about" ten-different things.

So if you're looking to rank for ten keywords, create ten top-notch pages around each one.

Now that we've got that out of the way, the remaining steps can be used as a little checklist to make sure your pages are well-optimized.

Step 2: Include Your Keyword In Your Title Tag (Once)

Your title tag is like your page's headline. It's by far the strongest signal that you can send to Google about your page's topic.

Ideally, you should work your keyword into a title that's also compelling for readers (that way, you'll get clicks from people who are browsing the search results).

For example, if you wanted to rank for "Miami Boat Rental," you could use compelling titles like:

▸ Miami Boat Rental: 5 Things You Need to Know Before You Go

▸ Why Miami Boat Rental Makes Sense for Your Next Company Event

▸ 7 Ways to Save Money on Miami Boat Rental This Summer

These describe what the pages are about to humans and include your target keyword without looking spammy.

Step 3: Mention Your Keyword in the Beginning of Your Content

To make your page's topic crystal clear for Google, you want to sprinkle your keyword into your content.

Keep in mind that this isn't keyword stuffing (which can get your site penalized). It simply means that you want to mention your keyword a few times. That's it.

And the most important of those mentions is at **the very top of your page**.

Think about it for a second:

Let's say you came across an article on CNN.com about a new presidential candidate named John Smith. The journalist behind the piece probably wouldn't hesitate to mention words like "presidential," "John Smith," and "running."

It makes sense that the most critical information kicks off any web page. That's why I recommend mentioning your keyword in the first 100 words of your page.

After that, it's just a matter of sprinkling your keyword into your copy once or twice more. You can mention your keyword more than that if it makes sense for your content. But it won't help you from an SEO point of view.

Step 4: Make Your Site Load Lightning Fast

Google has confirmed that they use a site's loading time as a ranking factor.

Although a sluggish site won't make or break your SEO campaign, it makes a difference. And considering how competitive most keywords are nowadays, every little bit helps.

You can evaluate your site's current loading speed using two free tools:

1. *Google PageSpeed Insights* (http://developers.google.com/speed/pagespeed/insights/): Gives information that you can use to

significantly improve your site's speed with changes to your HTML and images.

2. *WebPageTest* (http://www.webpagetest.org/): Actually loads your page with a virtual browser. Also provides insights that you can apply right away.

If you work with a web developer, I highly recommend working with him or her to boost your site's loading speed. If not, there are several WordPress plugins—like WP Smush It! And W3 Total Cache—that can help.

Step 5: Outbound Links to Trusted Sites

Google and other search engines want to send people to hubs of helpful information. That means sites that regularly link out to quality resources on other websites.

When it makes sense, include a few outbound links to non-competing pages in your content.

Step 6: Internal Link to Important Pages

Internal links help users find more information on your site.

But those internal links also help search engines get a better idea of which pages on your site are most important. The way search engines look at it, the more often you link to a page, the more important it must be.

That means you want to a) identify pages that you're looking to rank, and b) send a few internal links their way.

Create Compelling Content that Attracts Links on Autopilot

It's no secret that great content is the key that opens the door to links, social shares, and traffic.

But you may be wondering:

What the heck *is* great content, really?

I mean isn't "great content" subjective?

It is. But when I say "great content" I'm talking about content that does one thing and does it well: generates high quality backlinks to your site.

Content that accomplishes that lofty goal tends to have these four traits:

- ▶ It's highly targeted to a very specific audience ("6 Evernote Hacks to Increase Productivity" will do better than "6 Ways to Be More Productive").
- ▶ It has a visual component, containing images, screenshots, infographics, diagrams, or videos.
- ▶ It's awe-inspiring. "Good" or even "great" content doesn't cut it anymore. To get links today your stuff has to be jaw-dropping good.
- ▶ It's on a site with a clean, professional design (thousands of great articles are invisible online because they're hosted on ugly-looking sites).

And in this section I'm going to share five winning content templates with you that are downright link magnets.

1. Ultimate Guides

It's no secret that people today are busy—very busy.

Which means that the *last* thing they want to do is scour the web for information on a single topic.

Enter: ultimate guides.

Ultimate guides perform well because they curate all of the information on a given topic in **one** place. The content's USP is a very easy sell.

Importantly, whenever people mention that particular topic on their site, they'll link to *your* ultimate guide. After all, you created the "go-to" resource.

2. Absurdly Long List Posts

When someone sees a post like 200 ways to save money, they think, "Wow, this must be amazing," before they've even read the first sentence.

So the next time you're in the mood for a list post, consider upping your game so that your list includes 50, 100, or even 300 items.

It takes a lot more work than a top-seven list, but it will pay off when you have a piece of content that people can't help but admire and share.

3. Visual Content (Especially Infographics)

Humans are hard wired for images and visuals.

The fact is, images—in the form of infographics, diagrams, interactive images, quizzes, puzzles, and games—tend to outperform their text-based counterparts.

Why?

Sixty-five percent of the U.S. population classifies itself as "visual learners." So when you publish information in a visual format, you're satisfying a user base that's largely underserved by the web's mostly text-based info.

4. Industry Studies or Data

There's no denying it: People love to share data.

Whether it's data on the average person's shoe size, the number of calories in a meal, or the most retweeted tweet, unique data spreads like wildfire on the web.

And you don't need a double-blind placebo controlled trial to get your hands on this juicy data.

Polls and surveys are easy to use, dirt cheap, and give you enough data that you can easily publish your results in the form of a soon-to-go-viral blog post, infographic, or press release.

5. Systems and Case Studies

There's a dirty little secret behind blogs that grow like Jack's Beanstalk:

They publish *insanely useful* content that actually provides value to their target audience.

Sure, there's a place for "Here's my take on . . ." blog posts.

But content that actually gives people *a solution to a problem* will beat the "I think X is Y" articles 99 times out of 100.

First, identify problems that your target audience is having, whether it's filing their complex tax returns or losing those stubborn love handles.

Then provide a step-by-step solution to those problems (bonus points if you publish a case study of your solution in action).

Link Building that Works Today (and Won't Hurt Your Tomorrow)

On April 24, 2012, Google rolled out one of the most significant updates since the company's founding: Penguin.

Unlike those that came before it, Penguin zeroed in on shady link-building tactics such as mass web directory submissions and paid links from blog networks.

Although Penguin only affected around 3 percent of searches, the message from Google grabbed 100 percent of the online marketing community's attention: "Mess with us, and you'll get burned."

Fortunately, you don't need to throw the baby out with the bathwater. Yes, black hat SEO strategies no longer work (or more accurately, their benefits are short lived).

But that doesn't mean that you need to walk away from link building altogether.

There are four core strategies that work today (and won't get your site slapped down the road).

1. Link Building with Resource Pages

Resource pages are pages with a curated list of links (in fact, they're sometimes called "links pages").

Because they exist for the sole purpose of linking to excellent content, resource pages are some of the best link opportunities you'll come across.

First, find resource pages in your industry using these search strings in Google:

> KEYWORD + "useful resources"
>
> KEYWORD + "helpful resources"
>
> KEYWORD + inurl:resources

When you come across a page where your content would be a good fit, find the site owner's contact info and pitch your resource.

This email script works well:

Hi [name],

I came across your excellent list of [topic] resources today.

Great stuff!

I just wanted to give you a heads up that I recently published a [content summary].

It might make a nice addition to your page. Either way, keep up the great work!

2. Infographics

Infographics have exploded in popularity for one simple reason: They get results.

Results in terms of traffic, results in terms of brand awareness, and (most importantly) results in terms of link acquisition.

Here's a mini primer on link building with infographics:

1. Create a top-notch infographic based on something your target audience cares deeply about, whether it's a political issue, losing weight, or finding love. Emotional issues work well.
2. Find data to support your infographic's angle using Google search, Google News, and even Google Scholar.
3. Layout your data so that the most important info is at the top. This compelling stat will draw people in to read the rest of your infographic.
4. Publish the infographic on your site's blog.
5. Find a list of people (bloggers and journalists) who might want to share it. Email them and ask if they'd like to see it. If so, send it over. When they publish your work, they'll link back to your site.

3. Broken Link Building

Every day thousands of links stop working: URLs move, sites go down, and companies go out of business.

When you swoop in like a superhero and let another blogger or webmaster know about their broken links, they'll be more than happy to add a link to your awesome resource as way of saying thanks.

Here's the three-step process:

1. Find pages on the web that are a) on topic and b) have lots of links on them. Resource pages are perfect.
2. Use a browser-based tool like Check My Links for Google Chrome to quickly identify any broken links on the page.
3. Reach out to the person responsible for that page to let them know about their broken link. Gently pitch your awesome content as a replacement for one of the broken links.

Here's a word-for-word script:

Hi [name],

I came across your list of top 100 [topic] blog posts today.

Great stuff!

I just wanted to let you know I found a few broken links:

[URL #1]

[URL #2]

I also recently published a [short pitch]. It might make a nice replacement for [broken link].

Either way, I hope this helps you out!

4. Value-Adds

Value-adds takes the *quid pro quo* concept of broken link building to the extreme.

Instead of simply pointing out broken links, you actually go out of your way to improve the other person's site in a meaningful way.

Here are a few practical examples of what I'm talking about:

▸ Giving someone a unique piece of content, like an exclusive infographic or high-quality guest post.
▸ Improving an out-of-date resource on their site.
▸ Translating a piece of content to or from English.
▸ Transcribing a video and giving them the transcription for free.
▸ Creating a diagram that explains something from their article.

▸ Identifying a virus or malware and giving them the steps to fix the issue.

As you can see, there's a lot (and I mean *a lot*) of opportunity with this approach.

Summing Up

SEO is a lot like eating healthy: It's simple, but it's not easy.

You *know* that steamed broccoli is good for you. But getting your mouth to accept it over a bag of chips? That's a different ballgame.

It's the same story with SEO: You *know* that great content paired with targeted email outreach will land you higher rankings and more traffic.

But getting your team to execute? That's not easy.

It's much easier to bury your head in the sand and "forget SEO" or to publish "great content" and hope for the best.

But considering that very few people have stepped their game up in today's post-Penguin SEO world, the opportunity to do well with SEO has never been greater.

If you can find keywords that customers use, create well-optimized content around those keywords, and build links to that content, you'll cement your place at the very top of Google's first page.

CHAPTER 11

Email Lists
How to Create, Build, and Maintain an Engaged, Responsive List

Syed Balkhi

SYED BALKHI is an online marketer with design and development experience. He's the founder of WPBeginner, the largest free WordPress resource site, and List25, a website with over a million followers. Syed's work has been featured in *The New York Times, Wired*, Yahoo!, AMEX Open Forum, Mashable, Business Insider, *Huffington Post*, and more. For more information, visit www.WPBeginner.com.

In this Chapter, You'll Discover

▶ Why an email list is essential for every type of business

▶ How to grow your email list using opt-in incentives

▶ How to keep your subscribers engaged month after month

▶ Different ways to monetize your email list

▶ The all-too-common mistakes you must avoid

▲ ▲ ▲

An email list is simply a list of individuals who've signed up to receive information from you. It might be a list of email addresses, or you might also have their names and potentially other details, too.

Understanding Email Lists

One common but dangerous mistake many new online marketers make is to simply create a list in their regular email client. This has several huge disadvantages:

- ▶ You may well be limited, either by your email client or your ISP, in terms of how many emails you can send out at once.
- ▶ It's very easy for you to add people to your list who may not have chosen to receive information from you—leading to your emails getting ignored or marked as spam (and potentially even resulting in legal action).
- ▶ You will miss out on really useful features of email lists, like seeing who's opened your email, and being able to personalize messages by including people's names.
- ▶ Spam filters may block your emails (email service providers are whitelisted with many hosting companies and email clients).

So if you only take one thing away from this chapter, make it this: Always use a reputable email service provider to create your email list. These platforms give you access to a whole range of stats related to your emails, and they also ensure you build a list that complies fully with anti-spam laws.

The good news is that there are several different email marketing services to choose from, offering a range of features and prices. Three of the most popular are:

- ▶ MailChimp *(free up to 2,000 subscribers)*
- ▶ AWeber *($1 trial for 30 days, then $19/month for up to 500 subscribers)*
- ▶ Constant Contact *($20/month for up to 500 subscribers on "basic" package)*

It's easy to find reviews and comparisons of these three services online, and I recommend you spend some time looking around to see which is likely to suit you and your business best. While it's possible to move an email list from one platform to another, it's much easier to get it right the first time!

When you send out emails from a service provider, there are two different ways to do so:

- ▸ Autoresponders (known as "Follow-up series" in AWeber)
- ▸ Broadcasts

An autoresponder series goes out to each new person who signs up in the same order. (This could be daily, weekly, or anything you want.) You might use this to run a short course by email, or simply to send a series of beginner-friendly tips to new members.

A broadcast goes out to your whole email list at once. The people who joined yesterday will get it when you send it, just the same as the people who joined a year ago. If you're running a sale on your products, for instance, you'll use a broadcast.

Why Building an Email List Is Important

Some business owners feel that email is on the way out. They believe that instead of building an email list, they should invest their time in growing a large following on Facebook, Twitter, Pinterest, or another social network.

While social networks are definitely a powerful force online, they can't and shouldn't replace email lists. When you create an account with Facebook (or Twitter, etc.), you're at the mercy of that service. As some commentators have put it, you're essentially building on rented land—a practice often described as "digital sharecropping."

> *An email list is fully under your control. Like a website hosted on your own domain, it's owned and run by you.*

What if a particular network goes under? What if they change their algorithms (Facebook, I'm looking at you) and stop showing your posts to your followers—unless you pay?

There's also another really important reason why email lists still beat social media: Email definitely isn't dead. In fact, there are plenty of people who have an email address but no social media presence at all. Getting access to someone's inbox is still the most powerful way to reach them. This is why all social media networks require you to have an email account to sign up with their service.

Another great thing about email lists is that they level the playing field. Major brands use them, of course, but so do tiny start-ups and individual entrepreneurs. It doesn't cost much money or time to set up an email list—but you'll have the exact same access to a prospect's inbox as the biggest companies out there.

Growing Your Email List

Once you've chosen your email platform (MailChimp, AWeber, Constant Contact, or another solution) and set up a new list within it, you'll receive code to put an opt-in form onto your website. Normally, you'll be able to customize this form so that it fits in with your brand.

Ideally, your opt-in form should be as short and simple as possible. Every extra piece of information you ask for decreases the chance that someone will sign up. You may simply want to ask for an email address, not even a name, or you might ask for a first name plus an email address. Chances are, you won't need more information than that.

You may also want to include a line or two reassuring your readers that it's safe to sign up. They might be worried that you're going to send them a flood of spam or even sell their email address to someone else. (Perhaps they've had a bad experience in the past.) Many companies include a line such as *I will never spam you or give your email address to anyone else.*

Even then, people will need a nudge to sign up for your list. The best way to do this is to offer a special incentive. Free ebooks or reports have become very common, so you may want to do something different to stand out a little. Perhaps you could offer a 90-minute value-packed webinar (either live or as a recording) to new subscribers.

Another good incentive, if it makes sense for your business, is to offer a short course by email—perhaps four to eight weeks of weekly emails that lead the recipient through a particular process. You can set this up using the autoresponder feature of your email service provider. This can be an excellent way to get readers accustomed to opening your emails on a regular basis.

Once you've got your incentive in place, it's worth creating a special "landing page" for your email list. This is a simple, clean page with information about the incentive and about what people can expect on an ongoing basis (e.g., "weekly tips" or "a monthly round-up of industry news"). Of course, you'll also include your opt-in form on this page.

When you mention your email list on social media or in a guest post bio, you can easily link to the landing page—this is much more likely to get results than directing people to hunt in your website's sidebar or footer for the opt-in form.

What Should You Send to Your Email List to Keep People Engaged?

If you've created a blog, started a social media account, or even read a few articles online, you'll almost certainly have noticed that people reading online have short attention spans.

There are several reasons for this—including the fact that it's tougher to read on a screen than in print, and that many websites are chock-full of distractions. When you're communicating by email, you may have a slight advantage as there's less visual clutter in most people's email interfaces than on many websites, but you'll still need to compete with dozens, perhaps hundreds, of other emails for attention.

> It's essential that your email content be truly valuable.

It's easy to fall into the trap of thinking that email content is less important than, say, blog posts, because it's not (necessarily) published on your website—but this isn't the case.

Here's how to get your email content right:

- ▸ Spend time crafting your subject line, just as you'd carefully craft the headline for a sales page or the title for a blog post. We'll give you some concrete examples later in this section.
- ▸ Get the frequency of emails right. For many industries, daily is too much—your readers will feel inundated, and may quickly unsubscribe. On the other hand, once every three months is usually too little—people will forget who you are, and may trash your email or even mark it as spam, having forgotten they ever signed up for your list.
- ▸ Make your content truly worth reading. Ask yourself, "Would *I* open this email?" You might want to think about the questions or problems that your readers are likely to have, and create content to address those.
- ▸ Don't go over the top with design. Some marketers prefer to use plain text, others use flashy templates. While a bit of formatting helps make your emails attractive and readable, don't make the whole thing rely on images—these won't necessarily render correctly (or at all!) in everyone's email clients.

If you have a blog, you have the option of using your blog content for your email list—perhaps by sending a small snippet and teaser. (You can obviously add in extra emails, e.g., for a promotion.) This can certainly save time, but it's generally the case that joining your email list—and not unsubscribing!—is a lot more attractive for your audience if members of the list receive unique content.

The biggest challenge you face is often simply getting your email opened. Some marketers will go to almost any lengths to entice clicks (I'm sure you've had your share of dodgy emails telling you that you've won something), but unless you want a lot of spam complaints and unsubscribes, it's best to craft subject lines that clearly reflect your email's contents. On the flip side, a very bland, boring subject line will often mean your email gets ignored.

The easiest way to learn here is probably by example, so here a few bad subject lines:

"(no subject)"

Most email service providers will prompt you for a subject line if you leave the field blank (and may make it mandatory), but if not, do be very careful you don't leave the subject off altogether.

"ABC Corp releases new product"

This doesn't give readers much reason to care. Is there a particular aspect of the product you could emphasize in the subject line?

"Testing"

It's a good idea to test your mail out before sending, but be *very* careful to make any changes necessary before blasting it out to your list.

"June specials"

While this is admirably concise, it's not particularly enticing on its own and even if your company name shows as the sender (it should!), it lacks context. Why not highlight one particular special offer in the subject line?

And here are some much better ones:

"Looking forward to summer? Ten ways to stay cool while travelling"

Numbers work well in email subject lines, just like they do in blog posts, infographics, and other online content.

"Ends today—save $399 on a luxury Mediterranean cruise"

If there's a legitimate reason to invoke a sense of urgency, always do so: otherwise, people may not get around to opening your email.

"How to handle problem clients"

How-to posts are always popular, and if your subject line promises to help your audience with a pressing concern or problem, they'll be much more likely to open the email.

While it's not an absolute rule, most marketers suggest using lowercase (with just the first word capitalized) rather than title-case (all main words capitalized) for email subject lines. You may want to experiment with both styles and see which gets a better response from your audience. Definitely don't use ALL CAPS, though—you'll instantly look like a spammer.

Ways to Monetize Your Email List

Once you've built an email list, you'll want to put it to work by monetizing it. There are three key ways you can do this; I'll start with the simplest.

1. Promote One of Your Products or Services

If you sell products (digital or physical) or services, then obviously your email list is a good place to promote these. You'll want to find a balance here—too much promotion, and you'll turn away prospects who just needed a little more warming up; too little promotion and you'll be losing out on sales.

One useful technique is to create a footer that goes on every email with links to your most popular products or services, or simply to your online storefront. That way, every email you send will include this information—so readers will always have it at their fingertips.

Beyond that, you'll want to plan for regular promotional mailings, perhaps with different offers. It's a good idea to create a content calendar for your emails: Plan out what you'll be sending, and ideally create several emails on a topic related to your upcoming promotion. That way, you'll have prepared readers for the offer that's about to appear in their inboxes.

2. Sell Advertising Space

Just as companies pay to advertise on websites, they'll pay to be included in your emails. If you're using this technique, you may need to spend quite a bit of time building a large email list before you can attract advertisers.

You'll also need to be careful that you don't simply send out emails packed with ads—otherwise you'll find people unsubscribing in droves, and quite possibly marking your emails as spam (leading to future problems with deliverability).

3. Promote Affiliate Products/Services

This can be a better technique than selling advertising, as it doesn't necessarily require a large email list in order to be successful. As an affiliate, you can promote other people's products/services and earn a commission on any sales—ranging from a few cents to substantial sums.

As an affiliate, be careful that:

▸ You only promote products (or services) you genuinely endorse. It's a good idea to have used the product, or to have a personal connection with the service provider so you can be confident that what you're promoting is high quality.

▸ You match the products/services you promote to your audience's needs. This means thinking not just about topic area but also about price. Sure, you might get 50 or even 75 percent commission on a $1,997 online course—but if none of your readers can afford it, there's not much point you promoting it.

Although some marketers will advise you to build a large list before you think about monetizing, it's often a good idea to get some monetization in place early on (even if you're only making a few dollars from it). That way, you haven't conditioned your readers to expect that they'll always get lots of great free content without ever receiving a single sentence of promotion!

Five All-Too-Common Mistakes You Must Avoid

When you're new to email lists, it's easy to make mistakes. This chapter has warned you against some (like writing poor subject lines), but I wanted to finish off with a few final tips. These are some very common and understandable ones, but they can lose you a lot of subscribers—and money.

Mistake #1: Emailing Irregularly

You may well start your email list with great intentions, planning to send a weekly tip plus a longer monthly newsletter, but it's easy for business and life to get in the way. If months slip by without emails—only to be followed by a flurry of messages when you suddenly carve out some time—you'll be confusing and quite possibly annoying your subscribers.

Solution: Work out a mailing schedule and stick to it. Weekly, every other week, or monthly can all work well. If you decide to increase or decrease the number of messages, do so gradually (don't suddenly jump from emailing weekly to emailing daily).

Mistake #2: Forgetting to Promote Your Email List

When you launch your email list, you'll probably find yourself writing about it on your blog, encouraging your social media followers to sign up, getting other entrepreneurs to promote your opt-in incentive, and so on. As time goes by, though, it's easy to forget to actively promote your list—meaning that growth slows to a trickle.

Solution: Every few months, plan a new round of promotion. Write guest posts, update your opt-in incentive, or even encourage readers to forward your emails to friends (make sure you include instructions in your email footer along the lines of "If you received this from a friend, you can join us here . . .").

Mistake #3: Ignoring the "Snippet"

Some email clients, like Gmail, show a short preview of emails alongside the subject line. Unfortunately, many companies ignore this—leading to text like "Problems viewing this email?" or "ABC Corp logo" or worst of all, "Use this area to offer a short teaser of your email's content" appearing as the snippet.

Solution: Make sure the text at the start of your email is useful and adds to your subject line. If you're using plain text, you probably don't have a problem here, but if you're using a template and it has a special space for this text, be *very* careful to update it each time.

Mistake #4: Getting Upset by Unsubscribers

Every time you send out an email to a list, some of your readers will unsubscribe. While this is understandably disconcerting, you don't need to panic that you're doing something wrong. The fact is that some people will inevitably be clearing out their inboxes and reducing their subscriptions—it's nothing personal.

Solution: Look on the bright side. If someone unsubscribes, they were probably never going to buy from you in the first place—and now you're no longer paying to have them on your email list!

Mistake #5: Never Testing Emails

Your email service provider should allow you to split-test emails by segmenting your list and sending out slightly different versions—perhaps using different subject lines, or with and without personalization. If you never do any tests, you'll never know if a small tweak could've resulted in a much more effective email.

Solution: It's an especially good idea to test emails that go out repeatedly, rather than as a one-off broadcast—e.g., if you have an autoresponder series that begins whenever someone signs up for your newsletter. Any promotional emails are also great ones to test, as a small increase in open rate or CTR (click-through rate) can have a significant impact on your profit.

CHAPTER 12

Let There Be Links, But What Kind?

Eric Ward

ERIC WARD has been creating natural linking strategies for clients since 1994, when he founded the web's first link-building and content publicity service, called NetPOST. Eric publishes the strategic linking advice newsletter *LinkMoses Private*, and provides linking services, training, and consulting. In 2013, Eric wrote the *Ultimate Guide to Link Building* (Entrepreneur Press). Learn more at www.EricWard.com.

In this Chapter, You'll Discover

► Why links remain the key to your site's visibility

► How links can help or hurt your site's traffic and search ranking

► How to diversify links and maximize links to your site via social media

► Five simple techniques you can use to earn links to your site

▲ ▲ ▲

A crucial part of online marketing is links, and more specifically, attracting them—that is, seeking, earning, and attracting links to your site from related sites and social media users.

Links are important not only because they drive traffic, but also because they continue to be the single most credible metric used by Google and other search engines to determine a site's ranking.

Links are the fabric of the web. Links remain crucial to your success, but the "rules" of linking have changed over the years, and the humble link has become a source of confusion and frustration for thousands of online marketers.

Search engines pay extra attention to the types of links that point back to your site. Having the "right kind of links" can mean the difference between success and failure online. But as much as links can help you, they can also hurt you. Search engines can and have penalized sites for what they consider "unnatural" linking patterns. Google even gives names to their algorithmic updates, like "Penguin," which specifically targeted link spammers.

Link building is a general term used to describe a wide variety of techniques that can be used to ensure your content is linked to by others. Link building is a terribly inaccurate description of the approaches that savvy link developers and link marketers can use for generating links to clients' content. Content can mean anything from your site's homepage to an app you want people to download, to a Twitter profile page.

There are hundreds of different ways to build links. There's what some people call the natural, white-hat approach. More like public relations than SEO, this is where you have a website devoted to a particular topic, and you reach out to people who care about that topic and also have sites, to let them know about your site. The goal is that they'll choose to link to your site, either in a blog post, a resource list, or whatever. These are known as "earned links," and can be very powerful signals for search engines. The idea is that people who are passionate about a topic are more likely to link to higher quality content than to junk.

At the other end of the link-building spectrum there's what some refer to as "black hat," which is when you create your own manipulated collection of content, sites and links that you fully control, meaning they are not earned by merit, in hopes of fooling a search engine. This has been going on for as long as there have been search engines and is the main reason Google has put so much more effort into distinguishing which links they can trust or not trust.

> Google wants to recognize and reward good content with higher search rankings, but also wants to ferret out—and in some cases penalize—sites that violate their quality guidelines.

My nickname in the industry is LinkMoses, because I've been around forever, I focus 100 percent on linking strategies, and I'm vocal about not trying to manipulate search engines. Truly outstanding content does not have to resort to manipulation of links in order to get traffic. The strategies and approaches that are most effective are always centered on the content and outreach.

For example, on the content side imagine you have a site like Discovery.com. This site launches new content regularly. One week they may be launching educational content about global warming for kids, and then the next week they might launch an app for their *Animal Planet* show. Whatever content they're creating will appeal to a certain audience online.

The next step is identifying and reaching out to those people who are most likely to care. What people out there are teaching about global warming in their classrooms? What people are blogging about animal related apps? For any type of content there will be an audience of writers, reporters, teachers, librarians, and others that focus on that topic. The best link builders understand how to find them, and more importantly, reach out to them properly.

To Whom It May Delete

You can't short-cut or automate the outreach process, which is what so many marketers have tried to do. You can't outsource it to a third world country that sends out thousands of poorly written link requests.

I'm sure many of you reading this have received emails like I'm describing. And you delete them, just like I do. I don't respond to impersonal "To Whom It May Concern, Please Link to Us" requests. There are parts of the process where tools can help. Google, for example; if I'm doing a project for a site devoted to pediatric hearing loss, I can do a Google search for hearing loss websites, hearing loss content, hearing loss resource pages, hearing loss groups on Twitter or Facebook or Google+. Google is a tool that helps you get closer to that potential target site.

> The decision to link is a very human process.

Then you have to look at the target sites and make some decisions. Do you feel the site is of good quality? Can you reach the right person who can make the editorial decision about adding a link on their site to your site? What's the best way to reach them? It might not be email. It might be picking up the phone. This is why mass link building is not scalable with quality. The decision to link is a very human process.

Many people are interested in building links because they feel those links will help their search engine rankings. Each of the largest and most popular search engines perform link assessment evaluation or analysis to determine which sites should rank highest for any given search phrase. So yes, you can try to improve your rankings via link building.

The irony of this approach is that if you are successful, you have created a dependence on that search engine. What happens if you lose your rankings? This is what happened to hundreds of businesses after Google's Penguin, Panda, and Hummingbird algorithm updates.

When 90 percent of your site's traffic comes from Google's search results, and you lose that traffic, you are in trouble.

Diversify Your Traffic Streams

The best long-term linking strategies do not put all their emphasis on organic search results. In fact, the best scenario, the scenario you should be pursuing, is where your business can succeed regardless of what traffic you get from Google search.

> The best long-term linking strategies do not put all their emphasis on organic search results.

One example of this is partnering with another company to help each other. This is especially effective at the local level. A local company that specializes in pool maintenance and repair could have a section on their site with links to recommended local contractors for services like driveways, gutters, outdoor living spaces, landscaping, etc. These are not links for the sake of improved search rank, these are links for the sake of building awareness of your company, brand, and website.

Here's a real example from a past project. A Florida business sells scuba diving charters, training, and day-long dive trips to shipwrecks. Their website is very nice but simple. The company had tried for years to rank highly for local scuba/diving related terms. They'd paid for directory submissions, article syndication, and press releases. These tactics did not help their ranking at all. The problem was they competed with several famous dive shops and dive charter business websites, and those well-known dive charter businesses seemed to attract links without even trying.

Rather than try to fight deeply entrenched, well-known competitors, we decided to pursue a linking strategy that would take us directly to potential scuba enthusiasts behind the scenes. Forget Google searchers. We contacted every hotel within ten miles of their business and pursued a co-marketing arrangement where whenever someone booked a hotel room online, in the email confirmation the resort sent them, the following text was included:

> Thank you for booking your stay at the ++++ Resort and Hotel. Please find your confirmation information below. In addition to the many amenities offered here on site, we also are proud to partner with *****-scuba.com, where every one of our guests receives a 15% discount off scuba lessons, charters, rentals, and more.
>
> Print this confirmation out and learn more @ *****-scuba.com

One of the resorts that agreed to a partnership sends out roughly 100 email confirmations a day, or 36,500 *per year*. The scuba charter business was the only link in those 36,500 private email confirmations.

And here's a wonderful secondary benefit. This is stealth linking. Your competitors don't find your links by doing backlink analysis, because these links to the scuba site exist inside a private email confirmation, which exists inside your private inbox. This promotion started in 2008 and continues to this day. It has expanded into other areas like resort hosted scuba charters. As far as clicks and conversions are concerned, everyone involved is happy.

Remember this strategy had nothing to do with Google or search rankings. Still, some "trickle-down linking" also occurred because of this promotion, and the scuba site's search rankings did in fact improve. The lesson here? Forget about manipulating Google and you might just end up ranking higher on Google anyway.

The example scenarios I just described are two very different approaches to link building. I wish I could give you a strategy that would be a perfect fit for all websites. But the reality is every website needs a specific approach or tactic. If you run an e-commerce site that sells products I could buy anywhere, then I don't care where I buy it. Why would anybody link to that kind of content? There's 500 stores out there where I could buy the same exact tennis racket. So why is anybody going to link to one of those stores over any other store?

You're going to have to give people a reason.

Every site has its own linking potential, depending on its focus and its subject matter. Some sites have more than others. A website selling grain elevators in Iowa has a different linking potential than a site selling hotel elevators in New York.

There's any number of ways to build links to your site. Some sites pay others to link to them. Some paid links are considered to be spam and black hat, while others are considered to be perfectly acceptable.

If I'm an electrician and am looking for some used tools that typically are very expensive, I do a search on Google for used electrician tools and I land on a website that's called UsedElectricanTools.com (if such a site exists). If anybody sells used electrician tools, wouldn't it make sense for them to buy a link on UsedElectricanTools.com so they could reach the electrician looking for that tool? Of course. It's a perfect match and was not about search rank or manipulating Google. It's about the intent of the audience that's at that website. Who goes to UsedElectricianTools.com? Probably electricians looking for used tools. That's a natural, logical place to buy a link.

Social Media and Link Sharing

The biggest change that's happened on the web over the past ten years is that it has become easier for people to share links/URLs. Anyone who has an account on Facebook, Twitter, or Google+ can share a link in two seconds with hundreds or even thousands of followers, who can then reshare it, and in the span of a few hours, a link has the potential to pass in front of hundreds of thousands of people.

If you are not using social media and have not enabled sharing of your content, you are missing a linking strategy and traffic stream. Just ask Snoop Dogg. He has 11 million followers on Twitter.

Some content is of such interest it attracts links and shares and tweets like a snowball effect, that some call "going viral." But for most companies the main power of social media from a linking perspective is the ability to reach key influencers within very specific niches.

Once you get out there with new content, as people hear about it, find out about it, link to it, tell others about it, share it, tweet it, it has the chance to take on a life of its own and it can attract even more links. Trickle-down linking; links beget links.

But don't believe for a moment there's some social media strategy or tactic that you can use that anybody else could use in any sort of cookie cutter manner. You'll see sites selling social media awareness services and offering to "get you 5,000 new followers for $50." These services are, in my opinion, useless. You have to take the strategy and tailor it to the content of the site. Twitter and Facebook can both be used by any company, but *how* they use them will be much more important.

Some Techniques to Try

Where is link building headed? Nobody can predict the future, but based on what I've seen over the past 18 years, links are too useful for the engines to ignore. I think the engines will always be able to glean something from the worldwide collection of billions of links.

Aside from the engines, I suggest you start looking at links as pathways to your business, not just fuel for higher search rankings. It's fine to optimize your content for the search engines, because the reality is they do represent a tremendous opportunity for organic traffic. But this is the same for your competitors as well. I'm sure there are hundreds of truly outstanding personal injury attorneys in the United States, but Google can only rank one of them first. Are the rest supposed to give up? No.

Below are a few example link-building techniques that you can try. To see an amazing list, check out Jon Cooper's Complete List of Link Building Tactics at http://pointblankseo.com/link-building-strategies.

1. *If you are a local business go to https://moz.com/local/.* Moz Local offers a free tool that will give you instant feedback regarding the accuracy of your local business listings, and whether those listings are correct, consistent, and visible across the web.

2. *How-tos and tutorials.* People love to learn things, and it's quite easy to create tutorials, either in text, video, or both, that help

them. Whether it's a tool, DIY project, or anything else, showing people exactly how to do something is extremely helpful. To see a great example, go to Google and search on this exact phrase:

how to build a treehouse with your kids

Notice one of the sites listed in the results is www.instructables.com , which gives anyone the opportunity to create a tutorial for the world to see.

3. *Reach out to industry experts.* It's fairly easy to find experts in just about any industry. A few searches with the right keywords will help you. Invite these experts to participate in an interview on your blog. Interviews appeal to experts because interviews confirm their status as experts. And experts already have connections, followers, fans, and their own sites, blogs, newsletters, etc. Interviews attract links.

4. *Niche supplier or manufacturer guides and directories.* Almost every industry has some type of industry specific buyer's guide, and many industries have more than one. If you sell products or services that are a fit for these guides, it can lead to a link and more. It's exposure of your brand to the exact audience that would be interested in what you offer. Below are just a few examples I selected that illustrate the variety of these publicity and linking opportunities.

- *Firehouse Buyer's Guide.* An easy-access directory to the products, technologies, and services available to improve your delivery of fire, rescue and EMS related products. http://www.firehouse.com/directory.

- *The Pool & Spa Industry Search.* The information resource designed around its 3,000 members' and other industry professionals' requests, providing them a one-stop resource to find the products and information they need. http://poolandspaindustrysearch.com/

- *BeeSource—Serving the Beekeeping Community since 1997.* Beesource.com has over 14,000 registered members and is the most active online beekeeping community of its kind in the world. For the *Beekeeping Equipment and Suppliers Guide* go to www.beesource.com/

Surely if there's a supplier's guide for beekeeping, there's one for your industry as well. I use Google to look for them by using industry keyword plus terms such as *buyer's guide, suppliers, members,* etc.

5. *Subscribe to LinkMoses Private from Eric Ward.* OK, so I'm not above a little self-promotion. LinkMoses Private is an email-based newsletter that contains linking techniques that help with both click traffic and organic rankings today and for the long term. The goal of LinkMoses Private is to help you improve and sculpt a more effective inbound link profile. This involves recognizing the wide variety of linking opportunities that are available to you, from social media to the deep web, if you know where to look and how to pursue them. For more information, go to: http://www.ericward.com/lmp.

The advice I have given many times over the years remains the same. Pursue links you would want regardless of whether or not Google rewards you for them. Pursue links that help your business because of the relationships those links represent.

Leveraging
Apps

CHAPTER 13

How to Create and Implement a Facebook Strategy that Converts

Andrea Vahl

ANDREA VAHL is the co-author of *Facebook Marketing All-in-One for Dummies* and was the community manager for the Social Media Examiner for over two years. She specializes in running Facebook ad campaigns for businesses all over the world and is the co-founder of Social Media Manager School. She regularly writes for Copyblogger, Social Media Examiner, *iBlog* magazine, and other sites around the web. She also uses her improvisational comedy skills to blog as a slightly cranky character, Grandma Mary, Social Media Edutainer on her site at www.AndreaVahl.com.

In this Chapter, You'll Discover

▶ What is really working on Facebook to get fresh, targeted leads coming to your door

▶ Setting up a strategy that works with your busy schedule

▶ How to take advantage of tools like Facebook ads and contests and track your results

▶ Monitoring key performance indicators that will ensure returns on your investment of time on Facebook

Facebook is the largest social network on the web but many business owners and marketers still don't know how to take advantage of all Facebook has to offer. To complicate matters, Facebook continually changes their layout and their news feed algorithm to make it a moving target for marketers. Just when you get comfortable with what is working, it shifts.

Facebook Marketing Demystified

Some people talk about metrics such as the perfect time to post, the perfect length of post, the perfect way to post a link. But none of that matters as much as posting content that your audience cares about. Yes, there are strategies that work better on Facebook in terms of getting more visibility, but when you focus on providing good content consistently your audience will make sure they go out of their way to find you.

There is no doubt that Facebook is increasingly becoming a "pay-to-play" platform with pages getting less exposure in the news feed than they have in the past. But that should not scare marketers away. We'll touch on some of the ways you can take advantage of Facebook advertising a little later in this chapter.

> Think of Facebook more as a subscription model where you will need to invest some of your marketing budget each month but you can still take advantage of the organic reach that Facebook gives you.

Some people worry that Facebook use is declining, but many recent studies, including one from Pew Research, show Facebook use is increasing. All types of businesses are using Facebook, including B2B and B2C. You need to be online, and Facebook is still where it's at.

So where do you start? Or where do you restart if your efforts have stalled? I am a big fan of checklists and this checklist will help you make sure you have all your ducks in a row.

1. Optimize Your Facebook Page

Your cover photo is the first impression for your Facebook page. The cover photo also shows up in several ways on Facebook—if someone hovers over your page name in a post, in suggested pages, and in other places. If possible, have a tagline on the photo that states the main benefit of why someone should like your page. On Grandma Mary—Social Media Edutainer's cover photo we have "Social Media is waaay more fun with Grandma Mary!" People know instantly why they might want to like this page.

The next thing you want to optimize is your About section. Add your critical keywords here because this is indexed in Google and you get the chance to tell people more about what you do. Link to special places on your website you want to highlight and maybe even add some testimonials from happy customers in this section.

2. Have a Content Strategy

The biggest way people are going to interact with your Facebook page is through your posts. So you need to know what you are posting and how often. We'll talk more in a moment about what types of posts work best, but you will need to have a mixture of business news, tips, photos, links, and also humor. People are on Facebook to be social and have fun. If you have some humorous posts about your business niche, your posts will get comments, likes, and shares, which will then help your exposure on Facebook.

Having a content strategy also includes how often to post. Facebook posts do have a limited shelf-life of visibility and if you are only posting a couple times a week, you are in danger of dropping off your audience's radar. I recommend posting at least twice a day during the week to increase your visibility. That may feel overwhelming to some people, but when you create a content calendar of posts for the week, that task becomes more manageable. For example, you could post a helpful tip Monday morning and then a shareable quote Monday afternoon; then industry news Tuesday morning and something humorous Tuesday afternoon. See—it's not too hard when you get organized!

3. Interact with Others

One of the best ways to grow organically is to connect and comment on other complementary business pages. You can like another page as your page and then comment on their posts. Then that page's audience has the potential to see your name in the comments of that post, giving your page more visibility. But not only that, it creates good will with the other complementary pages, and they may be more likely to share and comment on your posts.

4. Use Your Personal Profile If Possible

Using your personal profile to help share your business news may not always be possible, but if you are the face of your business, people may be connecting with you personally. You can do things like open up your Follow button and create Facebook lists to help you manage your privacy with your personal profile. Your personal profile is more visible to your friends than your page, and by occasionally sharing your business news you have an increased chance of your most important announcements being seen.

Content that Works on Facebook

What type of content works best on Facebook? Make sure your focus is on your audience. Yes, you can post your sales messages, but you first have to make sure you are giving value.

> *Content that works best educates, entertains,*
> *or evokes emotion.*

Just because you are a business doesn't mean that you have to be serious all the time. Humor works extremely well and often has the highest number of shares and likes. But, of course, you need to balance that with value. Oreo does a great job of having fun while marketing their products (although it's easier to have fun when you are marketing a cookie).

Many brands are telling stories that evoke emotion as they advertise which are shared much more than a regular commercial. When you are posting something about your business, get into your audience's shoes and ask yourself, "Would I share that?" And use images in the post to help tell your story.

Ask questions as you post articles to try and start a conversation. But then make sure you return to participate in that conversation.

Using Facebook to Get Leads

Many business owners are interested in getting leads from Facebook, but how does that actually work? I typically teach people to use Facebook to target your perfect potential customers and get them onto your email list. Then let your emails do your selling for you.

> Focus on transferring your Facebook community to your email list. Social media will change, email is yours.

First you need to be clear on how your business brings potential customers in the door. Local businesses and restaurants may need to focus on actual foot traffic. Online businesses may focus on email marketing. For some larger B2C companies, a like or new follower may be valuable. Know what success looks like for you. Usually all businesses can benefit from getting an email address from a potential customer. You just need to have something valuable (a "freebie") to give someone in exchange for that email address. Here are some ideas for things you can offer:

- ▶ *Exclusive coupon.* Great for local businesses that need that foot traffic.
- ▶ *Free report or white paper.* This doesn't have to be very long, it just needs to offer valuable tips that your potential customer is interested in and that relate directly to your business.

▸ *Webinar or teleseminar.* Offer a short class or free call; this could be live or prerecorded.

▸ *Contest.* Use these throughout the year to give away something directly related to your business.

▸ *E-course.* Use a set of emails to teach some lessons. Use your automated email system to deliver the emails—one a day for 10 days, for example.

Now that you have developed your Facebook community that is interested in your information, post about your freebie with a link to the page where they can sign up. Post regularly about the freebie and also make sure you are occasionally offering new freebies to attract your perfect client.

If you haven't developed your Facebook community yet, you can use Facebook ads to target your perfect clients and advertise your freebie (or even your product). Free offers work very well on Facebook, and Facebook ads are very reasonable and extremely trackable. You can use things like "conversion pixels" to see exactly what each lead or sale costs you.

With Facebook ads, you can target your perfect customer through demographics and keywords. Then you insert the ad into the news feed, where it gets more visibility. When you use the conversion pixel, you can see exactly when someone purchased your product or opted in to your form on your website.

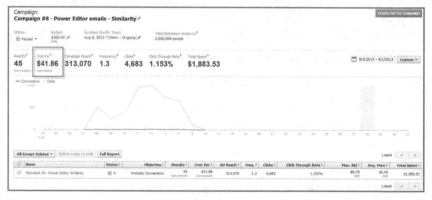

FIGURE 13.1

Consider using a separate email list or tags that you use when someone signs up to your list from Facebook so that you can then track any sales that come from that list. Then you can see the true benefits of using Facebook to get leads.

Fitting Facebook into Your Busy Schedule

One thing I hear frequently from business owners is how they don't have time to do social media or Facebook. Yes, it can be time-consuming but there are tools that can help you streamline your activities. And if you set up ways to measure your sales from social media, you may be more willing to spend time on Facebook because you know you are getting a return.

Here is a list of tools that can help you save time and find the perfect content to post:

1. *Facebook Scheduler*. Facebook has a way for you to schedule your posts. Using the Facebook scheduler is a great way to make sure your posts look good because they are using Facebook's own system. Sometimes when you use another third-party tool to schedule your posts, they don't pull the photo or the link information in correctly.

2. *Post Planner*. Post Planner is a third-party tool that works with Facebook, but they also do a great job with pulling in RSS feeds that you like, giving you the ability to easily share your favorite content as well as suggestions of topics to post about.

3. *Facebook Interest Lists*. Use these to put all your favorite Facebook pages in one group so that you can watch what is being shared on Facebook in your industry. You can then easily share that content with your Facebook community if you need a quick post.

4. *Activity Calendar*. Create a list of what you need to do on Facebook every week and schedule time in your day to get those tasks done. I have my activity calendar in an Excel spreadsheet, and I can see what I need to do daily, weekly, and monthly.

5. *Canva or PicMonkey*. Use these tools to create cool visual images to share. Easily create a list of tips, a photo with an inspiring

quote, or even a new Facebook cover photo with these tools. Professional-looking images are more important than ever in social media.

Using Facebook Ads and Contests to Get More Leads

I mentioned Facebook ads earlier in this chapter as a good strategy to get more leads, but I wanted to expand on that and also dive deeper into Facebook contests. Facebook ads have to be treated slightly differently than Google ads, if you are familiar with those.

You can target your perfect customer on Facebook by their demographic and the interest words in their profile, but they may not be ready to buy your product. On Google you are targeting your ads to keywords people put in the search window, so they may be more interested in actually purchasing your product or service.

That is why advertising freebies can work well on Facebook to get people on your email list. Then connect with them frequently with valuable tips in your follow-up emails until they are ready to buy your product or service.

You can track these opt-ins with conversion pixels. You just put a bit of code on the "thank-you" page of your opt-in sequence (usually the page that you send people to after they have confirmed their email address) and then the code sends a message to Facebook saying that someone who came from the ad made it all the way through the opt-in process successfully. Now you know exactly how much it costs you to get a lead from your Facebook ad. Then you can test different demographics and different ads to see which one converts the best.

One of my favorite Facebook ad tools is Custom Audiences and Similar Audiences. You can upload your email list of prospects and customers into a Facebook Custom Audience and create an ad directed at them so your email campaign is reinforced on Facebook. You can also create a Similar Audience from your subscribers. Facebook uses the demographics and interests of the people you've uploaded and expands that into a much larger audience of similar profiles (typically about one to two million people). Now you can further use interests and targeting to advertise to that group of people to really zero in on showing your ad to your perfect potential client.

Another effective tool in Facebook advertising is Website Custom Audiences. You put a bit of code on your website and you can then build an audience of all the people who have visited your website (they are added to the list only if they were also logged into Facebook at the same time). Then you can target an ad to that audience specifically. This can work well to reach people who have visited your website but maybe not opted in to your offer or purchased your product.

While these tools may sound a bit overwhelming, you don't have to get super fancy to have an effective ad campaign. My biggest tip for maximizing your Facebook ads is to do split testing. To do split testing right, change just one aspect of the ad at a time and measure how well that ad performs. So for example, you would first use the same ad and test which demographics and keywords work best for your targeting. Then when you had the best performing demographic, you would test how well a differing image worked or a different headline. Using split testing will help you find the best performing ad overall and reduce your cost per click.

Running a Facebook contest can also be a great way to get leads for your business. If you make the prize relevant to your business (either by giving away your product or service or something related to your product or service) then when people enter your contest you know they are interested in your business and not just winning an iPad (or some other prize).

The best way to run a Facebook contest to get leads is to use an application. Many great contest applications out there are inexpensive and easy to set up. Some of my favorites are Heyo, TabSite, ShortStack, Offerpop, Antavo, AgoraPulse, and Tabfoundry. They all have different features and capabilities so check which one fits your needs best.

Many of these apps have built-in statistics to help you track how well your contest converts entries. But you should also go a step beyond this and keep your list of entries separated in your email lists or tagged so that you can track if any of these entries eventually lead to a sale. After the contest is over make sure you are following up with all of the people who have entered your contest with a special offer. Even if no one does take you up on your offer right away, continue to send good tips and updates through your email list so that when they are ready to purchase your product, your company is the first one they think of.

Monitoring Key Performance Indicators on Facebook

Many businesses look at the new likes on Facebook as an indication of how well their social strategy is performing. While monitoring new likes isn't a bad thing since it indicates awareness and it can be the first step to your potential customer connecting to you, it isn't the only thing you need to watch.

> *You can't put Facebook likes in your bank.*

Of course, revenue from social media is the desired goal but sales can be hard to measure since people don't always purchase your product directly from a Facebook post. Maybe they opt in to your email list from a post, and then make a purchase six months later. If you can, keep your email lists tagged or separated in some way that can help you track your sales. Here are some other ways you can track email opt-ins or sales:

- ▶ Use conversion pixels in your Facebook ads.
- ▶ Use Google Goals to track when someone gets to your "thank-you" page on your website and track which site they were referred from.
- ▶ Use coupon codes that you use only for a specific platform to see which site provides the most sales (for example, one coupon code just for Twitter, one for LinkedIn, and one for Facebook).
- ▶ Ask how someone found you when they check out (they may not remember but sometimes they do).

Other key performance indicators you can use as measurements of success are things like engagement and website traffic. If you have a 100,000 likes on your page but no one ever comments or clicks "like" on your posts, you are probably wasting your time on Facebook. Dive into your Facebook Insights to get detailed analytics on each post. Watch how many people are commenting, sharing, or clicking "like," and track what works best.

You can also see specifically which posts are working best for your page in Facebook Insights. This can depend a bit on which types of posts you are sharing most often but checking in with these stats can show you what's working in general for you.

You can't only post things that get the most engagement, or we'd all be posting cat videos all day. But make sure you combine your best performing posts with the techniques that seem to be working for you. Did that post with the inspiring quote get a lot of shares? Figure out how to really relate that to your product or service in the next post.

You can track traffic to your website with things like Google Analytics or, if you are using WordPress, Jetpack Stats. You can even use trackable links by using link shorteners like http://bit.ly to take things a bit further.

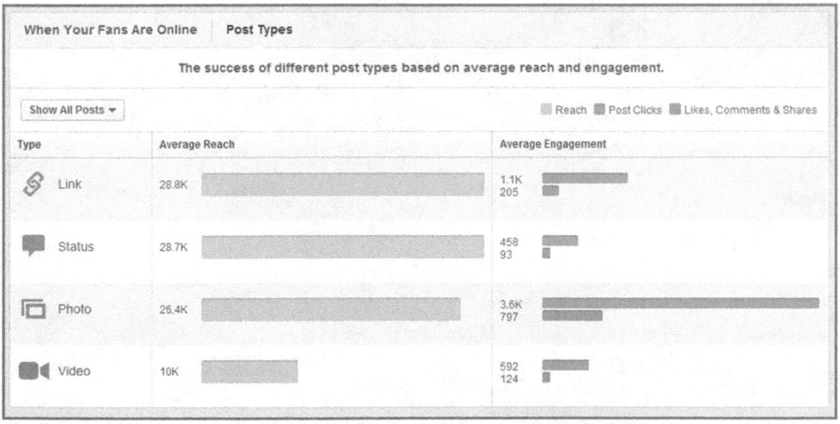

FIGURE 13.2

Whatever you do with your tracking, do it consistently. Spend some time doing some analysis on your stats so you can do more of what works best and spend less time doing things that aren't working. Facebook is an incredible tool and will continue to be relevant to marketers for a long time.

CHAPTER 14

Connecting with Clients, Getting More Traffic, and Making More Sales Using Pinterest Marketing

Beth Hayden

In this Chapter, You'll Discover

- ▶ Use Pinterest to connect with your target audience
- ▶ Harness Pinterest to drive massive traffic to your website
- ▶ Convert Pinterest users into customers

BETH HAYDEN is a social media expert, speaker, and author of *Pinfluence: The Complete Guide to Marketing Your Business with Pinterest*. Beth regularly contributes to the web's top social media blogs and is a senior staff writer for Copyblogger Media. Beth works with all kinds of businesses (from large corporations to solo entrepreneurs) to help them define and implement effective content marketing strategies. For more information, go to BethHayden.com.

▲ ▲ ▲

Social media sites and personal blogs are all aflutter with talk about Pinterest—the networking site that allows users to create online image collages, then share those collages (called "pinboards") with other Pinterest users.

In a sea of other social networking options, there are a number of reasons why you may want to pay attention to Pinterest—and possibly move it up on your list of marketing priorities. Check out these stats:

- ▸ Pinterest currently has more than 70 million unique visitors (as of 2014) and thousands of new users are signing up and using the site every day.

- ▸ Pinterest was named one of *Time* magazine's 50 Best Websites of 2011 and TechCrunch's Best New Startup of 2011, a heady honor in the super-competitive world of incredible startups.

- ▸ Most importantly—right now, Pinterest is driving more traffic to websites and blogs than Twitter, YouTube, Google+ and LinkedIn *combined*, according to content-sharing site Shareaholic.

Now, let's address a common concern, right from the start. You may have heard rumors that Pinterest is only good for marketing physical products (like jewelry or clothes) and that the social media tool can only be used to market to women. Maybe you're assuming that it can't possibly help you if you run a B2B company or a nonprofit, or if you sell knowledge products like ebooks or virtual classes.

But I'm here to tell you the rumors are untrue. Pinterest is great for marketing just about *any* product or service, no matter who your target audience is.

So when should you use Pinterest? Use Pinterest if:

- ▸ *You have an interesting story to tell with images and videos.* I could argue that most companies do, or that they could *create* an interesting story to tell. Even General Electric—not a company that would typically spring to mind as being able to do anything interesting with a Pinterest profile—has created cool pinboards like "Brilliance in Motion" (www.pinterest.com/generalelectric/brilliance-in-motion/) that tell their story in visually interesting ways. What kind of visual story can you tell about your business that will help your customers get to know you and humanize your brand?

▶ *You want to establish yourself as an expert on your topic.* Pinterest is a fantastic platform for content curation, and smart companies are using it for that purpose. If you regularly share content via tweets or Facebook updates, you can extend that sharing to your Pinterest platform by using pins and boards as a social bookmarking tool.

▶ *When you want to interface with your clients and work collaboratively with them in a visual way.* If you're a service provider and you regularly have opportunities to collaborate and brainstorm with your clients, Pinterest will be a fantastic tool for you.

You should probably NOT use Pinterest if:

▶ *Your lawyer advises you not to use it.* If you (or your attorney) object to the practice of pinning or repinning images from other websites, you can always just pin your own images—there are lots of cool ways to use Pinterest that way. But if Pinterest's potential legal issues make you feel squeamish—or if your lawyer has forbid you to use it—obviously you shouldn't start a Pinterest account.

▶ *You're an artist or photographer and you don't have an easy way for visitors to buy your work.* If you feature your work on your website, and you don't have a seamless way for people to buy your pieces online, you need to set up a shopping cart system before you get on Pinterest. Make the process as simple as possible; pinners should be able to easily click from a pin of your artwork to a sales page. And while you're at it, make sure you always watermark your images with your name and site address.

Interesting in learning more about using Pinterest for marketing? Let's dig into the details.

Getting Started with Pinterest

It only takes a few moments to create your Pinterest business account (which is a good idea, if you plan on using Pinterest for marketing purposes). Once your account is set up, you can create online collages ("boards") for different topics you're interested in, then add images and videos to your boards by "pinning" them. The interface is fast, slick, and fun.

A lot of the content on Pinterest (up to 85 percent, according to recent figures) is "repinned" from other users—so you can make yourself stand out by regularly introducing cool new content from outside websites and blogs. And always keep your target audience in mind when you're pinning—you want to regularly pin content that your prospects and customers will find useful, interesting, or entertaining.

> You can get a great little bookmarklet that lets you pin images from all over the web. This bookmarklet lets you put a "Pin it" button at the top of your web browser, so you can pin images quickly and easily as you come across cool and interesting content. Get it here: www.pinterest.com/about/goodies/.

Connect with Your Prospects on Pinterest

Once you've gotten the basics of Pinterest down, how do you use pinning to *really* connect with your target market? Here are five suggestions for using Pinterest to build genuine, lasting relationships with your prospects:

1. *Engage with other Pinterest users.* Tag other Pinterest users in any pin by using "@username" in your descriptions. You can use this feature to engage with customers, strategic partners, or industry

vendors. There aren't a ton of comments on Pinterest (and even fewer comments that tag individual users), so if you engage in this way, it can really help you build your following and stand out from the crowd.

Another suggestion is to regularly "like" other people's pins to give a thumbs-up when you want to recognize great content. This is an easy way to interact with other users in an approachable, personal way.

2. *Become an information curator for your niche.* Your job on Pinterest is to gather and display awesome content in your niche—and that makes you a *curator*.

In the real world, professional curators gather, organize, and display items for museums and galleries. Your job as an online curator is to do the same thing for your virtual audience.

Being a Pinterest curator means you pick the best images and then organize them in an interesting way that benefits your core audience. In other words, you cherry-pick all the best images related to your topic and pin them to your boards.

If you do a good job, it'll help you build your authority, and people will eventually look to you as the go-to source for cool images and content on your topic. When that happens, you can bet they'll come back to you again and again, giving you lots of chances to tell them about your blog or website (and convert them into customers).

So when you're pinning, pick the best information—the most educational, informative, and compelling content—to put on your boards, and users will flock to your Pinterest presence as a way to get information about your subject. That helps you become a trusted expert that they'll be happy to buy from, too!

> *You can pin photos from Flickr (flickr.com) or slide decks from SlideShare (slideshare.net), too!*

3. *Feature user-generated content.* You can start generating some goodwill with your community by featuring user-generated content on your pinboards.

   Set up a "Guest Pinner" program for your Pinterest account, and allow your best customers or star students to pin on certain boards.

   Give your guest pinners some general content guidelines (make sure they're clear on who your target audience is and the kinds of things your followers like), then add them as collaborators on the board and set them loose to pin images and videos. You'll be amazed what great content your guest pinners create, and they will also be delighted to get more attention for their own Pinterest accounts!

4. *Create boards for conferences that you attend.* Pinning can be used to network before, during, and after live events and conferences. Before the event, you can write and pin blog posts about what sessions you'll be attending and the people you're hoping to connect with (make sure to link to their pinboards or blogs, too!).

   During the conference, you can share photos and videos of sessions, presenters, and other attendees. After the event is over, do some post-conference pins to share your follow-up actions and talk about what you're hoping to accomplish with the knowledge you gained and the people you connected with.

   Here's another tip—conference pinning can (and should) be a collaborative effort. Create simple business cards that include instructions for getting invited to pin on the conference board, then share those cards with other attendees. You'll create amazing boards using this technique, and your fellow attendees will really appreciate your efforts!

Give 'Em More of What They Want

Want to find out what images and videos people have been pinning from your site?

You can find out by viewing your site's source page on Pinterest. Go to: pinterest.com/source/[yoursitehere.com] to see your source page. Just make sure you strip out the "http://www."

By checking out your source page on a regular basis, you can see which images (and what content) is resonating with Pinterest users. And once you know what pinners like, make sure to give them more of that!

Driving Traffic to Your Website from Pinterest

Pinterest can be a visitor referral machine for your website, and you can drive more traffic to your site by making your content as pinnable as possible. Here are some ways to actively drive traffic to your site:

1. *Make your content visually engaging.* In order for your web pages and blog posts to get pinned on Pinterest (and reap the benefits of being passed around on the site), your posts must include clear, appealing images. If you spend some time on the Pinterest site, you'll see what types of photos get repinned consistently; the pictures are interesting and compelling.

   To start getting traffic (and business) from Pinterest, you need to add images to every blog post, landing page, and sales page on your website—no excuses!

2. *Use photo badges.* A photo badge is an interesting image that has your blog post title superimposed on it. Check Figure 14.1 on page 186 for an example of a photo badge.

   Use Photoshop or free online photo editing tools like PicMonkey (picmonkey.com) to create beautiful photo badges.

   Once your photo badge is published with your blog post, make sure you pin it on one of your boards. You can use your badges on Facebook and Twitter, too!

3. *Make sure you've got a Pin It button on every page of your website or blog.* Make it easy for your readers to share your content on Pinterest. Get a free Pin It button for your site by going to the Pinterest "Goodies" page: pinterest.com/about/goodies.

4. *Figure out your Pinterest "peak times."* You want to think strategically about timing on Pinterest, and maximize your time in the

FIGURE 14.1

Pinterest spotlight by pinning your images when the greatest number of people will see them.

For most niches, that means you want to pin between 6 A.M. and 6 P.M. EST, but that's just a rule of thumb. The smart strategy is to look at the traffic stats for your own website to see when you consistently get the most traffic from Pinterest—then plan to pin during those times.

5. *Create tutorials and how-to content on your site.* Pinterest users love how-to content, so create tutorials and other educational content for your site, then pin that content to Pinterest.

6. *Use a clear call to action.* Featuring a "call to action" like "click here," "comment below," or "repin this," increases the engagement (repins, comments, likes) of a pin by 80 percent. So

include those calls to action in your pins to drive traffic to your blog posts or website!

Get More Pinterest Followers

Remember: The *quality* of your Pinterest audience matters a great deal more than the *quantity*. But if you're looking for some active ways to build your list of followers, here are some ideas:

1. *Follow other pinners.* This one sounds incredibly basic, but it truly is the quickest and easiest way to build a following. Many of the people you follow will follow you back, and your numbers will grow. Try to follow a couple of interesting new people every time you're on Pinterest.
2. *Pin consistently.* Pinning regularly—and pinning a LOT—is one of the very best things you can do to build your following. The more you pin, the more followers you'll get. So set aside a little bit of time each day to do some pinning.
3. *Actively seek out (and pin) new and interesting content.* The more original you are, the more followers you will get; so make an effort to find new things to pin (from your website and other online sources).
4. *Run contests.* I'm not a huge fan of using this technique all the time, but it can give you a boost in your follower count. Consider running a contest in which you ask your Pinterest followers to create a board on a particular topic, then choose the winner and give out a cool prize. The buzz will help you add followers.

Converting Your Followers into Customers

I'm going to let you in on a little secret.

The key to converting Pinterest followers into paying customers is getting them on your mailing list.

Pinterest is a fantastic tool. So is Facebook. So is Twitter. But if the people you're talking to and connecting with on these social media sites never visit your website or sign up for your mailing list, they're not likely to buy from you. And if no one is buying from you, all the time you spend on social networking will be completely wasted.

Email is a much more intimate and direct way of communicating with a prospective customer than any social media communication could ever be. Email messages are much more likely to reach their intended targets, because most of us check our email every day (many of us multiple times a day!). And though we complain about our email backlogs and being slaves to our inboxes, the truth is that we're still using email for a great deal of our day-to-day communication.

So if you want to convert someone from a pinner to a buyer, you need to get him or her on your list so you can follow up and get started on the process of getting that person to know, like, and trust you. It's a critical step in being able to convert Pinterest traffic to actual sales.

So how do you get them on your mailing list? You want to link to the best content from your website, and make sure there is an easy way for that person to get on your email list. Give something away (like a free report, free video, etc.) as an incentive to sign up for your list.

Then make sure you're delivering great content to your email list on a regular basis. And make offers, too—tell them what they can buy from you, what your services are, how your products are packaged, etc. Make it easy for them to go directly from your email campaigns to making a purchase from you.

Getting Pinterest users to open their wallets means giving them an easy way to sign up for your list; get to know, like, and trust you; and then buy from you. That's the critical formula that so many Pinterest marketers miss.

You can also highlight your best company stories on Pinterest. Pin pictures of your clients and paste their testimonials in the pin descriptions. Everyone loves seeing faces with testimonials—it makes them much more credible and friendly—so this is a great technique for gathering social proof about the awesomeness of your company and moving prospects toward the final finish line. Then you can link those pins back to a testimonials page on your website.

Pinning for Traffic—and for Dollars!

Pinterest has become a proven source of traffic for blogs and websites, quickly surpassing current favorites like Twitter and YouTube. While lots of folks are flapping their jaws about the impressive statistics of Pinterest, other companies are quietly using this fun new tool to pin their way to better customer engagement and a visually interesting brand.

My advice for marketers? Consider using Pinterest as part your online strategy for your business. And start creating a more compelling marketing message—one beautiful little pin at a time.

CHAPTER 15

Video Marketing
How to Win in a World Gone Video

Lou Bortone

LOU BORTONE is a video marketing consultant and online branding coach. A former television executive who worked for E! Entertainment Television and later served as the senior VP of marketing for Fox in Los Angeles, Lou provides services such as video production, brand development coaching, creative support, and video coaching. Connect with Lou at www.LouBortone.com.

▲ ▲ ▲

The web—and in fact the whole world—has gone video. Cisco Systems predicts that by

In this Chapter, You'll Discover

▶ Why online video is now an absolute "must have" marketing strategy

▶ Why video strategy is far more important than video technology

▶ The four pillars of video marketing

▶ How to get more comfortable being on camera

▶ Both on-camera and off-camera strategies for creating video

▶ How to leverage your content with YouTube and social media

2017, 90 percent of all web traffic will be video. Video has become the way we share, the way we communicate, the way we connect, and the way we sell.

Video has also become the way we search (YouTube is the second most popular search engine), the way we "surf," and the way we make buying decisions. Sixty-five percent of consumers will visit a brand's website and make a purchase decision after watching a video.

As an online entrepreneur, video marketing is your single most powerful tool for getting more visibility more quickly, so you can get your message out, attract your ideal clients, make more money, and have more impact. It's no surprise that ReelSEO reports 87 percent of online marketers are now using video to promote their products and services. It's also reported that your chances of getting a page-one listing on Google search increase by 53 times when you use video. You can also experience a dramatic 46 percent more conversion lift with video.

Video increases your visibility and credibility, it boosts your search engine rankings, and it rapidly accelerates the sales process. Video is clearly a more personal and familiar medium, and one that can truly create a strong and lasting relationship with your customers.

Video marketing is relationship marketing: crucial for connecting, building loyalty and developing the "know, like, and trust" factor which is so important when doing business online.

Strategy First

You may be surprised to learn that video marketing, or at least successful video marketing, is not about which camera to use, what's the best microphone, or even lighting and editing. That's production, not marketing.

To be effective with video, the emphasis needs to be on your *marketing* strategy. You must ask: What is the goal of the video? What business objective will it accomplish? Who will be viewing the video, and what do you want the viewer to do after they watch it? These are just a few of the marketing questions that must be addressed before you even set up a light or fire up the webcam.

Obviously, production is important (and we'll get to that), but it's still not marketing. Start with strategy and that will determine how much (or how little) equipment you need. So think strategy first, tools, equipment, and technology later.

Many video "newbies" make the mistake of stocking up on fancy equipment, high-end video cameras, or expensive software. Once all their gear is finally in place, they often have a "now what?" moment when they realize they've put the cart before the horse.

Thinking that equipment alone with help you produce great video is just like thinking that simply buying a treadmill or stair stepper will get you in shape. You still have to know how to use it and do the work!

Depending on your video marketing goals, you may not need a lot of equipment. It's more likely that you can get a great start just by using the video camera on your smartphone or the webcam on your laptop or tablet. Again, goals before tech.

Let's take Tania, for instance, a wellness coach who wants to build her online business and eventually sell wellness workshops and health-related products online. Tania's video goals include establishing her expertise in her niche and developing trust and credibility in her target market of health-conscious boomers.

Because she needs to build her online visibility and credibility, Tania decides to create a video tips series to post on YouTube and her blog. Since content matters more than quality to her audience, Tania doesn't need to invest in high-end equipment. In fact, she can simply use the webcam on her computer to record her health tips, and then do some quick edits in iMovie (or even using YouTube's onboard editor). No big production is needed here; just get those video tips posted quickly and consistently.

If Tania's goal were to get paid speaking gigs or appearances on TV news or talk shows, she may have taken a different approach and hired a professional camera crew to tape her segments. Production values would be more important for that more discerning audience. Let your strategy drive your technology requirements.

Your Video Plan: The Four Pillars of Video Marketing

As you create your video plan, you can use the "Four Pillars" formula to be sure you've got a solid structure for your video. They are:

1. *Purpose.* What does the video need to accomplish?
2. *Premise.* What is your message or story?
3. *Platform.* What type or style of video will you create?
4. *Promotion.* Where and how will you distribute your video?

Let's take a closer look at each pillar.

Purpose

This simply goes back to thinking strategically about the business goals for your video. You can use your video for creating awareness, increasing your visibility, building trust and credibility, generating leads, launching a product, growing your list, driving web traffic, selling a service—the list is almost endless. Understanding your objectives up front will determine your message, platform, and distribution.

Put your video goals in writing, like you would for any business plan. Here are a few sample video goals:

▶ Develop a video presence online to increase visibility
▶ Add an opt-in or welcome video to your homepage to connect with your prospects
▶ Create a "video tips" series on YouTube to establish credibility and expert status
▶ Post videos to build a promotional platform to sell books or info products
▶ Create a sales video to launch a product
▶ Create video tutorials or demos to sell as a product

Finally, be sure your video goals are part of your overall marketing plan, and not a "one-off" effort. Consistency is important and "one and done" videos rarely accomplish the task. Consider creating a video editorial calendar to integrate your videos into your annual business plan.

Premise

The second pillar for your video plan is to determine your message, script, or story. Your premise is how you will communicate your message and move your viewer to action. What do you want your viewer to do when the video is over? (You have to tell them that!)

Some video creators prefer to write a script or even storyboard their video to plan every shot. Others prefer to simply use an outline and ad-lib their script. There are no hard and fast rules, as long as you can effectively deliver your message in a way that motivates the viewer.

When developing your message or writing your script, keep in mind the very limited attention span of online viewers. Be clear, concise, and direct. Get to the point quickly and keep your video as short as possible. The vast majority of YouTube videos are under three minutes in length. (Obvious exceptions include training videos, webinars, and other long-form videos.)

Platform

What kind of video will you create? While you could argue that there are only really two types of videos—on-camera or off-camera—there are actually many different styles and options. Video has evolved into much more than the traditional "talking head" format. You'll want to find the platform that best fits your needs and personal style.

Most video creators default to the tried-and-true on-camera video, which can include the direct to camera video, a video interview with two or more participants, a video tips series, or a live webcast.

On-camera videos are usually best for when you want to make a more engaging connection with your viewers, or when you're promoting a more personal service and you wish to create more trust and credibility.

Off-camera videos, on the other hand, don't require you to be on camera, which can be a big benefit to the more camera-shy among us. Off-camera videos, often called "screencasts," can also be extremely effective when sharing a lot of information, such as during a video webinar or training video.

Promotion

The fourth and final pillar is promotion, or how and where will you distribute, share, and market your video online. Rule number one is to get your video off your hard drive and get it online. You'd be surprised how many entrepreneurs produce their video and never upload it! You've got to get your video in front of your audience and make it easy for them to find.

Determine where your target market is, and share your video there! YouTube and your own website or blog are the obvious choices, but think beyond YouTube and upload your video to as many outlets as possible.

YouTube is a great place to start, not only because they're one of the biggest sites on the internet, but also because they make it so easy to share and spread your video to other social media sites. Once your video is on YouTube, you can set up one-click sharing to Facebook, Google+, Twitter, LinkedIn, and more. You can also use the embed code that YouTube provides to get the video on your website or blog. In addition, YouTube will provide a link to your video so you can send it out in an email to your list.

Be sure to consider other social media sites that accept video, such as Pinterest, Instagram (15-second limit), SlideShare, and other video hosting sites such as Viddler or Vimeo. The more you distribute your video, the better chance viewers have to find it and watch it.

Last, be sure to make your video easy to share. If you want your video to be spread virally, make sure your video is compelling, relevant, and engaging. The most "shareable" videos tend to be short, fun, and topical.

Getting Ready for Your Close-Up

Now that you know the four pillars of video marketing, it's time to face the camera. First, you have to realize that you can't do video marketing without doing video and, at some point, that's going to mean being on camera. Appearing in front of the camera can strike fear into the hearts of even the most seasoned entrepreneurs—a condition I describe as "videophobia."

Most of us suffer some level of videophobia, and precious few actually relish the thought of talking into a webcam or smartphone. After all, unless we're actors, news anchors, or Kardashians, being on camera isn't something we do every day. It's outside our comfort zone. So, like any new skill, it has to be learned and practiced.

With that in mind, here are a few remedies to consider if you are one of the many business owners afflicted with fear of being on camera.

1. *Practice, practice, practice.* As the saying goes, all things are difficult before they are easy. But with time, patience, and persistence, video does get easier. It's often a matter of trial and error, so put in the time to practice and rehearse. Even the highest paid movie stars do a dozen takes to get a scene right, so why shouldn't you? Rehearse. Retake. Repeat.

2. *Get creative.* Get crazy. Get in character. Despite my 20-plus years in the television business, I was terrified of being on camera when I started doing online video. I had always been on the other side of the camera, so suddenly being the center of attention was scary. My solution was to hide behind costumes and characters. I put my kids in my videos, my pets, or props— anything to take the focus off me! Ironically, this worked like a charm and I became known for my wacky "LouTube" videos and crazy characters like Director Cecil B. DeMoron (see Figure 15.1 on page 198). It's a great way to lose yourself in the process and conquer your nerves. Think outside the screen and see what you come up with.

3. *Face your fear head on.* There's always the philosophy of "feel the fear and do it anyway," and "action cures fear." There comes a time when you just have to suck it up and do it. You may have to get outside your comfort zone to be on camera, but the result is well worth it. The more you do it, the easier it will become.

4. *Do an interview.* This trick works wonders, because it's always easier to do video when there are two people involved. When it comes to video, two heads are easier than one. Having a partner or co-host takes a lot of the pressure off you, and can

FIGURE 15.1 Put some "character" into your videos!

make the entire process more enjoyable. Google Hangouts (or even Skype) make it easy to do video interviews or "two-shots," even if you and your co-star are on different continents. Enlist a friend or colleague and have some fun with it.

5. *Relax and be yourself.* You do not have to be a celebrity or reality TV star to be on camera. YouTube has made it possible for anyone, anywhere, anytime to be on screen. People are watching videos to be entertained or educated. In many cases, they are looking to solve a particular problem. That means that it's your content that counts. Focus on your message. Share your story. Be yourself and do what comes naturally.

Of course, being on camera is not the only way to create great video. Even off-camera videos can be effective. Still, for making a connection and establishing that all-important "know, like, and trust" factor, there's nothing more powerful than appearing on screen.

Off-Camera Options

While on-camera videos are ideal for connecting with your audience and building your "know, like, and trust" factor, there are times when off-camera videos are more appropriate and, often, easier and more efficient. So whether you're camera shy or just having a bad hair day, there are plenty of options for creating compelling videos that do not require you to be on camera. Here are several resources for off-camera video creation:

1. *PowerPoint.* The first and perhaps most obvious option for off-camera video is the old tried and true Microsoft PowerPoint (or Keynote, if you're on a Mac). You can simply narrate your PowerPoint presentation, save it as a video file, and—*boom*—you've got a video!

2. *Prezi (www.prezi.com).* If you want to take your presentation to the next level by adding dynamic movements, zooms, and flashy graphics, then you may be ready for Prezi. This zippy presentation software allows you to get really creative with your presentations.

3. *VideoScribe (www.videoscribe.co).* VideoScribe is a fantastic resource for creating animated "sketch" videos and drawings. You can use their drop and drag features and become an instant animator. I really love this cool tool and use it a lot.

4. *GoAnimate (www.goanimate.com).* If you'd like to get even more creative with your cartoons, check out www.GoAnimate.com, where you can create and direct your own cartoon characters. You type, they talk! The possibilities are endless.

5. *Animoto (www.animoto.com).* One of the oldest and most popular video creation sites, Animoto provides templates or themes that you can use to create a photo montage using your pictures and text. You can also select music to accompany your montage masterpiece.

6. *Intro Designer (www.introdesignerapp.com/—available at the iTunes store).* This handy little iPhone app is just $3.99 and allows you to create slick "motion graphics" titles and effects, so you can create your own animated show opening. They've got 21 professional video templates to design your animated title treatments.

7. *Stupeflix (http://studio.stupeflix.com/en/).* Silly name, great resource. Perhaps named because it's stupendously simple to

create professional-looking videos with the cool themes the site provides.

8. *PowToon (www.powtoon.com)*. Last, but definitely not least, is PowToon, a veritable playground for creating sketch videos and custom animations. Everything you need to make a way-cool cartoon is at your fingertips with drag and drop simplicity.

With these easy-to-use resources, there are no more excuses to avoid video because you're camera shy. Using one or more of the "camera-less" options above, you can create great video without ever firing up the webcam. Explore and enjoy.

Being Consistent with Video Marketing

With so many on- or off-camera methods for creating video, you should have no trouble doing your first few videos. But video marketing, like any marketing, is not a one time event. Your video efforts need to be consistent and ongoing to get the most impact. Unless you want to succumb to the dreaded "one and done" syndrome, you will want to create a strategic marketing plan for using video regularly in your business.

As with any plan, you must begin with the end in mind. What are your business objectives for video? Is it to grow your list? Build your brand? Drive more web traffic? Enhance your credibility? Your goals will determine your direction. If you said "all of the above" to the video goals we just listed, here are some ideas for maintaining your video momentum:

▸ *Create an "expert tips" series to share your expertise.* Short, one- to two-minute how-to videos increase your credibility and expand your influence. You can even record these all in one session, and then post your tips video to YouTube once or twice per week. A tips series provides some consistency and gives you added visibility on the web.

▸ *If you have a blog, add a videoblog post every couple of weeks.* The search engines love video, and your readers will be treated to a dynamic change of pace from your traditional, written blog posts. Spice up your regular blog posts with video to make your blog more engaging. Extra bonus: Video is much more personal and compelling than print alone!

▶ *Get some face time.* Use a personal video message or video email to go "face to face" with your clients or prospects. Sending a video greeting, birthday wishes, or a thank-you video have much more impact than yet another regular email. Video email services like MailVu.com, Vsnap.com, and Eyejot.com make it point-and-click easy to record your video. If you want to stand out and be memorable, use video!

▶ *Make it an event.* Whether you're promoting a webinar or launching a new product, nothing makes a bold statement like video. Adding video to your promotional plans makes your webinar or launch look more like a special event. Again, it's the best way to break through the online clutter and make sure your message gets noticed.

▶ *Go live!* You can do a live webcast or offer a "Q&A" video session using free platforms such as Livestream, Ustream.tv or even Google Hangouts. These web resources make it easy to fire up your webcam and go live whenever you want. A live webcast is dynamic, engaging, and highly interactive. (You may want to do a test run first, just to get comfortable with the format.)

However you decide to use video, it will put your marketing on overdrive and accelerate your results. The secret is consistency and strategy. Make a plan and stick to it. Anyone can make one video. The real winners online will be those who make online video a regular part of their marketing efforts.

> *The best way to get more views for your videos*
> *is to make better videos!*

YouTube and Social Media

No discussion of video marketing would be complete without including YouTube and social media. After all, YouTube and video are practically synonymous, and the reach and influence of the video hosting site is incredibly powerful.

YouTube is the second most popular search engine (second only to owner Google) and has over one billion unique visitors every month. Over six billion hours of video are watched monthly, and 100 hours of video are upload to YouTube every minute! To put the video giant's reach into perspective, Nielsen reports that YouTube reaches more U.S. adults ages 18 to 34 than any cable network.

You can use YouTube as the headquarters and "hub" for your videos, since they will host your videos for free, and they provide an excellent platform from which to promote and share your videos. YouTube is the ideal website for increasing your online visibility, making connections, and expanding your social presence.

Take advantage of YouTube's dominance by posting your videos there first, and using it as a hub to share and spread your video. Use the easy, one-click sharing options to send your video from YouTube to Facebook, Twitter, Google+, and even LinkedIn. Just connect the accounts once and one-click sharing is enabled. You can continue to share your video by emailing the link, or by using the embed code that YouTube provides to add the video to your own website or blog. YouTube is the ultimate "upload once-share everywhere" platform.

YouTube may be the biggest "social" network for your videos, but it's certainly not the only one.

You might be surprised to learn that Facebook is the third largest site for video viewing online. Facebook is not only where many people are discovering videos, it's also a great place to post video for audience engagement, and the perfect platform for generating comments and starting conversations. Facebook is very video-friendly, and it's ideal for posting your videos of up to 20 minutes in length.

Twitter also drives video viewing, so be sure to promote your video via Twitter. In fact, one auto-shared tweet results in six new YouTube sessions! Remember to shorten your video links to make sharing easier.

Also, when sharing your video from YouTube to Twitter, viewers can pull up and watch the video directly in Twitter.

Pinterest represents yet another opportunity to make your video more visible. Just take a screenshot of your video, "pin" it to the appropriate board in Pinterest, and link the photo back to your video. When people click the image, they'll be taken back to your video. Even better, if you pin your video from YouTube to Pinterest, the video will play right within Pinterest.

Finally, video creators often forget that you can get even more social exposure by adding video to LinkedIn. The easiest way to add some visual appeal to LinkedIn is to add the SlideShare.net app to your LinkedIn account (LinkedIn owns SlideShare), then use SlideShare to add your presentations—and videos—to your LinkedIn profile. Adding video to LinkedIn via SlideShare makes your profile pop and gives you yet another platform to share and spread your videos.

Combining video and social media is all about leverage. Save yourself tons of time and give your videos a better chance of being seen by sharing your video to as many platforms as possible. With so many "cross-sharing" opportunities, it's never been easier to spread your video. And the more places your video is seen and shared, the more visibility, credibility, and profitability you'll enjoy!

Video marketing has become a vital resource for you to use to build your brand and grow your business. If you want to win in a "world gone video," you've got to develop a video marketing strategy that will keep you relevant and fully engaged with your clients, colleagues, and prospective customers. There's no better time for you to tap into the most powerful marketing tool on the web.

CHAPTER 16

LinkedIn Prospecting Strategies that Convert Connections into Clients

Viveka von Rosen

VIVEKA VON ROSEN is the author of *LinkedIn Marketing: An Hour a Day*, contributing expert to LinkedIn's official "Sophisticated Marketer's Guide" and is known internationally as the "LinkedIn Expert." She is the CEO of Linked into Business and co-founder of Linked Prospecting, and she also hosts the biggest LinkedIn chat on Twitter. For more information: www.LinkedIntoBusiness.com.

▲ ▲ ▲

This chapter will walk you through the step-by-step strategies you can implement today;

In this Chapter, You'll Discover

▶ Why you need to be on LinkedIn

▶ How to create, customize, and optimize a profile that will draw prospects to you

▶ The best ways for finding your target prospects

▶ The best ways of engaging with your target prospects

▶ The best ways to stay top of mind with your target prospects for more referrals and sales

▶ Some simple yet effective company page strategies

saving you time and getting you better results when prospecting on LinkedIn.

Why You Need to Be on LinkedIn

Are you, like many professionals, still not convinced of the power of LinkedIn? Here are some LinkedIn stats that might change your mind:

LinkedIn is the largest business-focused social media site. Many businesses that resist traditional social sites like Facebook and Twitter will venture into LinkedIn. In fact, according to HubSpot, LinkedIn is 277 percent more effective for lead generation than Facebook and Twitter.

The "Sophisticated Marketer's Guide to LinkedIn" (find the complete guide at: http://business.linkedin.com/content/dam/business/marketing-solutions/global/en_US/campaigns/pdfs/Linkedin_SophGuide_011614.pdf) shares the following stats:

- ▸ LinkedIn is the number one social network for driving traffic to corporate websites
- ▸ LinkedIn members are 50 percent more likely to engage with a company they engage with on LinkedIn
- ▸ Ninety-one percent of marketers use LinkedIn to distribute content
- ▸ LinkedIn drives more traffic to B2B blogs and sites than Twitter, Facebook, and G+ combined
- ▸ Ninety-three percent of marketers rate LinkedIn as effective for generating leads
- ▸ Sixty-five percent of companies acquired B2B leads through LinkedIn

Whether you are in marketing, content marketing, B2B sales or not—these numbers should inspire you to polish up your profile and start engaging on LinkedIn!

Creating a Profile That Attracts Prospects

It's important to remember that your profile is your online branding, so you need to make sure that your profile has cohesive branding to your website and other social presences. Make sure you're using the right logo and make sure that your employees are using the right logo. You might want to create some standardized copy as a template your employees can use (if you have employees) in their profiles.

Another thing to remember is that LinkedIn is like a website, and just like you wouldn't want spelling or grammatical errors on your website, you want to make sure that your LinkedIn profile is free of errors as well. One way to get around this is to create your profile first in a word processing document to catch spelling and grammar errors. Creating your copy in a word processing document will also allow you to count and do some basic formatting. If anything happens and you lose your profile, at least you've got a copy of it. And it will be much easier to rebuild.

Another tip is that your LinkedIn profile is very similar to Google in that if you have the right keywords in the right places, you show up better in a search. You probably already know what your keywords are, but keep it simple.

One of the best places to find keywords are other people's profiles. Type your keyword (or keyword phrase) into LinkedIn's Smart Search and see who shows up. Go into their profile and check out their skills section. These are pretty relevant LinkedIn terms and they're actually quite good search terms.

LinkedIn also recently released a new keyword suggestions feature to its Premium members, which will actually suggest keywords to you as you create and/or edit your Summary section in your profile. But it is a paid feature.

Create a list of keywords and prioritize it. You'll be putting these keywords in your:

- ▸ Professional Headline (LinkedIn gives you 120 characters, including spaces, to work with)
- ▸ Title fields (100 characters)
- ▸ Experience and Education description fields (1,000 characters)
- ▸ Summary section (2,000 characters)
- ▸ Interests (1,000 characters)

Professional Headline

Your Professional Headline is the area right underneath your name; the 120 characters that describe who you are and what you do. Most people will just have their "Title" at "Company" (because that is LinkedIn's default). They don't take the time to describe who they are, what they do, and whom they serve. This is a great place for a tagline and a few keywords.

FIGURE 16.1

Your picture, name, and Professional Headline are usually what people see in most communications on LinkedIn, whether you are responding to a group update, sending a message, inviting someone to connect, or using the introduction feature. So invest the time to make your Professional Headline engaging.

Title Fields

Most people only put their current titles in the Title field, but you can expand this section (100 characters) to really describe all your roles above and beyond your current title, adding a few keywords if relevant. For an example, feel free to take a look at my profile: LinkedIn.com/in/LinkedInExpert.

Description Fields

A lot of people just skip the description field of their Experience section, but I would strongly urge you not to! You have 1,000 characters in the description area to plant those keywords. As you describe what you do for the company and what the company does, these keywords are going to naturally settle right in. And with LinkedIn's new search algorithm, the description section of your Experience is more important than ever!

Summary Section

In the Background section of your profile, there is something called the Summary. Make sure to use the most of this 2,000-character field to expound on who you are and what you do. I always recommend that you keep the Summary section customer-facing (as in "What's in it for them?"). It's OK to list your features, but what difference do you make to your customer or your prospect? Be clear on what it is that you do but—more importantly—how does that benefit your prospect?

Create your Summary in a word processing document; use formatting, bullets, and don't be afraid of white space! Chunk those bits of information up into bite-size pieces your prospects can digest. And use your spell checker, too. I can't tell you how often I read profiles with spelling errors. This is your professional online representation—so make sure it is spelling error free.

Interests

The Interests section, found at the very bottom of your profile under Additional Information, is the only section on LinkedIn into which I recommend you blatantly dump your keywords. You have 1,000 characters to add both personal interests (hiking, biking, walking, judo) as well as the list of keywords you created. Just copy and paste it in, and make sure you separate each keyword or keyword phrase with a comma so that the words are searchable.

If you just get the right keywords in these four sections, you have a much, much better chance of your profile showing up when someone does a search on them. Since LinkedIn actually drives more traffic than Google+ and Bing, you need to make sure that you, not your competition, is being found by your prospects!

Finding Your Prospects

The second thing we're going to do is talk about the best ways to search and find prospects on LinkedIn. We'll be looking at:

▸ Who to search for
▸ LinkedIn's advanced search
▸ Boolean search
▸ Saved search

Advanced Search

LinkedIn recently came out with its "Smart Search," but quite frankly, I don't think it's that smart! I often don't find the results I'm looking for and prefer to use LinkedIn's Advanced Search. It is found just to the right of the Smart Search box. (The tiny, light gray link that says "Advanced.") The Advanced Search is available to everyone no matter what membership you have, whether it is premium or not.

Once you click on the link, a new page opens and you'll now have the ability to search by:

▸ Keyword (which is essentially the Smart Search above)
▸ First name
▸ Last name
▸ Title or potential title
▸ Company
▸ School
▸ Location

When working with LinkedIn it is so important for you to know who your target market and prospects are. You must be clear on your "buyer" or "purchaser persona." Ardath Albee writes about buyer personas in her great book *eMarketing Strategies for the Complex Sale*. Or, if you just want

FIGURE 16.2

a quick, free template, you can download HubSpot's resource: http://offers.hubspot.com/free-template-creating-buyer-personas.

If you don't know who your ideal buyer or prospect is, stop reading now and look at these resources.

Once you're clear on who these individuals might be, it's just an easy cut and paste into these different search fields on LinkedIn.

- ► What keywords would your target buyer have in their profiles?
- ► What would their titles be?
- ► Where would they work?
- ► Where did they go to school?
- ► Where would they live?

Whether you have the free account (that gives you access to the fields on the left side of the page) or the premium accounts (that give you access to the fields on the right side of the page) please consider using the Advanced Search on LinkedIn.

The results will be much more accurate and relevant to you—and with the free account, this becomes very important since you only get to see the first 100 results.

Boolean Search

Even with the Advanced Search, we don't always get as accurate a result as we would like. In order to more fully refine a search, consider using Boolean logic or Boolean search strings.

As with all things written on LinkedIn, if you can create these Boolean strings first in a document file and then cut and paste them into the different fields on LinkedIn, you'll find them easier to manipulate and save. One of the things that you'll notice in LinkedIn searches is the old adage "garbage in, garbage out." If you create your search first in a document, it's much easier to catch that "garbage." Most times, if you don't get any results, it's probably because there is a spelling mistake somewhere in the search.

Boolean search uses a series of "modifiers" to help you refine your search. These modifiers include:

- ▸ + and "" to hold search phrases together
- ▸ OR when you are not sure of a title or keyword
- ▸ AND to definitely include a search term or phrase
- ▸ NOT to exclude a search term or phrase

+ or " "

If you are doing a search for a Chief Executive Officer and don't use the little plus sign (+) between chief and executive and officer (chief+executive+officer) or you didn't put that phrase in quotation marks, then LinkedIn will search for a bunch of "chiefs" and a bunch of "executives" and bunch of "officers." Your result is going to be much less targeted than if you had used the + sign or the quotation marks around the phrase: "chief executive officer."

OR

If you are just not quite sure about whom you are looking for, then OR becomes your best search friend! Maybe I want to work with the head of a company. What does the head of the company call him or herself? Did they choose CEO OR "chief executive officer" OR founder OR owner OR partner OR co-owner OR co-founder OR . . . If you didn't use OR and put the wrong title in the title search field, then you lose the opportunity of seeing everyone who might be a good fit. You can use the OR modifier in both the keyword and Title (and company) fields on LinkedIn.

AND

Use AND when you want to clarify an audience or a niche. If you were looking for a CEO OR owner OR founder OR partner AND you wanted to make sure to only search for people in the legal industry, you would simply add AND legal AND law AND lawyer AND law firm to your search. If you are not sure what keywords you want to add, you can always use parentheses to hold options together. Your search might look like this: CEO OR chief+executive OR founder AND (legal OR lawyer OR law).

NOT

I think the most important modifier is NOT. (You'll learn this over time.) When you get your search results, you might see a lot of competitors show up (or employees or job seekers or consultants). If you are not interested in any of those folks as prospects, you can erase them from your list by using NOT. You might want to add: NOT consultant NOT jobseeker NOT <your company name>. The use of NOT will definitely target and clarify your results.

So your Boolean search will look something like this:

CEO OR chief+executive OR founder OR owner AND (legal OR lawyer OR partner NOT consultant NOT consulting NOT job+seeker NOT Seeking+employment.

Once you get your results, quickly look through them and then continue to modify your search until you get the exact results you want. Create your Boolean search strings first in a document, and that way you can save them, edit them, and continue to search on those particular search strings until you find results that really work for you.

Saved Search

Once you create a search that gets the results you want, save it. At the top right of your screen you will see a "Save Search" link. You can save three searches with a free account and more with premium accounts.

What is so cool about the saved search is that every week LinkedIn will pull up anyone new who falls into your saved search and send you an email with their names. LinkedIn will literally send you a list of prospects! You can delete your searches, you can change them up, and you can save new searches.

Engaging with Prospects

Once you have found your prospects either through the Advanced Search or through a Boolean search, how do you reach out to them? That's where LinkedIn comes in. LinkedIn gives you all the tools you need to reach out and engage with these people:

- ▸ Invitations
- ▸ Introductions
- ▸ Messages
- ▸ InMails

Invitations

Your first option is inviting a new prospect to connect (as long as you see the blue connect button on their profile). When possible, always include a personal note and customize that invitation. It looks much better and gets a much better response rate. Many people won't even open an invitation if no personal note is included.

Once you have found a prospect and click on the blue connect button, then you'll have to choose how you know them. The best option to invite someone to connect is through a shared group (you'll see the group option if you do indeed share a group).

If you don't have that option but that person has their email address listed somewhere in their profile, then choose "Other" and put that email address in there.

If that option is not available, you can always do "We've done business together." And choose your company. It's not the best option, but if it's your only one then fess up to not actually knowing them. You might customize your invite to read something like this:

> Hi John—we haven't worked together, but I am an avid reader of your books (OR I admire your work. OR I see you are an influencer in this industry. OR I see you work at this company that I admire. OR I'd love to interview you for my blog post. OR I see your name online all the time. OR I did a search on this and you showed up.) and I'd love to connect.

You only have 300 characters, but if you have the room, you might include: "If you feel you received this in error and don't want to connect, please just ignore this invitation." You can't put a phone number and email address in there, but at least sign with your name. Just your first name will work.

Introductions

Sometimes, asking for an introduction is the best thing to do. Now, an introduction, if it gets passed along, does not mean that you are connected, but it does mean that you can now engage with that person. (Plus you'll get their email address, and sometimes their phone number.) The Get Introduced link can be found in the dropdown to the right of Send InMail. So if you don't have the blue Connect button, or even if you do, but you don't want to just invite that person to connect, you can just click on the dropdown arrow and you'll see the option to Get Introduced. Once you click on that a new page pops up and you'll see the people you have in common. Choose the person that you feel most comfortable with to be the Introducer.

Before even using the Get Introduced link, however, you might ask your shared connection if he or she is willing to pass along the introduction *before you actually send it*. If I wanted to connect with

Prospect Rachel and Connection Ken knew us both (which I will know because LinkedIn shows me so). I would just send Ken a message asking, "Hey, would you be willing to introduce me to Rachel?" And when he says yes, I'd then use the Get Introduced tool.

Remember, when you ask for an introduction, tell them why you want to be introduced and then give them an out. For example:

> Hi Ken, I was hoping you would introduce me to Rachel. I was searching on business development professionals in the Denver area, and she came up very high in my LinkedIn search. I noticed you're connected to her, and I would love it if you would be willing to introduce me

Similarly you will want to address your sought-after connection, too!

> "Hi Rachel. As I said to Ken, you came up really high in a search, I noticed that you're active in the Denver Metro Chamber of Commerce. Would love to connect with you further. Would you accept an invitation from me?"

Just don't use the introduction to pitch your wares: "Hi Rachel. I'd love to speak at the Denver Metro Chamber of Commerce, will you hire me?" That's not going to go over very well, so start working on that business relationship first. Let them come to you with the request to use your products and services after you've built a relationship with them.

Messaging through Groups

When you find a connection on LinkedIn, check to see if they're a member of any groups. If you happen to share a group with that person, you can just send them a message through the group. Or you might have to join a group so that you can send them a message through that group:

1. In your prospect's profile, click on the group name you share (or join one).
2. In the group, click on the tab that says *Members* (not search).
3. Also don't click on the Member button because that will either have you join or leave the group.
4. In the page that opens you'll see there's a search bar.
5. Type in your prospect's name OR.
6. Do a simple Boolean search in the search box.

Because you share a group with that person, you should have the option of sending them a message or inviting them to connect.

Even though it's an extra step, I recommend you send a message asking a person if they're willing to connect (and why you want to connect with them). You have more characters to work with in a message as opposed to an invitation, so you have more opportunity to tell people why you want to connect with them.

Once they reply that they are willing to connect, you can send them the connection request through the group.

InMails

Finally, when all else fails, you can definitely send an InMail. It's $10 per InMail for a free account, three free InMails with the basic premium account, and it goes up from there. Just be aware: No sales pitches! That rarely works well. What you're trying to do is get them to accept an invitation to connect or at least land an email address or a phone call. Don't pitch your product or your service in your first InMail.

Staying Top of Mind with Your Prospects

Once you have developed your network, you can use LinkedIn's tools to stay top of mind with them in a quick and easy way. I recommend using:

- ▸ LinkedIn Sharing Bookmarklet
- ▸ LinkedIn Pulse
- ▸ LinkedIn Publisher

LinkedIn Sharing Bookmarklet

One of the tools I really like on LinkedIn is called the Sharing Bookmarklet (www.linkedin.com/static?key=browser_bookmarklet). If you're using Chrome, Safari, or Mozilla Firefox, all you have to do is pull that little Sharing button into your browser toolbar. (It's similar to Hootsuite's sharing Hootlet or the Bufferapp sharing link.)

The Sharing Bookmarklet allows you to share content from anywhere on the web with your LinkedIn audience:

▸ As an update

▸ As a tweet

▸ As a post to groups (be careful with this, though)

▸ As a message to individuals

LinkedIn Pulse

This is the other tool I like using to share good info with my network (and stay top of mind with them). Select publishers and influencers specifically create this content for LinkedIn.

Pulse can be found under Interests (click on the Pulse link), or you can find it on your homepage. On Pulse, you can also follow specific channels of info, certain publishers, and Influencers. There's a channel that talks about women and business, a channel that talks about marketing, a channel that talks about accounting. Basically, for any type of industry there's a channel on it.

So if you're looking to share content with your market that is helpful and useful, you don't have to look any further than LinkedIn Pulse.

LinkedIn Publisher

Publisher allows those of you who are content curators to share your blog-length posts with your network on LinkedIn. Apply to get Publisher here: http://specialedition.linkedin.com/publishing/.

What I love about Publisher is that the posts show up under your profile (like your old Activity Feed used to). And posts are searchable under the Smart Search.

You know you have LinkedIn Publisher when you get an email from LinkedIn telling you that you have it, or you have the little pen in your updates field.

Here are six steps to creating a post:

1. Create some new content or repurpose an existing blog post.
2. Add formatting, hyperlinks, images, bullets, media, etc.
3. Save it.
4. Preview it. You want to catch any whack-a-doo formatting.

5. Post it to your network.

6. Share it!

Last Thoughts

When it comes to doing business on LinkedIn, the question I get asked the most is, "How can I use LinkedIn more effectively?" Especially from new users who have some experience with social media (Facebook, Twitter, etc.) but have been resistant to LinkedIn because it just doesn't make sense.

People see a new platform (at least new to them) and think that they are in store for a giant learning curve. But the truth is, LinkedIn is just a tool that allows you to do what you already do in business—more effectively. Yes, you need to learn how to use the platform, but you don't have to create a whole new series of business strategies as well. LinkedIn's mission statement is: "To connect the world's professionals to make them more productive and successful." That's how we should be using it.

CHAPTER 17

Google+
A Social Media Toolbox for Every Business

Stephan Hovnanian

STEPHAN HOVNANIAN, web strategist at Shovi Websites and author of the *Google+ Pro Tips* ebooks series, specializes in dissecting trends, techniques, and best practices related to web design and online marketing, and then making them applicable to businesses. Stephan's goal is to help your business find and use the best tools to build a better, smarter web presence. For more information: www.stephanhov.com

▲ ▲ ▲

Google+ takes social media to an entirely different level, enriching the Google

In this Chapter, You'll Discover

▶ How to leverage Google's "social layer"

▶ What Google brings to businesses

▶ How relationships and influence affect social signals and search rankings

▶ How Google+ can be used for collaboration and content marketing

▶ How to identify key areas and build a following

▶ How to establish a routine to incorporate Google+ into your marketing and social listening products that so many of us use every day. Use this information to take your entire web presence up another level with Google+, and future-proof your online marketing strategy.

Note: Privacy on Google+ works in a way that allows the user to control the visibility of a post by sharing it publicly or to a specific set of users (circles). For the purposes of this chapter, we are assuming that all sharing is done to a public audience, which is what most businesses and marketers should choose, unless they have a specific cause to share with a limited audience.

What Google+ Offers Your Business

To understand what Google+ offers businesses and marketers, we need to understand what Google wants from Google+. Think back to the earlier days of search when, if you wanted to have a page rank highly for a particular keyword, all you had to do was run through a checklist of mechanical techniques that fooled Google into thinking your page was about that term, and that you were such an authority for the term that Google would recommend you as their number-one result.

Now, think back to how we found answers to our questions (and companies to work with) before the internet: Human qualities such as reputation, customer service, and a quality experience were the factors that recommended one over the other. We even do this today, asking our own trusted circles for advice and recommendations before a purchase.

These qualities still heavily influence our decisions as consumers, as well they should, because factors such as trust and reputation are harder to fake.

In an effort to improve the quality of the search experience, Google has long been moving toward using these human, less mechanical, more semantic qualities in its algorithms. This is where Google+ comes into the picture.

To use an example, let's say you are a reclusive niche blogger with a single web page about a movie review. In the mid-1990s, your web page might have ranked number one for the title of the movie, because it was really easy to buy backlinks, optimize the page mechanically for those keywords, and cast a wide enough net that Google's algorithm *thought* you were the authority on that topic.

Today, you wouldn't rank at all for that movie review. Why? There are professional movie reviewers who blog about the movies they watch. They have earned a reputation in the public's eye by appearing on talk shows, being featured in editorials (online and offline), and playing host to conversations around their social posts about movies, by building and interacting with an online community. This sounds like real life, doesn't it? Legitimate authorities in a subject area will always enjoy greater success and opportunity than their lower-quality counterparts.

How does this all tie back to Google+? Well, Google+ is the glue that intends to bring the human side of doing business to the online world, specifically in search.

As a business owner, you provide a quality product, great customer service, and your website is (hopefully) optimized to convert visitors to buyers. Your social and content marketing outposts are aimed at building authority and reputation online, and to get people talking about (and recommending) you naturally.

When you connect your business to Google+ and create conversation around your brand throughout their platform, you are injecting the human elements of doing business into Google's understanding of who you are, what you do, and what they should recommend you for to their searchers. In time, they will see you as the authority and begin to recommend you over the reclusive niche bloggers we talked about earlier.

However, Google+ isn't completely about search rankings. The trust, authority, and recommendations you are building toward your search goals while being active on Google+ are obviously important. But, you cannot build the trust, authority, and recommendations without making connections with people. The rest of this chapter is going to explore how you can use the Google+ platform to connect, collaborate, and market, with a suite of very powerful tools.

Relationship Marketing and Social Signals

Google+ is structured in a way that offers two key benefits to marketers and businesses: It allows them to easily build relationships with one another, and it impacts their web presence by passing social signals.

Building relationships, from a mechanical standpoint, is quite easy on Google+. The open nature of the platform allows users to comment on public posts, whether or not they have that user in their circles. The open, asynchronous format is similar to Twitter (I can talk to you without having to follow you), compared to other networks which require users to establish a connection first before being able to interact with each other.

So a user can go onto Google+, type in a keyword, hashtag, or the URL of a web page they like, and find existing discussions about those very topics into which they can inject themselves and meet others who share that same interest. If the user is happy with the discussion, she can add the participants (the user who shared the post, as well as the commenters) to her circles and participate on more of their posts.

When it comes to seeking out the most influential users on a particular topic, the best technique is to look for the most active conversations and the ones with the highest number of shares. Typically, interacting on that user's posts can expose you to a greater audience than the user who never gets any comments.

Communities are also a good place to build relationships. Community owners and moderators are typically active and worth connecting with. The fact that most communities are topic-oriented means you will have members with common interests, which is great for prospecting and networking. Commenting on community posts will earn you visits from community members to your profile, where they will learn more about you and potentially add you to their circles.

How do these relationships play into social signals back to our website? Each Google+ profile has influence in its own right, and for certain keywords. Knowing this, be cognizant of how and what you share on Google+ to help train it about your areas of expertise. Anyway, should you build a relationship with a user who has an established reputation on a certain subject, their share of your content will count as a stronger recommendation than someone who has no authority on the subject matter (in Google's eyes).

The idea holds water in real life, and if you recall from earlier in the chapter, Google is trying with Google+ to emulate the real-life trust and connections we build with each other. If I wrote an article about a movie theater experience for my blog, and a professional movie blogger caught wind of it and shared it, that's quite an endorsement, isn't it? These signals pass to our Google+ posts, our profiles, and our web pages, and Google has begun to weigh the social interactions surrounding a piece of content (or entity) as a measure of reputation and trust. The types of interactions are considered as well, meaning a "like" or +1 will not factor as heavily because of the low level of effort and lack of context surrounding the action; a comment, share, or a completely separate link to my article, on the other hand, require increasing levels of effort and as such are weighed more heavily.

This is why buying social signals is not a viable strategy anymore. The return on investment for low-value signals—or even higher value signals from users with no reputation—is unacceptable. Without a high level of authoritative discussion surrounding your content, you will have a hard time ranking in search and building a reputation as an authority in your field. This authoritative discussion and reputation can only be earned naturally.

So far, we've talked about the human aspect of Google+ and how the platform can be used to build your reputation and subject matter authority. Now, let's dig into some of the marketing-related areas of the platform, so you can use it to grow your business.

The Google+ Content Marketing Toolbox

As social media platforms go, Google+ certainly offers the broadest set of tools and features for content marketing. Highlights include:

- ▸ Long-form posts, complete with basic formatting, such as bold, italics, strikethrough text, nested formatting (bold + italics), and support for special characters, including arrows, hearts, and more; in other words, basic blogging is feasible using Google+
- ▸ Generous real estate given in the streams for photos and videos; combined with built-in video editing via YouTube, and built-in

photo editing via Snapseed, visual media can deliver a striking message

▸ A robust tool for events, which syncs instantly with Google Calendar

▸ Communities for topical, focused, and targeted discussion

▸ Hangouts on Air, live broadcasts that save to a user's YouTube channel and can be combined with an event to create a rich, immersive, live experience to connect face to face with people and brands

▸ Interactive post types, such as shared circles and embedded documents from Google Drive, can create networking and collaboration opportunities right in the stream

▸ Hashtag support that lets you easily discover related terms and influencers; this is fantastic for research, general discovery, and brand building

Combining any or all of these features can easily fill out a content creation schedule for a company, which is why Google+ can also seem overwhelming to newcomers. However, there is one more feature within Google+ that is a content marketer's dream: *Every post on Google+ is a unique URL and can be indexed in search.*

How do we take advantage of this? Every social network has its unwritten rules regarding how to write for its users, and Google+ is no exception. The long-form posts and openness make for quality discussions, so take advantage of this to create additional content that can be indexed in search when you share a link to your website. In other words, after you publish a blog and post it to your website:

1. Write up a similar introduction with an engaging title.
2. Add three to five hashtags that relate to the subject matter.
3. Share it on Google+ with a link to your blog post.

In a way, you are "double-dipping" for that blog post: The original web page gets indexed of course, as does your Google+ post—two opportunities to drive social signals and traffic to your website through search.

Now let's take things one step further, shall we? Armed with complementary "social" content that links back to your website, you can create a suite of Google+ posts that have an opportunity to create engagement and social signals across the entire platform, all of which lead back to your website.

Reimagining content that begins on Google+ is also very easy to do. Let's use a Hangout on Air as an example. Each Hangout on Air (HOA) will most likely have:

1. An event page on Google+
2. Several shares of the event page to encourage people to RSVP
3. Microcontent, such as a photo of the guest, or a link to a related blog post, shared on Google+ in conjunction with a call to action about the event
4. A share of the YouTube video after the event is over, usually with a short recap
5. A blog post to complement the show, which will also be shared on Google+

That's five unique pieces of content surrounding one topic. A sixth could be a shared circle of all the attendees to the event as a gesture of thanks for watching (the publicity could encourage more to participate next time). In each piece of content, you have the ability to use keywords, +mentions (tagging people), hashtags, calls to action, and links to related content to drive traffic, engagement, and social signals. Not to mention the amazing amount of content you can get out of a live discussion, which could lead to future blog posts, or segments of the original video edited down and repurposed.

All of that content can be created on Google+ to market your idea, and then cross-promoted to other channels to amplify your reach even further. Which brings us to the next section of this chapter.

Grow Your Following on Google+

Chances are good you have a healthy following on at least one social network by now. Chances are also good that you put time and effort into building that following. If you are starting out on Google+, you have to do the same thing. Your efforts are supplemented by the interconnectivity of Google+ to all of Google's products, which means more of your existing connections can find you on Google+ as you both become active in one form or another.

Now that you are ready to put the time in, here are some simple ways to grow your following on Google+:

- ▸ *Cross-pollinate your content* by taking advantage of the fact each Google+ post is a public web page. Tweet your Google+ event links to drive traffic from Twitter over to the live Hangout on Air. Pin your Google+ posts to Pinterest boards. Email links to your Google+ content within your newsletters. Include Google+ posts in any of your curation methods (you can even embed certain types of posts on your blog).

- ▸ *Add follow badges* for your business page and profile to your website. These badges are configurable to meet the design specs of your website, and allow a visitor to add you (or your business page) directly to their circles without visiting Google+.

- ▸ *Import contacts or others' shared circles* to your own circles. Those users will get a notification that you added them, and hopefully reciprocate. Be sure your profile is complete and explains what people should expect of your Google+ presence, so you can deliver value to them right out of the gate.

- ▸ *Tell people you're on Google+!* Add the logo to your brochures, social profiles, display ads, author bios, you name it. Talk about Google+ outside Google+, at networking events, Twitter chats, and anywhere else there's a crowd of people who want to connect with each other.

Beyond these techniques, there are two critically important ways to grow your following on Google+. The first is to **be active**. Not just active with posting and sharing content, but active on other people's posts. Inject yourself into as many relevant conversations as you can on a daily basis, leave thoughtful comments, make human connections, and watch your engagement grow on your own Google+ posts. As you create deeper connections with other users, your influence over them (and theirs over you) grows with respect to personalized and recommended content.

The second is to be follow-worthy. This means a complete profile, a sense of purpose, and professionalism when you post, and a desire to interact with those who interact with you. Google+ is not the place to employ megaphone marketing tactics. Remember, try to emulate how we build connections in real life.

A Simple Daily Google+ Marketing Routine

The rich content creation features we talked about earlier in the chapter make for a more time-consuming approach to Google+ than other networks, but like any network, these best practices are important to get the biggest return on your time and investment. Having said that, how can a time-strapped individual or business create a routine for Google+ that lays enough of a foundation to see consistent engagement, follower growth, and traffic to their website?

First, you must have a content plan, and the sources from which to deploy it. This means setting up your Google+ circles in a way that emulates feeds that you can hop in and out of for posts to share. Be sure to bring content into Google+ from the outside, such as RSS feeds, Twitter lists, or email newsletters. And, of course, there's your own content to share with your audience. Lastly, if you're ever at a loss for ideas, you can always search on Google or within Google+ itself.

Armed with your content plan, each day you can populate your Google+ profile with shares of others' posts, new posts of your own, and posts/shares within communities. Three to four posts per day (total) is adequate, and in some cases can be scheduled using third-party tools. Test whether more or fewer posts results in better engagement; the good news about Google+ is that posts do have a healthy shelf life compared to other networks, so velocity and volume can be tuned down.

Next, you are going to enter your communities and look for relevant posts to leave insightful comments on. Five to ten comments should inject you into enough conversations to get you a steady flow of new followers. Welcoming newcomers to communities with follow-up questions is also a very easy way to strike up a relationship.

Commenting on the posts of influential or active users will also help build credibility and gain attention.

Last, during the course of the day, you will want to stop into Google+ and respond to any notifications or brand mentions (you can bookmark searches in Google+ like you would on other networks, and discover conversations around your brand or articles where you weren't tagged). **In other words, interact with everyone who is interacting with you!**

During the course of the week, you will want to pepper in some circle management and prospecting. You can prospect using Google+ search; just look for keywords or hashtags related to your target customer and either circle users or engage on their posts to build up a relationship. Keeping your circles small and curated will help you stay focused when you are browsing the streams on Google+.

In this chapter, we learned why Google+ can be so powerful in building authority and reputation for ourselves and our business. We covered some of the mechanical ideas for marketing and growing a following. We established a routine, since consistency is important to building authority. Going forward, as you integrate Google+ into your marketing strategy, be mindful of how your strategy should emulate real life business, and you will find yourself awash in opportunities.

CHAPTER 18

How to Attract Leads and Drive Sales with Podcasting

Jason van Orden

JASON VAN ORDEN is co-host of Internet BusinessMastery.com, the longest running podcast about internet business. He has a passion for helping people use online media to attract attention, make an impact, and get paid to do what they love. He speaks internationally about podcasting and internet marketing and has spoken at some of the largest conferences in the world. Jason is the author of the Amazon bestselling book, *Promoting Your Podcast*. To learn more about how to amplify your message and profit from your expertise, visit JasonVanOrden.com.

In this Chapter, You'll Discover

- ► What it takes to create a podcast that stands out in the crowd
- ► Simple tools that produce professional podcast quality on any budget
- ► How to get maximum exposure in iTunes for faster audience growth
- ► Proven strategies for using podcasting to build your lead list and boost sales
- ► How to track audience growth

When I first read the word *podcasting*, it immediately grabbed my curiosity. That was 2005. "Did you mean . . . ?" was Google's reply when I searched for the term. Google still didn't know what podcasting was. Podcasting has come a long way since then.

Podcasting's Payoff

The number of people who have listened to a podcast grows steadily every year. Companies like Apple have trained consumers to download and consume mobile audio and video content. The proliferation of smartphones and other mobile devices with broadband connections has made podcasting an ideal channel for claiming the attention of targeted prospects and getting them to buy from you.

The podcast that I co-host, Internet Business Mastery, has generated seven figures in sales for products priced from $100 up to $6,000. Our students use podcasting to launch authoritative brands and create five- to six-figure income streams with podcasting. This includes topics ranging from career advice to illustration, finance to foreign language, pregnancy to project management and many more.

In this chapter, I'll give you a plan for using podcasting to generate more revenue for your business. The purpose here is not explain the technical details of creating and publishing a podcast. I have a free step-by-step tutorial at HowToPodcastTutorial.com that will help you with that.

My goal is to share with you my best strategies to help you create a show that stands out, attracts a large audience, and converts them into buyers. Please note that while I focus here on audio podcasting, the principles apply to video podcasting as well.

The Secret to Standing Out in the Crowd

It used to be that by simply launching a podcast you would attract an audience. So few shows existed that listeners happily subscribed to any quality show related to their interests. Today, the selection has grown significantly. Don't let that scare you away from podcasting. There's still plenty of opportunity to create a popular show. If you spend a little time to craft a show that is truly unique, you'll already be ahead of 90 percent of the podcasts available in iTunes. Here are my three top tips for creating a podcast that will stand out.

1. Target a Specific Audience

The biggest mistake I see new podcasters make is not defining their audience carefully. A show that is made for everyone ends up reaching no one. Precise audience targeting makes it much easier to get listener attention. It's also much easier to sell to an audience when you've precisely targeted their unique needs.

> To stand out, create a podcast that targets a very specific audience with at a very specific pain or desire.

A podcast that talks about general fitness is too broad in its scope. A better approach would be to specifically help pregnant women stay fit during pregnancy and then lose the baby weight after birth. An alternative effective approach would be to target men who have more than 50 pounds to lose. A good rule of thumb is to niche down two additional levels in the topic and/or audience.

2. Differentiate Your Format

Download iTunes at iTunes.com. Browse the podcast directory in the iTunes store. Listen to half a dozen shows related to your topic. Note what they do well. Find out what is still missing. One tip is to read the most critical reviews to find what is missing for the audience. Use this information to set your show apart.

Choose a format that is different than other shows in your market. If most of the other shows use an expert interview format, consider a format that consists of short tips, step-by-step tutorials, or answers to listener questions. If all the other shows are 30 minutes or longer, you could consider a format that is under 15 minutes.

3. Be Consistent

Your show should become a habitual part of your listener's routine. They'll listen to it on their commute, during a workout at the gym, or while walking the dog. This means you need to publish frequently and consistently. A good rule of thumb is to start with a weekly release. Also, release on the same day every week.

Professional Production at the Right Price

Speaking of standing out, your show has about ten seconds to make an impression on a new listener. Both the quality of your content as well as the production quality of your show contribute to this first impression.

If the audio quality doesn't meet minimum standards, listeners will hit the stop button and never come back. They have plenty of other quality content to choose from. Don't let that scare you. You can get a professional production without breaking the bank. All you need are a few key tips.

Four Simple Ways to Get Professional Audio Quality

1. Buy a Good Microphone

Don't use a cheap microphone. A quality mic is an investment that pays off. Head to your local music supply store or electronics retailer. They will point you in the right direction.

Many top microphone manufacturers now make models specifically for podcasters. Blue and RØDE are two companies that make affordable microphones that are very popular with podcasters. Expect to invest at least $75. Get a USB microphone if you plan to record directly into your computer. Not only is this the easiest set up, it also gives you the highest quality audio.

2. Use a Pop Filter

A pop filter looks like an embroidery hoop with a pair of nylons stretched over it. If you've ever seen a pop star recording in a studio then you've seen them singing through a pop filter with the microphone on the other side.

Two Simple Ways to Get Professional Video Quality

The audio production tips in this chapter apply to video as well. Get a good mic to record audio. Use a pop filter. This will be a foam cover that fits over the mic rather than the hoop-shaped filter we talked about earlier.

Edit and brand your video podcast. You have both the audio and video element now making it even more important. Here are two more simple ways to get professional video quality.

1. Use an External Microphone

Do not use the built-in microphone on your video device. The mic attached to your video camera is not sufficient to capture quality audio. Watch any home video recording of a birthday party and you hear a lot of echo from the room because they use the mic attached to the video camera. This is a sure sign of amateur video production. If your audio quality is bad, it doesn't matter how great your video looks.

Anyone whose voice is heard on the video needs to speak into a microphone that is placed close to them, not several feet away on the camera. These means using a lapel mic that attaches to their shirt or a shotgun boom mic that is held over their head (out of the camera's sight).

Visit your local electronics or music equipment retailer. They can help you find a microphone that plugs directly into your camera to get high-quality audio. There are even adapters that allow you to plug a lapel mic into your iPhone.

2. Let There Be Light

High-quality video needs light, lots of light. Without enough light, your video will look flat or grainy. Shed more light on your subjects to really make your video pop. The best method for this is called three-point lighting. YouTube is full of great tutorials on three-point lighting.

The purpose of the pop filter is to get rid of nasty breathy sounds that our mouths make when we say words starting with letters like "p" or "t." We don't notice these sounds in everyday conversation. However, a microphone picks up these small bursts of air really well.

Not only is it distracting for listeners, it's a sure sign of an amateur production.

Get a pop filter that mounts to your microphone. It's usually attached to a small flexible arm that allows you to place it about an inch in front of the mic.

3. Edit Your Show

Don't expect yourself to nail a recording in one take. My co-host and I have been recording podcasts since 2005. We still make mistakes and have false starts. Record your show in sections. Use as many retakes as you need. Then send it to someone for editing. You can also learn to edit it yourself using a free program like Audacity. Editing your show removes the pressure to be perfect while recording. It also makes for a clean finished product.

4. Create an Audio Brand

Radio has given listeners certain expectations about what a professional show sounds like. A professional show has an intro, theme music, and an outro. This is your show's "audio brand." This serves as an instant cue to the listener that you are serious about your content. It gives the audience confidence that you won't waste their time.

> The show intro is the perfect place to include a short tagline that tells new listeners what your podcast is about and why they should keep listening.

Promoting Your Podcast

While Apple didn't invent podcasting, they certainly put it on the map. The iTunes' podcast directory is the primary place that people go to find podcasts. This does not mean that only Apple users can find and consume your podcast. Listeners find and consume podcasts through any number of devices, mobile applications, and desktop web browsers.

However, Apple's iTunes is the first place to promote your podcast for maximum impact.

Search Engine Optimization for iTunes

The iTunes store is essentially a search engine for content. Users go there on a daily basis to find music, movies, TV shows, books, apps, and podcasts that are relevant to their interests. Like with any search engine, iTunes' objective is to offer a user the content that he or she is most likely to enjoy.

The podcast directory is one section of the iTunes store. iTunes users can also use the application to subscribe to their favorite podcasts. That way new episodes download automatically to their iTunes library.

Within the podcast directory, there are three primary places that listeners look to find shows. You need to show up in each of these places.

First, users can search the iTunes Store for keywords that interest them. The search bar is found in the upper right-hand corner of the iTunes desktop application. You need to show up at the top of the results for searches relating to your show's topic.

Second, users browse the categories and subcategories of the podcast directory. Each of these categories has *New and Noteworthy*, *What's Hot*, *Top Podcasts*, and *Top Episodes* lists. These lists are updated frequently based on the latest iTunes store activity.

> The shows that get ranked and featured for any given topic are the ones that are the most relevant to the topic and provide the most authoritative (or popular) content.

Getting Maximum Exposure in iTunes

How do you make sure your show is seen as relevant and authoritative?

The secret to doing this lies in your podcast feed. If you don't have a feed yet, then set one up. The easiest way to do this is with blog software like WordPress. Then make your feed iTunes-ready using a service like FeedBlitz.com or a WordPress plugin like PowerPress.

An iTunes-ready feed contains key information (also called tags) about your podcast. The podcast directories, like iTunes, use these tags to create your show's listing. These tags also greatly influence when and where you show up in the directories.

To establish your show's relevancy, the podcast title, author, and description must contain the kind of keyword phrases that your target audience is likely to search for. This is how iTunes knows what topics your show is about.

The authority (or popularity) of your show is determined mainly by two factors.

1. The number of people who have recently clicked the subscribe button for your show inside the iTunes store.
2. The number of new, written reviews that your show has in iTunes (especially reviews with five-star ratings).

A Successful Podcast Launch Campaign

When your show first appears in the iTunes directory, it's important to leverage your network to get new subscribers and written five-star reviews. It's most effective if this occurs within a one- to two-week period. Turn to your family, friends, email list, social media following, and professional colleagues to help you out. The goal is to land in the *New and Noteworthy* list and possibly the *What's Hot* list, too. This gives your show an initial boost of new listeners. Then continue to encourage your following to subscribe and review your show to maintain and grow your ranking.

> Your show needs to regularly get new
> subscribers and five-star reviews in iTunes in
> order to attain (and keep) a high ranking
> in the podcast directory.

How to Measure Audience Size and Growth

How many people listen to my show? It's a question every podcaster wants to know. Unfortunately, the technology doesn't exist yet to track if someone listens to an episode or how much they listened. The best approximation of your audience size is the average number of downloads that each episode gets. Your media host should provide an accurate download count for an individual episode (audio or video file) over a given period of time.

It's important to note that a "download" is not limited to someone saving the audio or video file to their computer. When someone streams an episode through a media player on your site, on a mobile device, or in a directory like iTunes it is also counted as a download in your stats. Also keep in mind that a download doesn't indicate a listen. Someone could download an episode and never press play. Even so, the numbers still give you a relative indication of your audience's growth over time.

In order to correctly interpret your download stats, it's important to understand how and when listeners tend to download your show.

The Life of a Podcast Episode

When you first release a new episode, there is typically an immediate spike in the number of downloads. This is a result of those that are subscribed and have set their podcasting application (on their computer or phone) to automatically download new episodes of your show. The rest of your audience will download or stream the show in the coming days and weeks. To get a real sense for the size of your audience, you need to look at the number of downloads for an episode after it has reached its "plateau."

Typically, one of our episodes reaches 30 percent of its total downloads in the first day, 60 percent after the first week, and 90 percent after 30 days. From there, downloads continue to trickle in as new listeners discover the back catalog.

Your past episodes will continue to pull in new listeners and downloads forever. That's the beauty of creating content that lives online. For the purpose of measuring your audience size, the number of downloads in the first 30 days gives you the best indication of your currently active audience. It's normal for download numbers to fluctuate up and down from episode to episode. Some topics will appeal better to your listeners than others. To measure the growth of your audience, chart the average "30-day download number" of each episode over time.

Podcasting Profits

Once you attract an audience, it's time to leverage that attention into profit. Your podcast attracts new, targeted traffic for the top of your sales funnel.

> *The most effective way to make money from your podcast is to use it as the first step in a multi-step sales funnel.*

Before a prospect is ready to buy from you, you need to establish credibility, earn trust, and remove potential objections. This is the first objective of your podcast. The second objective is to turn a listener into a qualified lead. This could be mean getting them to opt in to your email list or call for a free consultation. The exact call to action depends on your sales process.

In each of our episodes, we invite our listener to go to FreeVideoGift. com to get started today creating their ideal business using our step-by-step checklist. This URL takes them to a landing page where we invite them to sign up for our email list. This business checklist is the incentive to sign up. Once someone subscribes, we follow up with an automatic email series that moves them toward a sale.

As you plan the call to action for your podcast, keep in mind that a listener is likely on the go, consuming your content from a mobile device. Create an invitation that is easy to remember and take action on, given these circumstances.

Also, a podcast doesn't work well for time-sensitive promotions. This is because a podcast "lives" forever. Someone could listen to your podcast years after it is produced. Keep this in mind when planning the call to action for your podcast.

To summarize, use your podcast to drive leads for a direct-response sales funnel. Create an easy-to-follow call to action that brings new leads into a follow-up system. The podcast does the pre-selling, your follow-up system does the selling.

Tracking the ROI of Podcasting

Tracking sales that result from your podcast is similar to tracking the effectiveness of any direct-marketing ad or campaign. You can trace sales back to the podcast if you're smart about how you set up the call to action.

We use the FreeVideoGift.com URL uniquely for our podcast. We don't use that address for any other source of traffic. Our site metrics track how many email subscribers and buyers arrive from that URL. We know that any sales tracing back to that URL came from the podcast. You can do similar tracking by using a unique phone number or coupon code in your calls to action from the podcast. By carefully tracking your calls to action in this way, you can compare the investment into your podcast against other sources of traffic.

The Bottom Line

Imagine seeing your brand listed right next to trusted brands, such as NPR, Dave Ramsey, or Oprah. This is the kind of authority that comes with producing a podcast. You attain instant authority. Authority brings trust and influence. Influence translates into changing the lives of others *and* getting paid really well to do it. By using the tips in this chapter you will already be ahead of the vast majority of podcasts. The results will be immense.

To help you with the technical aspects of creating and publishing a new podcast and getting into iTunes, I've created free step-by-step resources. Visit HowToPodcastTutorial.com, sign up for the email newsletter, and I'll send you a checklist for launching your profitable podcast.

I look forward to seeing your podcast at the top of the charts in iTunes.

CHAPTER 19

Instagram for Business
How to Brand Your Business and Build a Loyal Following

Sue B. Zimmerman

In this Chapter, You'll Discover

▶ How to brand your business and build a loyal following on Instagram by observing a few simple, easy-to-remember steps on page 244.

SUE B. ZIMMERMAN, aka The Instagram Gal, is a master at Instagram for business. She teaches entrepreneurs, business execs, and marketing professionals how powerful for business Instagram can be. Sue B. is the founder of the online Instagram course Insta-Results, the author of the number-one ebook *Instagram Basics for Your Business*, a speaker, and a business coach. She is also the founder of SueB.Do and Sue B. Zimmerman Enterprise. Learn more at www.suebzimmerman.com.

How to Brand Your Business and
Build a Loyal Following on Instagram

1. Find beauty everywhere you are and in everything you do.

2. Engage with other users and brands on Instagram.

3. Curate visually appealing images that are informative, resourceful, and fun.

4. Use hashtags to find followers, find prospective clients, and to converse with others interested in your industry and vice versa.

5. Implement a call to action (CTA) in every post.

6. Tag other Instagram users to help amplify your message.

7. Analyze your data through statistics programs to guide your strategy.

8. Leverage Instagram's integration with Facebook and other social media platforms to help save time and reach more people.

Remember scoffing at Facebook as a legit promotional platform for business? It was just some website some student at Harvard designed to connect college kids. You may even recall the first time you saw someone conducting a phone conversation on the street with a mobile phone. "What could be so important that guy couldn't wait until he got back to his office?"

In the same spirit that now counts Facebook and wireless technology as standards in marketing and business support, just take another look at Instagram. Seriously.

In 2014, Instagram reached 200 million users with 25 percent of Fortune 500 companies posting on an average of 5.5 times per week. And, out of the top 100 brands that post on Instagram (like Pepsi, Starbucks, Coach, Nike, just to name a few), 43 percent of them post daily with photos and videos.

Can I Really Build My Brand with Pictures?

Brands are adopting Instagram in a visual way, creating a personality behind the brand that goes beyond just words, product pictures, sales, and offers.

And yes, many have well-known products to celebrate in images. But consider the Boston Celtics. They don't have frothy lattes and sleek leather tote bags to show off. They use Instagram to create an intimacy with their fan base and celebrate the culture of their franchise and their amazing city. Here are some ideas for making Instagram work for your business, no matter the industry.

Instagram for Products-Based Businesses

Just, for instance, real estate agents have photos of graceful porticos and sparkling outdoor kitchens to post. A jewelry company can serve up shining images of gleaming gemstones and funky bracelets.

Instagram for Service-Based Businesses

Instagram can be a showcase for ideas other than seemingly tangible items or products, like other things in which your company is engaged. Put a face on your business by revealing an insider's look into the people behind the service. For instance:

- Community event participation
- Employees participating in 5K races for charity
- Awards dinners and the recipient of the Best Customer Service Representative of the Year
- Halloween costume contests
- Pics of the team at an industry networking event

By thinking beyond the tangible and more about the "intangibles" that can be posted to Instagram, creativity may start to fly. *A picture is still worth a thousand words.*

My Story and How I Found My Ideal Client (and Many More) on Instagram

You may be wondering how I, Sue B. Zimmerman, became known as The Instagram Gal (or The Instagram Expert). I started teaching other business owners how to use Instagram for business because I know firsthand what an amazingly effective social media platform it can be.

In my *spare time*, I am the proud owner of SueB.Do, a seasonal retail store located on Cape Cod. SueB.Do carries product lines of preppy fresh clothing, jewelry, and accessories representing the beauty, fun, and character of the Cape, inspired by the places where I am the happiest: summers with my family on Cape Cod, Martha's Vineyard, and Nantucket.

Direct-to-consumer is the business model I thrive on, powered by my personal connection to customers, word-of-mouth buzz, and social media. I sell SueB.Do products at craft shows, home parties, trade shows, and philanthropic events in the Boston area and on Cape Cod. *And I grew my own retail business by 40 percent just by using Instagram to connect with my customers and potential clients.* Understanding that power, I unleashed my knowledge and my successful theories and began to educate others on how to use Instagram for business.

Watching my own brick and mortar retail business grow and my product sales increase, I realized no one was educating other business owners on how to use Instagram! I literally jumped right in and became the Instagram Gal.

I started sharing posts about how to use Instagram for business with tips, ideas, and generally becoming a resource for those wanting to learn. I strongly encourage everyone to have a hashtag strategy (we will cover that later in this chapter), and because I hashtag keywords that I want to use to attract followers, I met one of my ideal clients through an Instagram post. A local luxury real estate agent from my hometown was looking for ways to boost her presence on Instagram and found me searching through hashtags: #Instagram and #Wellesley. She contacted me to learn more and soon became a $30,000 client, and, even better, became a friend and an invaluable member of my tribe (those who help promote and share my message on my behalf).

But I digress. What I am trying to impart is that Instagram works for brands and businesses. It's not just a personal platform for sharing cute baby photos and silly pictures of your cat. I know firsthand that you can build your book of business on Instagram, as well as create and nurture authentic relationships, quite simply, through a photo.

Find Beauty Everywhere You Are and in Everything You Do

Instagram is about sharing life's beauty through creative and sharp images. This applies to both product- and service-based businesses. While product-based brands have an advantage over service-based brands, there is a unique opportunity to show off creativity within. Show how the company sees the world and make it meaningful to people.

For all businesses, it is so important to share the company story through its history, day-to-day activities, philanthropies, events, behind the scenes, and more. Highlight staff, clients, and partners by showing followers the company's core beliefs through images.

The cool thing about Instagram is that it is chronological so it really shows the brand's development and growth. When the company showcases milestones, prospective clients and customers can easily review the timeline of events through a series of images and interactions with its followers.

Engage with Other Users and Brands on Instagram

Instagram users—and social media users in general—tend to forget that social media is more than just posting. For example, when attending a networking event with a room full of potential clients or referral sources, an attendee wouldn't stand up at the podium and announce their goods and services or latest offer and walk out the door. Rather, the attendee would most likely have a goal of what they intend to accomplish, who they want to meet, and how they want to engage with them. The attendee also knows that networking is about being social, interacting with others in the room, engaging in a mutually beneficial conversation, and lastly, follow through.

These same rules apply to social media, and in this case, finding the ideal client on Instagram. It is imperative that you use Instagram to do one of two things: 1) start a conversation; 2) join a conversation.

1. *Start a conversation.* On Instagram, every post you make is starting a conversation. It should be more than just a pretty picture though; use the post or comment area to ask an

open-ended question and give a call to action. This will encourage others to respond, which will allow you to continue a dialog to offer your expertise or insight as well as learn from your audience.

When searching through other Instagram users' posts, use the opportunity to ask a question, share a thought or tip, or bring others in on the conversation (by tagging them to alert them to the dialogue). The more engaging you are, the more other users are attracted to you and will pay more attention to your posts. When you are actively engaged on others' posts, you will no doubt attract new followers.

2. *Join a conversation.* When scrolling through Instagram and you find a dialogue you feel you can contribute to, jump right on in! The users will appreciate your insight, your wit, or your tips, and you will most likely gain new followers. How do you just join a conversation, you ask?

When you are following other brands that are relevant to your brand's unique goals and objectives, users who are thought leaders in your industry, or businesses who share like-minded views and values, you will find plenty of opportunity for joining a conversation. Therefore, be sure to follow other brands and businesses that you support or want to learn from, or ones for which you can provide value.

If you want to join a conversation that isn't in your immediate circles, you can go find one. By using hashtags, you can see who is talking about what you want to talk about, too! For instance, if you are a real estate agent, go to the "Discovery" tab, type in #realestateagent, and see who is posting, talking about, interested in, looking for, and leading the industry. You can narrow this down by location or stick with worldwide. When you find a user or business that is starting great conversations on Instagram, it is acceptable to chime in. And, not only is it acceptable, it's expected and welcomed. Use it as an opportunity to engage with those you might never have been able to reach.

Curate Visually Appealing Images that Are Informative, Resourceful, and Fun

When creating a content strategy for Instagram, there are a few simple rules to keep in mind. Ensure your photos and images are sharp, professional, and clean. Do not post irrelevant images that will lose the follower's interest. *Every post should bring value to the follower!*

Does your post share a tip, tell a story, give an idea, empower a thought, or highlight a company milestone? Then, it's probably good to go.

Also, do not be afraid to be real or raw. Your makeup and hair team doesn't always need to be on standby; in fact, people relate more to your true self or your brand's behind-the-scenes raw footage.

Your posts must also show variety so that you do not bore your followers. If you are having trouble coming up with ideas, create branded promotion days like: #throwbackthursday or #teamtuesday or #mondaymantra. See what other Instagram users are doing to leverage the promotion.

There are also apps that can help with creating a variety of stylized images. Photo collage apps, video collage apps, filter apps, and graphic design apps will help boost your creativity and shake things up (in terms of content) a bit.

Use Hashtags to Find and Converse with Followers, Prospective Clients, and Others in Your Industry

What is a hashtag, anyway? A hashtag is a symbol (#) that is put in front of a word or group of words to designate a search term or discussion topic.

For instance, if you are looking for an investment property in Boston, you might search #realestate #boston and see what comes up. You might find an agent specializing in the Boston area, a property that was just listed, a property that was just sold, or a broker who is located in or around Boston.

Again, remember this is how I found my ideal client. She was looking for an #Instagram #Expert and she lived in #Wellesley. (Can you believe we were practically neighbors and never met?)

Consider creating 30 hashtags for your business that are either branded, product or service related, location or community based, and keyword driven. Consider the words that potential clients will use in their searches to find you. If you are a massage therapist, for instance, you may want people to find you by searching these key terms:

#massage #massagetherapy #massagetherapist #relief #healing
#stressrelief #certifiedtherapist #deeptissue #city #location

While they may find you searching for a service they are looking for, you might also find them first, which presents an opportunity for you. For instance, a user posts a harried selfie after a long day of work. Perhaps their post says, "Long day at work. I need a #massage. Stat." You confirm their location is in a reasonable radius to your office, and you comment on their post: "Tough days are so stressful and add tension to your neck and back. I can help . . . call and mention this post. I will give you 10 percent off your first visit. I have some openings tomorrow if you're available."

Try using hashtags and take note of how they will change your entire strategy. Instagram users welcome 20 to 30 hashtags per post; while Twitter users generally handle 2 to 3; and Facebook users tolerate 1 to 2 hashtags per post. This allowance of so many hashtags on Instagram offers brands the chance to touch more followers, prospects, and fans by broadening the reach.

Like I always say, hashtags are the magic of Instagram.

Implement a Call to Action (CTA) in Every Post

Posting on social media involves so much more than just finding content to post. It is about engaging and building authentic relationships online so that others build you up and help you create social relevancy. When content is simply posted and there is no engagement, it is essentially doing nothing for you or your brand. The goal is to attract engagement so that you can build your loyal following, amplify your message through social sharing, and get people to react.

On Instagram (and any social platform), creating a call to action on each post will cause your followers to engage in a variety of ways.

And just about any way is a good way. A call to action is a statement or question that asks your followers to do something, which can range from (in a very generic sense):

▶ Answer this question

▶ Take this poll

▶ Share this post

▶ Tag a friend

For instance, if you are attending a conference in San Diego that has a lot of social buzz, one way to engage with followers and other attendees or speakers at the conference is to post: "I am so excited about attending this @nameofconference! Who else is going and who are you most excited to meet? #conferencename." The following people will see this post: Your followers and anyone following #conferencename and @nameofconference. Those who see the post may be equally as excited and comment: "I can't wait to meet @speaker1 and @speaker2 and you @suebzimmerman!"

How does this affect your engagement? First, the more engagement you receive (e.g., a comment), the more people will engage and the more people will see your posts. Second, the commenter has just tagged three people in their comment which means those three people are likely to respond and also tag two to three people. Those two to three people will tag and comment, and your message has been amplified exponentially!

When you ask someone to take a poll, you are encouraging engagement and asking others for their opinions and insight. People love to talk about themselves, and they love to know you are listening! A call-to-action poll or questionnaire will allow you to learn more about your client or prospective client and allow them to feel heard and/or become part of the (your) process.

Tag Other Instagram Users to Help Amplify Your Message

As mentioned previously with regard to discussing calls to action in your Instagram posts, tagging other users on Instagram helps reach a broader audience. The person you tag will be notified, and on Instagram, they don't have to follow you and you don't have to follow them to be tagged and alerted (unlike some other social media platforms like Facebook).

Other users love to know their message is being shared and broadcast through loyal followers, so it will often elicit a reaction from the person tagged. Often, Instagram feeds move quickly so the tagged user may miss their spotlight on your account! So it is great to alert them of the post or comment. Also, if they are famous or have a very large following, you may consider not only tagging them, but hashtagging them as well. This way, no matter how they are alerted, they won't miss one or the other. For instance, "Hey @suebzimmerman, did you see this #InstaAwesome post? #suebzimmerman #instagramgal #instagramexpert"

Tagging someone encourages them to engage as well. And again, when they engage, you receive more attention to your posts.

Analyze Your Data through Statistics Programs to Guide Your Strategy

Social media statistics and reporting can drive your efforts and your success! If you are not using the data that is readily provided to you, you are missing out on opportunities to grow your brand in a really strategic way. For Instagram, an amazing tool to track your activity is through Iconosquare (www.Iconosquare.com).

Iconosquare sends you email reports about your account's metrics, including number of likes, comments, and what types of posts people engage with most. You can also learn what time of day most people react to your images, which day they are online most, and which of your followers engage with you most. This information can help you determine your content and posting strategy rather than going blind, resulting in lost time, money, and effort.

For instance, posting at 2 P.M. for most brands is going to get little engagement. However, if you post at 7 A.M. or 7 P.M., when people are starting their day or winding down, you will get more engagement. The data will show that your followers engage most at those times of day and are on Instagram at those times of day. If the goal is to get more engagement, then using a strategic posting strategy will help leverage that objective.

Iconosquare will give you a "score" based on percentage of people who love your posts, engage with them, and share your message. Track this score to determine your growing success.

Also, Iconosquare offers resources on running contests and promotes existing contests should you decide a contest is right for your brand. You can also learn from others by searching for names of users and/or hashtags. If a thought leader in your industry has a ton of followers and engagement, it is important to follow them and learn from their strategy and marketing plan.

Leverage Instagram's Integration with Facebook and Other Social Media Platforms to Help Save Time and Reach More People

One of the beautiful things about Instagram, other than being able to share amazing images with a different fan base, is the ability to share a post across multiple platforms. Instagram integrates with Facebook, Twitter, Tumblr, Foursquare, and Flickr. When you set up Instagram, it allows you the opportunity to set up its share feature to these various platforms either automatically or per post.

Whichever settings you choose, the best recommendation is to share your post later. Give your post time on Instagram to generate activity and engagement. Then share to your Facebook or Twitter feeds to generate even more interaction. Remember, the more engagement you receive, the more relevancy Instagram (and all social platforms) will give your post, which means more people see it. The more people who see it, the more they will react, share, comment, and like.

When sharing to Facebook, you can share either to your personal profile or to your business page. Many users think you can only share to your personal profile, but this is not the case. Go into your settings and change the landing page of the Facebook profile. If your linked Facebook profile has business page admin rights, it will give you the option to connect to any one of them.

Remember, whichever setting you leave it on is the same setting it will return to when you make your next post. When you toggle images between accounts, be sure to check the settings first.

Instagram users aren't always the same as Facebook or Twitter users, and they typically aren't online at the same time. Use this opportunity to share your post with MORE people! Cross-promoting on multiple platforms will magnify your message to hundreds, possibly thousands more followers.

Also, a Twitter bonus! When you share your post from Instagram to Twitter, it does become a live hyperlink. This means it has search engine optimization benefits if you are promoting your website as well. When more people click, more people see it, which means more traffic to your site.

Instagram is a powerful platform that can be used as a branding tool for your business. Sharing visual content about your brand allows followers to learn more about you in a more personal and relatable way. When you use Instagram with purpose and strategy, you can build your brand and your following in a really fun and profitable way. I will see you on Instagram…and when I do, tag me and tell me you read this chapter in this #InstaResourceful book!

Sue B. Zimmerman, aka #InstagramGal @suebzimmerman

CHAPTER 20

It's Time to Add Twitter to Your Core Marketing Strategy

Kim Garst

KIM GARST is the CEO and founder of Boom! Social, a leading social media marketing firm in Tampa, Florida. While Kim maintains a strong presence on most social media sites, she is recognized as an industry-leading power Twitter user, a position she has used to propel herself up the *Forbes* list of Social Media Power Influencers as well as the Social Media Examiner list of top social media blogs year after year. Visit www.KimGarst.com to learn more.

▲ ▲ ▲

In this Chapter, You'll Discover

► Your evolution from "hating" to "loving" Twitter

► The return on investment (ROI) of a single tweet

► A basic strategy for viral Twitter growth

► Your blueprint for becoming a Twitter master

► A timeline and your investment in the world's most powerful social media marketing tool

Twitter has woven its way into our daily lives and now is commonly accepted by consumers and used by most brands, at least the smart ones, as a tool to at least support, if not replace, other marketing efforts. Twitter also remains the fastest growing of the top-tier social networks. Still, many marketers do not understand or know how to harness its power.

Forget all of your preconceived notions about Twitter and instead embrace it as the "140-character-at-a-time" marketing dynamo that it is.

Your Evolution from Hating to Loving Twitter

Can I make a guess? At least half of you reading this chapter either hate, loathe, or reluctantly tolerate Twitter. I get that. I was right there with you for the first year I was on the site. You have to understand what Twitter is, why it is important, and how to use it correctly before you can appreciate its immense power. Once you do, you will love it forever, just like I do, promise.

Let me try to explain where the evolution takes place. Strictly from a business standpoint, Twitter is the most undervalued, misunderstood, and underutilized of all of the major social media sites. The executives, business owners, marketing directors, and "traditional" media who say you cannot effectively communicate in 140 characters and that the "Twittersphere" is just a noisy waste of time are usually the same ones who have not taken the time to develop a basic Twitter skillset, craft a Twitter strategy (yes, an actual Twitter strategy), or thought about how social media as a whole should be integrated into their marketing platform and plan. They are typically the same people who believe that sales and marketing success is simply a function of ad placements, repeat impressions, and price competition.

I do not blame them. For so many years, "push" marketing was the norm and it worked. It is, however, being replaced by a different type of marketing, "pull" marketing. With pull marketing, the consumer gets to talk back. They get to publicly ask questions and communicate with thousands—make that millions—of consumers around the globe in real time. The company no longer controls the conversation.

Great customer service experiences are passed on for the world to see as are mistakes, errors in judgment, and examples of companies being self-serving, greedy, or ignoring their customers. Twitter is simply one delivery vehicle, call it a megaphone or international virtual town square, for making our collective voices heard. If you are in business and do not care what we, the consumers, think then stop reading now.

Ready for the magic? You go from hating to loving Twitter when you realize that it is not a place to talk, but a place to listen and really communicate. It's not a place to push your products and services, but a place to provide value. You give, give, give, and, like good karma, it comes back to you tenfold.

Good Karma Coming Back Tenfold (aka–The ROI of a Single Tweet)

Good things happen to me on Twitter every single day.

If you make the commitment to GIVE on Twitter without keeping score or expecting anything in return, guess what happens? The laws of the universe hold true and good karma is returned. Sounds hokey, right? I am telling you that it's true.

I will give you one example how *one* tweet and *one* follower can change your life.

I received a tweet from Kathi Sharpe-Ross. I did not know it at the time, but Kathi is the founder and president of the Sharpe Alliance, an integrated brand building and promotion company based in the Los Angeles area. (Her clients over the years have included Coca-Cola, Super Bowl XXXII, Quincy Jones, and the World Cup, to name just a few.) I tweeted back to Kathi, not because I read her LinkedIn profile or thought I could get something out of her, but just to say "hi" and thank her for reaching out. We tweeted back and forth over the next few days, and she told me she wanted to meet me and had a project she thought I might be interested in. Coincidentally, I was scheduled to be in Los Angeles in the next couple of weeks and we met.

Here is where it gets crazy. Kathi's company was selected by the National Association of Professional Women (NAPW, www.

napw.com) to help them manage and promote their annual national networking conference in New York City. NAPW has over 400,000 members and is one of the largest and most well-respected professional organizations in the world. The conference itself was sold out at 1,200 attendees, with hundreds more on the waiting list in case a ticket opened up. Kathi was helping select speakers for the event. Long story short, Star Jones was the master of ceremonies. The keynote speakers were Arianna Huffington and Martha Stewart. There was an all-star panel discussion of leading business women tucked in the middle that included Lesley Jane Seymour, editor-in-chief of *MORE* magazine; Desirée Rogers, CEO of Johnson Publishing; Monique Nelson, CEO of UniWorld Group Inc.; and ME!

Really? Me? Three years ago I would have been lucky to get a ticket to the event. Now, I am on the stage in front of 1,200 super-sharp women entrepreneurs, on a panel tucked in between two female

FIGURE 20.1 From left to right: Lesley Jane Seymour, Desirée Rogers, Star Jones, me, and Monique Nelson.

business icons surrounded by a group of this country's leading female business superstars and everyone wants to know what I think about the power of social media and how it can be used for business.

All I could think (and if you watch the tape of the event you can hear me say) was, I am showing you the power of social media *right now*. I am here, in front of you, among these amazing women because of social media. My voice never would have been heard, or amplified, without this amazing set of community-building tools we call social media.

Thank you for "following" me, Kathi Sharpe-Ross, and for reaching out to me on Twitter. Does anyone doubt the power of a single tweet or a single follower now?

A Basic Strategy for Viral Twitter Growth

I can already hear the critics saying, "Yeah, well that was a one-time thing," or "It only happened because you were famous." Ladies and gentlemen, I *made* myself famous—primarily using Twitter—and you can, too! It was *not* a one-time thing. It was a well-executed strategy that was centered on a commitment to help people and provide value.

In the beginning I did that and picked up a new follower here and there. The word spread that I was someone who helped people learn to use social media as a business-building tool, and more followed. Today, I have hundreds of thousands of followers on Twitter and a second-level following (followers of the people who follow my followers) of over 300 million. I am retweeted or @mentioned, on average, every 45 seconds. My Twitter following grows organically by 400 to 500 new followers a day!

Guess what happened to my core strategy? Nothing! I still give, give, give, and provide value every single day. The scorecard is now, however, clearly in my favor.

Your Blueprint for Becoming a Twitter Master

By now you should be sold on the value of Twitter and the need to add it as a major part of your social media marketing efforts, if not your entire traditional marketing plan. Also, hopefully, you want to know how to do it. There are lots of resources to learn Twitter. There are open Facebook groups (kind of ironic, right?), tons of YouTube videos, an endless list of online Twitter "experts," products, coaches, consultants, and more.

Of course, I cannot possibly tell you everything you need to know about Twitter here in just a few pages, but I can give you some of the guiding principles, techniques, tips, and lessons learned to get you pointed in the right direction.

If you are brand new to Twitter, ready to make a serious commitment to harnessing its power, and want to build a strong, large, valuable Twitter following fast, take the following steps.

Start with Strategy

Name something that does not usually go better with a little planning. Yet time and time again I see people and companies dive into Twitter without any idea what they are trying to do or accomplish. Here is how it usually goes. They open a Twitter account, immediately start tweeting before they learn the basic skills and Twitter etiquette, push products, hop into conversations they know nothing about or are not part of, follow everybody they can until they figure out that you are capped at 2,000 people you can follow until 1,819 follow you back, start unfollowing people to clear up space to follow more, and find automated tools to do a lot of the manual labor, which, unfortunately means spamming people to death. WHEW! Then they quit, say Twitter is worthless, and join the throngs of people who think it is a stupid waste of time.

Sound familiar, or at least plausible?

If you are learning Twitter from somebody and they are not starting with strategy, run! Answers to these questions (and several others) are critical components of a Twitter strategy:

- ▸ What are you trying to accomplish with Twitter?
- ▸ What is the "value" you bring to the conversation?
- ▸ What types of people to do you want to connect with?
- ▸ How do you feature your products and services without being pushy?

- ▶ What is your plan for eventually moving people off of Twitter and to other places (like your email list, Facebook page, telephone, Skype) to deepen the relationship?
- ▶ What resources are you prepared to commit to building a successful presence?
- ▶ What tools will you use to measure success?

Twitter without strategy equals failure. I see it all of the time.

Learn the Basics and Build a Strong Page

Know what a hashtag is, why it is important and how to use one. Invest in a quality, branded Twitter skin and profile photo. Understand your privacy and security settings, understand Twitter's basic terms of service, learn basic "Twitter-speak"; know the difference between an @mention and a direct message. Understand retweeting and why following back is important. Above all, optimize your profile. That means building out a strong profile, adding links, and including the proper keywords.

I am sure the list of "basics" is longer, but you get the idea. What you are trying to do is be able to be found on Twitter, make a great first impression when you are found, and know the lay of the land and rules of engagement right from the start.

Look, Listen, Observe, Search, and Follow

Twitter has over half a BILLION users. Over half of those are active users, and they are tweeting on just about every topic under the sun. As in the real world, in each market niche there are already established thought leaders and experts. Use Twitter search and advanced search to find the people and topics that are important and related to *your* niche or market space. Once you find them, watch the conversations and observe the leaders and key players. Pick up on the general tone, subject matter, and topics being covered. When you feel comfortable, start following these people. As you follow them also add them to a Twitter "list." A Twitter list is simply a sorting mechanism created by Twitter that allows you to follow all of the tweets from your selected group of people in a single stream. You can have multiple "groups" of people sorted in whatever fashion you choose on separate lists.

The goal of this step is to become a part of the existing Twitter sub-community that revolves around your business in a very nonobtrusive way. Imagine a real-world situation where you were the outsider in an already established community. How would you act? You probably would not come in acting like the big shot, offending the established leaders and pushing what you had to sell. It is the same way on Twitter.

Contribute, Add Value, Support, and Participate

So far you have established a credible Twitter page, learned the operational basics, lingo, and rules, and very quietly inserted yourself into not just *any* community, but the *right* Twitter community and shown deference to the established leaders. Now, start having conversations. Do not rule every topic. Just add when you have a good point, question, or can add something of value. When you see something you like from another member, retweet it, or send them a message. When you see great content from another source, do not be afraid to share it. Always give credit where credit is due and be polite. Continue to follow people who you find interesting, valuable, or important in your niche.

If you do all of this, an amazing thing will start to happen. People will reach out for your advice. They will retweet your tweets and pass along your content. Most importantly, they will follow you once they realize you are important to them and already follow them.

Execute, Build Relationships, and Scale

With the above completed, *now* you are ready to scale and begin executing the components of your Twitter marketing strategy. Want to be the top social media blogger in the world? Develop great content, be consistent, provide value, and use a link to every blog post you write with a cleverly written tweet. Me, I have over 400 blog posts written and I tweet one every hour or two. Want to drive traffic to your website? Want to increase your Facebook page likes, or promote a contest? You can do it all with Twitter!

BUT do not forget for one second that Twitter is a place where people choose to have conversations with you and be part of your community. Skip the relationship-building piece and fall back into your "push" marketing mentality and you will watch your community leave you for greener pastures. Stay authentic, keep it real, provide value, and value relationships, and you are going to do much better than "just fine"; you are going to start achieving the goals you set, you know, the ones in your Twitter strategy.

Wow, that sounds like a lot, right? People are always looking for shortcuts. I can promise you that what I just outlined *is* the shortcut. It is a lot more effective and ultimately takes a lot less time than just randomly approaching Twitter with no plan.

A Timeline and Your Investment in the World's Most Powerful Social Media Marketing Tool

The question I probably get most often is, "How long do I have to spend on Twitter each day to get dramatic results?" My first piece of advice is to make a serious commitment to developing a Twitter strategy, identifying the resources at your disposal, learning the basics, and establishing a strong base. That is probably a 30-day process. From there, plan on spending about an hour a day 5 days a week for another 60 days. That is probably a 100-hour commitment altogether. In that hour per day, spend 20 minutes reading, learning, retweeting, and listening. Spend another 20 minutes passing along other people's content while also weaving yours in. Spend the last 20 minutes following quality people and otherwise managing your community growth.

I say to do that for 60 days. What happens then? Well, then I am not going to have to make any recommendations on how you manage your Twitter account. You will see the results for yourself, and my guess is that the bigger problem will be how to get you NOT to be on Twitter all of the time.

CHAPTER 21

So Many Choices!
How to Determine the
Best Sites and Content Strategy for You

Bob Baker

BOB BAKER helps musicians, authors, and creative entrepreneurs use their talents and know-how to make a living and make a difference in the world. He is the author of the highly acclaimed *Guerrilla Music Marketing Handbook* (which appeared in the movie *The School of Rock*). Bob's other books include *The DIY Career Manifesto, The Guerrilla Guide to Book Marketing*, and more. Learn more at www.Bob-Baker.com.

▲ ▲ ▲

In this Chapter, You'll Discover

▶ Where to spend your time and money online so you get the most bang for your buck

▶ The types of content you should post as social media updates and messages to your fans

▶ The three E's of communication and the four sensory modes of communication

▶ How to tailor all of the many online marketing options to your strengths and personality

By now your head should be spinning with marketing ideas you have gleaned from this book. You have at your fingertips hundreds of ways to use Facebook, YouTube, LinkedIn, Google+, Twitter, Instagram, blogging, podcasting, email, and more.

You're ready to get busy promoting yourself online like a superstar!

But then confusion and overwhelm set in as you quickly realize you don't know where to start. The two most common questions that come up at this point are:

▶ What sites should I focus on?

▶ What do I post and share online with my followers?

Those are great questions. Inquiring minds want to know: What sites will deliver the most bang for your buck? How can you make the best use of your time? And what do you communicate to your fans, friends, followers, and subscribers? Not knowing the right answers keeps a lot of self-promoting entrepreneurs from doing anything at all. Can you relate?

Unfortunately, there is no one-size-fits-all, easy-button answer. The best strategy for you will be much different than the best strategy for someone else. The key is to tailor your online marketing plan to your strengths and personality.

To help you figure this out, let's break down this confusing topic into its most basic components. Doing so will help you clear away the fog and gain clarity.

The Three E's of Communication

I've had a passion for the written word since childhood and have spent a good portion of my life sharing my ideas with people in many forms. From this perspective, I can tell you that there are primarily three reasons that we communicate with other humans.

To Educate

With this basic form of communication, you impart information. This includes giving people facts they need to know, instructions on how to do something, directions, or some similar exchange of knowledge.

As a self-promoting businessperson, you might educate people on how to solve a problem, where to find the best resources on your topic, when your next product will go on sale, what steps you took to accomplish something, and more.

To Entertain

Here your goal is to give people a temporary mental vacation or just a good reason to smile. One age-old form of entertainment is telling great stories. Instead of delivering a dry list of tips, describe a real-life experience that illustrates the point you want to make, complete with interesting characters and plot twists. Do that and you will definitely entertain your followers.

You can also give people that brief mental vacation by posting a funny quote, sharing a witty observation, or uploading a silly photo of something strange that caught your eye. Give people something that will amuse them for a couple of minutes, and they will be more likely to remember you.

To Enlighten

With this type of communication your aim is to either inspire people or get them to think differently. Your goal is to give them an emotional charge that makes them feel better.

> You should keep these three communication goals (educate, entertain, or enlighten) in mind whenever you post a status update or send a message to your fans. If you can solidly accomplish just one of them, you're doing well. But often you can combine themes and inspire and entertain people while you educate them. Then you'll be firing on all cylinders.

You can accomplish this with something as simple as an inspiring quote or as involved as a 900-word blog post about how you overcame a personal challenge. You can post links to interviews and videos (created by you or someone else) that include empowering messages and much more.

The Four Sensory Modes of Communication

Now that we've explored the three basic types of things to communicate, let's dive into the vehicles you'll use to deliver your messages. Many of these may seem obvious, but if you take the time to consider the subtle differences, you'll make better choices and reach more potential customers online.

Here are the four basic methods you have to communicate online: text, audio, video, and still images.

Text

Yes, the good ol' written word is probably the most common way to get ideas across online. This category might include short tweets you post on Twitter, status updates you add on Facebook, articles you post to a blog, email messages you send to fans, and more. If you can write even moderately well, this is the easiest and most common way to communicate online.

The thing to consider here is if you truly enjoy the writing process. Some entrepreneurs venture online because they have an important message to get out, not because they feel compelled to express themselves through the written word. Keep that in mind as you look over these four options.

Audio

This mode of communication is obviously absorbed by the ears. If you have a decent speaking voice and are comfortable doing it, you might record yourself offering helpful advice or delivering a commentary on your topic. If you are a musician, then audio (sharing your songs) will obviously be a big part of your online strategy.

It can also include spoken-word messages to your website visitors or social media followers. Imagine how you would feel if you received an email from one of your favorite experts that included an audio option. In addition to the normal text information included in the email, you found a link that said "Click here to listen to a special audio message."

Wouldn't that be more engaging than simple text?

Another option would be to produce your own podcast, which is basically an online radio show (covered earlier in Chapter 18, "How to Attract Leads and Drive Sales with Podcasting"). More time and technical skills are required with a podcast, but it is a good audio option to consider.

Video

The third communication mode involves reaching people through their eyes via video content. As you may know, video has become one of the most popular ways that people absorb information online. If you aren't using video of some form on a regular basis, you are missing out on some great opportunities to reach new customers and create stronger bonds with existing ones.

There are many ways you can communicate using video. Some of your choices include: simple talking-head recordings of you speaking directly into a webcam, interviews you conduct with other experts and entrepreneurs, instructional screencast tutorials, interviews with raving fans, sneak peeks at life on the road or "backstage" at a live event, a visual tour of your office or workspace, and more.

Visual (Still Images)

While video is king, don't overlook the visual impact of still images. These can include shots taken from your latest promotional photo shoots or live events. They can also be still photo versions of some of the video ideas in the previous paragraph: Pictures of you with your fans, life on the road, your workspace, etc.

Additional ways to use visuals online: Upload images of your products, business cards, T-shirt designs, stage banners—anything that will catch the attention of distracted fans online and motivate them to spend a few extra moments seeing what you're up to.

This is something I've really been focusing on recently. Every time I publish a new blog post or audio podcast, I create an image to go with it—often with the headline embedded in the photo. I post this image on social media every time I link to the content it represents. People notice these visual updates much more than they do simple text-only updates.

> Key Point: You can really only reach people online in one of two ways: through their eyes or through their ears. With the ears, that usually means spoken-word or musical content. With the eyes, it can be written, still image, or video content. Until someone comes out with internet smell-o-vision, taste sensors, or a touch screen that touches you back, that's what you have to work with. So make the most of your options.

What's Your Communication Style?

There's a good reason I gave you the preceding lists related to online communication. I want you to use this basic knowledge to start determining the types of content you will post online, along with the best formats to use.

Here's the big question you need to answer: *What is your strongest communication mode or style?* Answering that will help you determine the best way to communicate online.

Are you a good writer? Do you have a passion for the written word? If writing is your thing, then text-based forms of communication may be a big part of your future. If you dread writing and consider it a burden, or if your grammar skills are horrendous, then you probably won't make a text-based blog a big part of your marketing game plan.

Are you a good conversationalist? Can you express yourself well verbally when speaking off the cuff? Do you sound natural when reading from a script or prepared notes? Have you ever dreamed of hosting your own radio show? If you answered yes to any of these questions, then audio messages or a podcast would be an effective way for you to deliver your message.

Do you have graphic design skills? Do you enjoy photography or art? If so, then maybe you should focus on presenting yourself visually.

What about video? When you speak into a camera lens, do you look and sound natural? Or do you feel awkward? Have you ever dreamed about being a roving reporter? Or does the idea of being captured on video horrify you? How you answer these questions will help determine how you use video content and how often.

There's no cookie-cutter right answer here. Some people mumble through social conversations but are brilliant and engaging with the written word. Some people never honed their skills at prose but are powerfully effective when speaking into a microphone. Even if someone is articulate using the spoken word, that doesn't mean it will translate well to an on-camera presentation.

Your job right now is to determine where your strengths lie in these areas. Then make a commitment to using the communication mode that suits you the best.

A word of warning: Your current discomfort level with one mode or the other should not be confused with your potential ability. It's quite natural the first time you hear a recording of your speaking voice or see yourself on video to be surprised: "Oh my, do I really sound like that?" or "I hate seeing myself on camera."

If you have an inner feeling that either audio or video communication is right for you, start getting practice out of the public eye by yourself. I did a lot of on-camera work in college classes and personal projects with friends long before I hosted a local cable music video show many years ago. When I moved to the more public platform of the video show, I was far from perfect. But by then I had moved past the early awkward stages of speaking into a camera. And by doing it regularly, and carefully watching and learning from the playback of my recorded segments, I continued to get better.

So make the best use of your existing communication strengths, and take steps to hone the skills that you feel will serve you best. Knowing what your strongest skills are in these areas will help you answer the following common question.

Since I Have Limited Time, What Sites Should I Focus On?

If the written word is your strength, then perhaps Wordpress.com, Blogger.com, or Tumblr.com would be best for you.

If it's spoken-word audio, you might make Soundcloud.com or your own podcast via iTunes and Stitcher the main focus of your efforts.

If the video format is your thing, then YouTube.com or Vimeo.com would be obvious sites to invest time in.

If you have a flair for design and creating eye-catching images, then Pinterest and Instagram would probably suit you best.

> *Important note: Even if you choose one or two sites or mediums to dominate, you should still have a presence on many other social sites and use them to direct attention to your core format.*

Great. You're totally onboard with everything you've read to this point. But you may still be asking the following.

Now that I Know My Ideal Communication Mode, What Do I Post?

Don't feel bad. It's a common question, often followed by statements like "I don't have anything to say," or "No one cares what I'm doing." And it's this uncertainty that leads many businesspeople to either do nothing (not an option for you) or to start making lame announcements like "Hey, my new coaching program starts in two weeks—register now!"

You can do better. And you will do better once you read the following list of content suggestions. Note that "content" here refers to anything you create: text, audio, still images, or video. Keep in mind that just about all of the examples that follow can be created in any of those four formats. So as you look over the list, think about how you can apply each idea to your communication style and strength.

Original Content

This is obviously stuff you create yourself from scratch. It might be a blog post about an experience that inspired your new service or a short video asking people to come to your next speaking event in a certain city. It can be a review of your favorite new book, a commentary on something that's hot in the news, or photos of your recent trip to a historic location related to your topic. If it was written, designed, or recorded by you, it's original content.

Curated Content

This is something that a lot of self-promoting entrepreneurs overlook. You don't have to actually create everything you share with your friends and followers. Who has that kind of time? One thing that smart online marketers do for their fans is "curate" content—which is just a fancy way of saying that they find helpful stuff their customers might enjoy and link to it.

For example, I'm best known for being a source of music marketing ideas for independent musicians. Therefore, a lot of my social media updates are simply links to helpful articles, blog posts, videos, and podcasts on music promotion. Some of them I wrote or recorded myself but many were created by other people.

By doing this, people in my target audience come to view me as a trusted source of solid information on my topic. I act as a filter that helps them find some of the best content out there on music marketing, whether I produced it or not. And, over many years of consistently doing this, my reputation is enhanced.

You can do something similar. Whatever your specific topic or genre is, you can start pointing people to the best articles, reviews, videos, interviews, and events related to what you write about. Doing so, you'll attract more targeted fans.

Of course, you'll also sprinkle your updates with links to your own activities. But by thinking beyond your own immediate needs and positioning yourself as a resource on your topic, your notoriety will grow a lot faster than it would otherwise.

Questions

One of the big buzzwords in recent years has been "engagement." That means you ideally want people to interact with your messages and not just silently view them from the sidelines. One of the most direct ways to inspire engagement is to ask a question.

If you're a life coach, you might ask "What is your favorite personal development book?" If you're a romance expert, it might be "What's your favorite love story of all time?" If you're a musician, consider "Quick! Can you name seven songs that have a color in the title?"

You can also ask silly questions, such as "If you came back as a crayon, what color would you be?" (I actually asked this question on Facebook once and got dozens of comments.)

Fill in the Blank

Similar to questions, another powerful thing you can post is a sentence that you ask your fans to complete in an unexpected way. Examples: "Early to bed and early to rise, make a _____" or "I love the smell of _____ in the morning." I find it helps to actually include "Fill in the Blank" at the beginning of these types of updates.

Personal Updates

While many of your updates and messages to fans will be related to your business, product, or service, you should also consider sharing glimpses into your personal life. This shows you are human and will help fans feel they know you as a person as well as an entrepreneur. Only you can decide how much to reveal about your family, your home, and your personal beliefs, but an occasional peek at your private life could help you bond with your followers.

Funny or Heartfelt Observations

If you have a sense of humor, share your wit online. Oftentimes the funny things you say to your friends or to yourself should stay private, but sometimes they may be worth sharing with fans. Whether it's a comment about someone you are stuck behind in a grocery store check-out line, or your opinion of the quarterback's lousy performance in the big game, consider posting some of these humorous things online. The same thing applies to more serious and touching experiences you have. If you're laughing, smiling, or crying about something, there's a good chance other people will, too.

Quotes

When you're really coming up blank for something to post online, you can't go wrong with a funny or inspiring quote. Even though it seems at times they are overdone, I can tell you from my experience, quotes get shared and commented on a lot. There are countless websites dedicated to quotes, so you won't have any trouble finding good ones with a quick search.

> Tip: When it comes to posting funny or inspiring quotes online, don't forget to create or share visual quotes—images with the quote text over a colored background or photo. These get viewed, liked, and shared more often.

Straight Promotion and Sales

I saved this for last, not because it's unimportant, but because I wanted to put it in its proper place. Some aggressive promoters think that everything you post online should be selling something. That's a shortsighted attitude. Other timid businesspeople are afraid to market themselves or sell at all. That's a poor strategy, too.

The key is finding a balance. I don't suggest you get too worried about percentages, but a basic rule of thumb might be: For every 10 things you post, make three of them promotional in nature—letting fans know where they can purchase your product or service, asking people to sign up for your free email list, announcing an upcoming workshop, etc.

Keep the Communication Flowing

Even if you don't think you have much going on in a given week or month, continue to post regularly and stay visible throughout your social networks.

If you disappear for months until you have something big and bold to promote, you will have to reacquaint yourself with your audience. You will have to work that much harder to remind them of who you are and why they were attracted to you in the first place.

But if you consistently post helpful new content of your own, point people to the best links related to your subject matter, and engage them with questions, fill-in-the-bank statements, quotes, and witty observations, they will be more involved with you and much more likely to jump in and support you when you have something really big to promote and sell.

Now that you've finished this chapter, I hope you have a lot more clarity and direction on what websites and social media outlets to focus on—and what kind of content to share regularly with your growing fan base.

CHAPTER 22

What You Need to Know about Mobile Marketing

Kim Dushinski

KIM DUSHINSKI is the author of *The Mobile Marketing Handbook: A Step-by-Step Guide to Creating Dynamic Mobile Marketing Campaigns*. On her website, www.mobile marketingprofits.com she provides mobile marketing insight, tools, and resources for businesses, marketers, and mobile marketing entrepreneurs.

▲ ▲ ▲

Think of ten people you know. When was the last time you saw any of these people without their cell phone within arm's

In this Chapter, You'll Discover

- ▶ Why and how you should check your mobile statistics
- ▶ How to make your website work for mobile visitors
- ▶ Making sure your email marketing is fully mobilized
- ▶ How to how to be found by mobile searchers
- ▶ Integrating text messaging into your online marketing
- ▶ Whether to build a mobile app for your business
- ▶ Three things not to do with mobile

reach? Your customers are the same way; and through their cell phone they have a portable online access point with them at all times. Mobile marketing is online marketing; it is just that your customers are using a different device to find and interact with your business. And you can have this interaction with them more frequently and easily.

It is wise to have your customers' online mobility firmly in mind as an integral part of your marketing strategy and not to think of mobile as a separate strategy. Everything you learned in every other chapter of this book is applicable to mobile marketing because your customers are using mobile devices to engage with your business. In this regard, mobile marketing is not something you choose to do—your customers are already doing it with you.

Knowing Your Mobile Statistics

It is important to know how many of your customers are interacting with your business via their mobile devices so you can prioritize your mobile marketing strategy within your overall marketing mix. It is also helpful to have this data should you need to persuade others within your business about the importance of adapting to mobile.

One of easiest ways to check your mobile traffic is to log in to your Google Analytics account. Once you are inside the admin dashboard, go to Audience > Overview > Mobile > Overview. You will see the percentage of visitors who are viewing your website from desktop computers, mobile (smartphones), and tablets.

You can also find out what kind of mobile devices your site visitors are using. Go to Audience > Overview > Mobile > Devices to see the list of devices and the percentage of your mobile visitors using each one. This data is important if you decide to build a mobile app for your business because you will know which platform to work with first based on your audience.

An easy way to find out how many of your potential customers are seeking your type of business using their mobile devices is to log in to your Yelp business account. If you have a physical location for your business it is likely you have a Yelp listing whether you built it or not. Be sure you have claimed your listing and then go to your Activity dashboard.

In the lower right-hand corner, you will see a statistic showing how many of your Yelp profile visitors were on a mobile device. This information will tell you more about the type of business you are in than your specific business. Some industries will have a much higher percentage of mobile visitors (restaurants, nightclubs) than others (professional services).

The important part about knowing your mobile statistics is that it gives you perspective about the importance of your mobile strategy. If you do not have a sound mobile strategy in place, you are virtually ignoring two out of every ten potential customers.

Making Your Website Mobile Friendly

Given that your website is the core component of your online marketing and it is likely that a substantial percentage of your site visitors are visiting via a mobile device, you want to make that experience as good as possible. Despite the small size of their device (usually a smartphone), consumers expect to have the same online experience with you as they would via desktop.

The easiest way to do this is to build your site in a responsive manner. This means the site's design will scale to fit the device, but the content will remain the same. For WordPress users, getting a responsive design can be as simple as building your site with a responsive theme. The best thing about responsive design is that you have just one website; you don't have to keep content up to date on different sites. The downside to responsive design is that the exact same content may not be ideal to each type of visitor.

Another option for your website is to build a stand-alone mobile site and redirect mobile visitors to it instead of your desktop site. This option is good when you have the ability to offer mobile-only features that don't work as well on desktop sites, such as submitting a just-taken photo. The beauty of this choice is that you can build your site specifically for each device.

It is best to give your visitors the option to select
which version of the site they wish to use.
Go ahead and serve the mobile version first to
mobile devices, but provide a way for them
to display the desktop version if that is what
they want. And do not make a mobile visitor
automatically redirect to your mobile app
without giving them the choice
to stay on your website.

Having a dynamic website, one that provides mobile-specific content and a mobile-friendly display to mobile visitors while serving the desktop version to those with fuli-size monitors is the ideal. The key to this working is to know what your visitors most need from your business when they are mobile (hours, location, click-to-call phone number, special offers, etc.) and provide that to them when they are mobile. The tools to easily build a dynamic site are not yet commonplace, but they will be, just as responsive themes used to be few and far between, but are now typical.

Mobilize Your Email

You will not likely be able to tell through analytics how many of your email recipients are reading your emails on their mobile devices, but suffice it to say it is nearly all of them. It may be surprising to you to know that many people unsubscribe from email lists whose emails do not work well on their mobile device.

If you depend upon email as a critical marketing tool in your marketing mix, then you must make sure your email reads well on mobile.

Here are some tips to mobilize your email:

▸ Use a one column design.

▶ Make sure any images you use are a small file size.

▶ Keep text to short paragraphs and write emails easy to read quickly.

▶ Use lots of space around clickable links to accommodate finger-tip-size clicking.

▶ Ensure all outgoing links open in a mobile-friendly environment.

> *If you expect to sell through email marketing, your shopping cart must offer mobile friendly ordering. If your about-to-be customers click through to buy and the order form doesn't work well, you are likely to lose the sale. Check your ordering process on mobile all the way through the process to the sale to make sure it works well.*

If your email service provider offers mobile-friendly templates, you can choose one of the templates they have made. If not, you will need to design your own inside their template design tool or have one created for you.

You can also use mobile to build your email list. If you are speaking to an audience, you can get opt-ins from the stage by mentioning your free giveaway and telling them to grab their phones and sign up now to get it. They don't need to wait to get back to their computer to do it. Just be sure that where you send them to sign up is a mobile friendly web page. Some email service providers offer a text-to-opt-in feature. That works even better.

Three Things about Mobile Search

One of the most common uses of smartphones and tablets is searching online. Just like with desktop search, the biggest player in mobile search is Google, so you want to make sure you take advantage of all the ways to work well with them.

First, if you are a local business with a physical location, you must give full attention to your local business listing on Google Places. When a mobile searcher is looking for a local business, Google serves up their Maps listings near the top of the search. Build your listing as robustly as possible. Add photos, videos, a full description, hours, and any other details you can. It is the best free way to be found by local searchers.

Second, you need to know that Google sends mobile searchers to sites that use responsive web design, sites that use dynamic web design (different content and different design to mobile sites), and those that have a separate mobile site (https://developers.google.com/ webmasters/smartphone-sites/details). While their algorithms are not an open book, when Google says responsive web design is their "recommended option," it seems prudent to go with that option in order to maximize your organic mobile search traffic.

Third, mobile search result advertising is a great way to be found. If you are already doing AdWords advertising, you are already doing mobile advertising because it is incorporated into your ad spend. You can choose to minimize your mobile ads or use them exclusively. Knowing your mobile stats will help you prioritize. Having a mobile-friendly website will give your mobile search results advertising the ability to work.

Integrating Text Messaging into Your Online Marketing

One of the most powerful tools of mobile marketing is text messaging. The best way to incorporate texting with online marketing is to use your online efforts as a way to get opt-ins for your SMS text message list. Then you can use text messaging as a way to reach your audience outside their full and overwhelming email inboxes.

Text messaging is very similar to email marketing in that you have to give people a reason to opt in and then you need to create value for them in your messages so they stay subscribed. It is unlike email marketing in that people almost always read every single text message, and they do it very quickly. Email hasn't seen that kind of response since we used to sign guest books on websites we visited.

> *Text messaging must only be done with explicit permission via an online sign-up form or by texting in from their phone to opt in. You cannot use cell phone numbers you have gathered previously. You cannot rent or buy a list of cell phone numbers. You must create a text message campaign and entice people to participate by permission.*

After you have built a list of opt-in subscribers by creating a compelling reason for them to sign up, you can send text messages to your list with the kind of information you promised them when they enrolled. You can only send them as many messages as you said you would. If you say five messages per month, then you cannot suddenly start sending twice a week messages because you are having a promotion.

Text Message Content Ideas

- ▶ Short tips or strategies your audience can use
- ▶ Mobile coupons
- ▶ Reminders of webinars or other events
- ▶ Announcements of product releases
- ▶ Meetups at events

To Mobile App or Not to Mobile App

It may be very tempting to jump into building a mobile app for your business, but given the financial and time investment involved it is smart to consider first whether or not a mobile app is the right match for your business. The single most important factor in this decision is whether or not your app will provide a way for your customers to do something repeatedly. More specifically, it must be something they want or need to do repeatedly.

If the mobile app you have in mind will simply tell customers about your business, give them your location and hours, a list of services and provide special offers to them, then you don't need an app. You just need a mobile-friendly website.

People will only download an app they see as beneficial to them; usually it is either useful or entertaining. They will only keep it on their phone if they find they use it regularly. Otherwise it will be deleted.

If the mobile app you have in mind will give them access to their account with your business, entertain them in a way that also congruently markets your business or in some other way engages them repeatedly, then you can consider moving ahead with a mobile app.

A different way to take advantage of mobile apps is to advertise inside other apps. The key to this working is to be congruent. Don't try to advertise your professional service inside a gaming app. When someone is playing a game they are not looking for a virtual assistant.

What NOT to Do with Mobile

Do not use QR codes unless the action caused by the code is 100 percent mobile friendly. You can have the code send people to a mobile-friendly landing page or to watch a video, but do not send people to a desktop homepage.

Do not send any text message without explicit and documented permission.

Do not think of mobile as a separate marketing tool. Mobile is completely integrated into your customers' daily life, and they don't think of it as something separate. They just use it to do what they want. Be ready for that by assuming that whatever you do in your marketing will be accessed by mobile visitors.

With the continual improvements and proliferation of mobile devices more and more people will be using cell phones and tablets as their first choice in consuming information online.

Let the principles in this chapter guide you to optimizing your online marketing to the millions of mobile users so you can fully tap the power of the internet to grow your business.

CHAPTER 23

How to Build an Award-Winning Blog in Six Months

Ian Cleary

IAN CLEARY had 20 years' experience in the technology industry before focusing his efforts on digital marketing and social media. He is considered one of the global experts in social media technology and, within six months of launching his social media tools and technology blog, it was named as one of the top ten social media blogs in the largest and most recognized annual global social media blog awards. For more information, go to www.razorsocial.com.

▲ ▲ ▲

In this Chapter, You'll Discover

▶ How to differentiate your blog from the competition

▶ The essential elements for sustaining a growing blog

▶ Building and leveraging relationships with key influencers

▶ How to deliver quality, consistent content that gets shared

▶ Why email marketing is still your best friend

▶ How to capitalize on every visit to your website

▶ The importance of monitoring the impact your content has and optimizing your process

In August 2012, we launched a marketing technology blog focused on social media tools and technology. By January 2013, we were listed as one of the top 10 social media blogs in a global competition run by Social Media Examiner.

Winning in this competition was not luck. We followed an approach to blogging that can be followed by any new blog that is starting out or by existing blogs that want to dramatically improve on their traffic and reputation, even in a crowded market.

Your blog is the magnet that attracts traffic to your site and, if you use the right approach, this magnet will keep drawing more and more traffic that will result in you becoming recognized in your industry, building amazing business partnerships and setting up systems for the low-cost acquisition of customers for your business.

Can you achieve similar success and see rapid growth in your blog and business over a short period of time? Absolutely. Let's get started.

Research Your Market to Identify What Makes Your Blog Different

There are millions of blogs around the world so it's very difficult to stand out unless there is something unique about your blog. Identifying a niche or something that helps differentiate your blog from other competitor blogs makes a massive difference in accelerating your blog's growth.

This involves some research to find out who your competitors are, what they are writing about, what gaps exist in areas that they don't write about, and how popular the content they create is.

It starts with creating an Excel spreadsheet for your research:

▸ Search Google for keywords relevant to your product or service to see who appears regularly. Check out their content and see what they write about.

▸ Research the competitors that you already know of. What content do they write about?

▸ Use OpenSiteExplorer.org to rank you and your competitors. This tool ranks websites and pages of websites out of 100. The higher the scores, the harder it will be to beat the competitor in search results when you are competing for the same keywords.

▸ Add a column in your Excel spreadsheet for the estimated traffic of your competitors. Use tools like Compete (www.compete.com), Quantcast (www.quantcast.com) or SEMRush (www.semrush.com) to get estimates.

▸ Use Ahrefs (www.ahrefs.com) or similar tools to find out which blog posts on their website have the most links pointing to them. Content that is popular will be linked to by other websites.

▸ Use SocialCrawlytics.com to analyze the volume of social sharing on your competitor's blog content. Popular content gets shared a lot.

In our case, we noticed, from research, that our competitors sometimes wrote about social media tools and these were very popular posts, but they didn't focus all their attention on that area. By focusing all our attention on this area, coming up with much better content and delivering content from a different angle, we ended up with really popular blog posts. We began to own and dominate the niche very quickly.

Put Down Strong Foundations

It's really important that you build your blog on a reliable platform that is supported by good infrastructure.

Building Your Platform

WordPress is a blogging platform that is used by over 20 percent of websites worldwide. It's a safe bet for your platform as it's supported by a huge community around the world.

Whichever platform you choose, work with a top development team that understands not just design and technology but also conversions. There is no point in having a nice-looking website if it doesn't convert into sales for your business.

Your hosting provider is also a key player in your blog's success. Here are some key requirements for your hosting provider:

- ▶ Fast speeds guaranteed with unlimited bandwidth available (i.e., if you get a rush of traffic there will be no limits imposed)
- ▶ Managed service. What happens when your site gets hacked? If you do not have the skills in-house, make sure your hosting provider can provide a managed service (or find a relevant partner) so that if things do go wrong, there is someone there to fix them.
- ▶ CDN. A CDN is a content distribution network. If you want to build a global audience, you need to ensure the fast delivery of your content, irrespective of where in the world your site is hosted. A CDN will automatically distribute your content around the world and keep it in sync. When someone accesses your content, they will be sent to their nearest location in order to ensure maximum speed.

Build Your Content Strategy

From your initial research, you will have started to formulate ideas for the content you want to write about. But it's extremely important to have a content strategy in place before you write anything at all. Producing content is very time intensive, so you need to minimize your time commitment and maximize the effectiveness of the content.

- ▶ *What are you going to write about?* It will be based on your niche, and topics within this niche. What format will the content be in?
- ▶ *When will you write?* It's important to get into the habit of writing, and that usually means defining specific times and days that you always write.
- ▶ *Who is your target audience?* Developing personas that identify who you are aiming your writing at is essential. The persona should include the type of person they are, where they work, how old they are, etc.
- ▶ *What optimization will you do on the content?*
- ▶ *Which channels are you going to distribute the content to?*
- ▶ *Your team.* Who will be involved? As well as writing, you may need people involved to edit, produce graphics, help with content distribution, etc.

▶ *Measurement.* How are you going to measure the impact of your content?

Build Relationships with Influencers

Relationships are a key part of the success of any blog.

> You can have the best content in the world, but
> the cream does not rise to the top unless
> you help it get there.

Without a plan for building relationships with relevant people in your industry, your blog will not get the growth it deserves. The influencers can be people or websites which, of course, have people at their core.

Influencers online typically have a large audience, they are connected to many other influencers, and people take action based on what they share and talk about. Leverage their audiences to get your content in as many relevant hands as possible.

How Do You Find Out Who the Influencers Are for Your Industry?

From your research you will have come across competitors that you may want to develop relationships with, and other websites that may be coming up all the time in search results.

Use tools such as LittleBird (www.getlittlebird.com), GroupHigh (www.grouphigh.com) or Twtrland (www.twtrland.com) to help you make a list of key influential people in your industry. When someone is influential, they are followed by other influencers.

▶ LittleBird produces a list of people, ordered based on who has the most influencers following them. This can be a very useful way to identify influencers.

▶ GroupHigh is very focused on bloggers, so if you want to find the top bloggers in your industry you can filter based on topics and then view a lot of detail for each blogger.

▸ You can also use social media analysis tools, such as Twtrland, to identify influencers on channels such as Twitter.

How Do You Build Relationships with These Influencers?

The best way of building relationships with influencers is by helping them!

▸ *Share their content.* Set up systems to make sure you find their new content and can share the best of it. For example, create a list of influencers within Twitter and add it as a column in Hootsuite. Now, you can track the influencers' activities and look for opportunities to interact. Add their websites to Feedly, which is a tool for reading and subscribing to blogs. Through Feedly's integration with an application called Buffer you can automatically schedule the content sharing.

▸ *Comment on their blogs.* Most people are lurkers and don't comment, so bloggers really love getting comments.

▸ *Profile them on your blog.* Ask them for an interview. Influencers like doing interviews! By interviewing them, you get a chance to speak and interact with them and get to know them. Group posts where you ask a question or series of questions to different influencers and profile them all in one post works amazingly well!

▸ *Guest post for them.* Influencers have very little time and they have high demands for content. The majority will allow you to guest post, but it depends on your approach. Be a subscriber, interact with them, understand what content their audience likes and then approach them.

Produce Quality, Shareable Content

It's great if you can produce a lot of content, but don't ever sacrifice quality for quantity. If you can only produce one quality post a week then don't be tempted to write two poor ones instead!

Write High-Quality, Popular Content

I advise a lot of companies to write long, detailed posts. This is not the case for everybody, but my reasoning is that it's very difficult to write great content in a couple of hundred words. Great content is what people talk about, share, and link to. So if you can't write a masterpiece in a couple of hundred words then write longer, more detailed content.

In research by Neil Patel, it was found that the majority of blog posts in the top ten search results are more than 2,000 words. Google doesn't only look for long content but, in terms of links and shares, this is content that has done really well.

Which articles are going to get the most links, shares and attention? An "Introduction to Online Advertising," at 300 words, or "The Ultimate Guide to Online Advertising" at 2,000 words?

One good tactic for getting a lot of attention is to do a group post that includes information from some of your influencers. We did a group post where 54 influencers told us their favorite WordPress tools. We included a picture of each person and then shared it out on social media channels. Most of the influencers will also share the post with their followers so you get a lot of extra attention, shares, and links to the post. This post got massive attention, links, shares, etc.

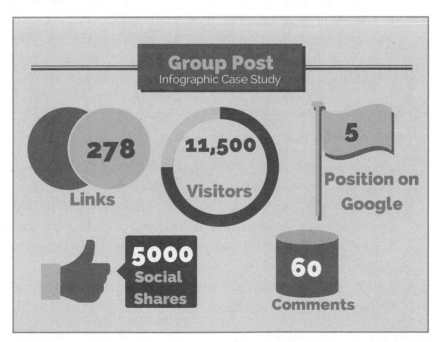

FIGURE 23.1

Infographics work really well, and our trick is to reference lots of influencers and/or tools in each infographic. We referenced over 30 tool providers in an infographic and, of course, they shared it like crazy and created blog posts sharing the infographic with their audience.

But never post an infographic without a full blog post explaining the infographic. This is just an image for Google; you still need a good detailed blog post.

Get Eyeballs on Your Content

After going to all that trouble to produce a fantastic piece of content, you need to give it a fighting chance to be seen by as many people as possible.

Optimize Your Content for Google

You do not have to be a search engine optimization (SEO) expert to optimize your content for Google. In fact, sometimes being an expert can be a disadvantage because you over-optimize, which sometimes leads to Google penalties.

There are two sides to optimization: on page and off page. On-page optimization involves changing elements within your website, and off-page optimization is about getting links back from external resources.

On-Page Optimization

Here are the basics that you need to consider:

1. When you write a post, check Google Keyword Planner (Long Tail Pro is a good alternative) to identify keywords to target.
2. Find out how competitive it is to rank on these keywords. Use tools such as SEOMoz keyword difficulty tool, which will give you a very good idea where you will appear in search results after writing the article.
3. Ensure these keywords, and other similar/relevant keywords are referenced in the following:
   a. Title
   b. Description

    c. Heading. At least one Heading 1 on the page

    d. Web page name

    e. Content. Include these keywords and other relevant/related ones

If you're on WordPress, use the Yoast WordPress SEO plugin to help make it easier to optimize your content.

Off-Page Optimization

This is about link building, but one of the best forms of link building is getting links naturally. You achieve this by having great content and building strong relationships through social media and other channels. But until this happens organically, you will need to do some promotion. See the section "Promote your Content" that follows for some tips.

Optimize Your Content for Social Media

This is an area that has become increasingly important. When your visitors share content out to their social media channels, you can add relevant information that tells the channel more about the content.

For example, Twitter cards allow you to describe your content. You can tell Twitter the main image for any given piece of content and, when that content is shared, the image you have specified is the one that is displayed within Twitter streams.

Promote Your Content

When you build strong relationships and grow your presence on social media, you naturally get links. But if you want more backlinks, you need to reach out to relevant people and tell them about your great content.

So how do you promote your content?

1. *Share new content automatically to your own social media channels.* Set up a tool—such as Dlvr.it—that will automatically monitor your blog for new content and then distribute it to relevant channels.

FIGURE 23.2

2. *Encourage social sharing when people see your content on your blog* (e.g., use social sharing plugins such as Flare).

3. *Reach out to relevant people.* Use a tool such as BuzzStream to track all your interactions with the people you reach out to. If you find people who promote your content, these are people you may want to reach out to again.

4. *Pay for promotion.* You can run some advertisements to ensure your content gets seen. Jason Miller, an expert marketer, talks about the importance of reaching beyond the audience you attract through organic means. You don't want to be delivering to the same audience all the time.

5. *On some channels (particularly Twitter), you need to send your new posts multiple times, and always create different wording to describe the new post.* This gives more people a chance to see the content. SocialOomph is a great tool for this and works

particularly well for evergreen content that you should continuously share.

Build Up Your Email Marketing

Over 70 percent of the people who visit your website will never come back. Frightening? Absolutely. So how do you encourage people to return? You convince them to subscribe to your email list and then you can prompt your subscribers every time you publish a new blog post.

Your email list is extremely valuable. From day one of your blog, set up an email marketing tool such as MailChimp or AWeber and put subscription boxes on your website to encourage sign-ups.

How do you increase the rate of sign-ups? Well, there are various tricks involved in increasing your sign-up conversion rates.

- ▶ *Social proof.* People are very much influenced by people of authority, what other people similar to them do, and anything that shows them they are not alone. For example, on Andy Crestodina's site, Orbit Media, he shows how many people have subscribed to his blog. This is over 5,000 people so that is social proof.
- ▶ *Provide an incentive.* Why don't you provide a free guide to everyone who signs up? This must be high quality, but free guides that are relevant to your target audience help with conversion rates.
- ▶ *Be pushy.* You have to be pushy to get people's attention, and there are various ways of being pushy:
  1. *Bold colors and calls to action (CTAs).* You need your opt-in boxes to be prominent on the page. Big, bold colors, strong headings, and a very clear call-to-action button.
  2. *Opt-ins in multiple places.* You don't just put an opt-in box in the right-hand sidebar—what about at the end of blog posts? What about feature images that take the full width of the page? And the "About Us" page, where people are really showing an interest?

3. *Pop-ups*. When someone is browsing through your site, you can have a pop-up that appears after a certain time or when they take a particular action. These pop-ups can be annoying but, if done well, they can substantially increase conversion rates. Syed Balkhi developed a popup tool called OptinMonster. You can set this popup to only appear on "exit intent," which means that it pops up when the mouse has moved off the main screen (i.e., when your website visitor is about to exit). This pop-up can achieve very high conversion rates.

When someone signs up to your email list, it's really important to try to establish a relationship with them. You are building a community, not just a list. If you do not get many sign-ups on a daily basis, consider sending them a personal email when they do join your community.

For our first 500 subscribers, I sent a personal message thanking everyone for signing up and asking them some questions about who they were and what they did. As well as building relationships, it was excellent research, as I knew exactly who was signing up and what they were looking for.

Convert and Sell

So by now, you have a highly effective blog that is attracting traffic and you are building a community through social media and through your email subscriber list, so it's time to sell.

Your email subscribers may not be ready to buy immediately, but you need to nurture them over time. As you build up your subscriber list, consider moving from an email marketing tool to a marketing automation tool, such as InfusionSoft, Ontraport, or Marketo. These tools help you automate the process of nurturing your subscribers and, ultimately, generating sales.

People buy from people they know, like, and trust, and there's no better way of building this than through a blog.

Optimize and Monitor Results

If you're not analyzing the results at least on a weekly basis, you will not achieve your potential. You need to monitor what content did and didn't work, the conversions you got from your traffic, where the traffic came from, and how engaged people were when they arrived.

One key thing to track is the links you are using. You can include information within a URL that describes what you are sharing and where you are sharing it so that you can see which links get the best results. Google provides a tool called Google URL Builder, and this allows you to add information to any URL (web address). In Google Analytics, you can then track what happens to these links.

Beyond Google Analytics, you can consider tools such as Mixpanel or KISSmetrics, which help you to analyze the steps in your purchase funnel and track visitor behavior. You should also look at social media analytics with tools such as Simply Measured (simplymeasured.com).

Get Out of the Office!

It's still extremely important to get out of the office every so often and meet with the people with whom you are building relationships—customers, influencers, and subscribers; you can only do so much online. Despite the success we have had with our articles, some of the most important business relationships happened after meeting people in real life. But we would never have had these meetings in the first place without the blog!

Final Comments

A blog is a hugely powerful way of attracting relevant traffic and converting that traffic into business. But it's not simply a case of writing any random content. You need to write strategically, build relationships, and promote your content, while building a repeatable process that drives repeatable results.

Take your blogging seriously, and it will produce amazing results.

CHAPTER 24

How to Build a Loyal, Die-Hard Following of People Waiting for Your Next Offer

Craig Valentine

CRAIG VALENTINE, MBA, an award-winning speaker and trainer, has traveled the world helping speakers, executives, and salespeople turn their presentations into profits. He is the 1999 World Champion of Public Speaking for Toastmasters International, winning out of more than 25,000 contestants in 14 countries. Craig is also the author of several books, including *World Class Speaking*. For more info visit: www.Craig Valentine.com

▲ ▲ ▲

In this Chapter, You'll Discover

▶ Six keys to earning an income and rapidly grow loyal customers

▶ Leveraging your content to thrill your prospects and customers

▶ An automated system for growing your list and exploding your profits

▶ Establish communities around your products and programs to create momentum and free up time

▶ Gain extra income by letting your products sell your products

▶ The formula for becoming an online marketing superstar

By now you've seen what kind of mindset is needed to become an online marketing superstar, you have picked up tools to get traffic, and you have gained an understanding of how you can leverage apps to build your business. The question is, once you get all of these new prospects and customers, what can you do to have them become loyal, die-hard followers, waiting and anticipating your next offer?

Recently I sent out two emails (each one week apart) to my entire list of subscribers, and they led to more than $75,000 in revenues. Why did I receive that kind of result? It's because my list of subscribers were anxiously awaiting the launch of the course.

Tease Them Before You Tell Them

As a professional speaker I usually try to tease my audience for the message they are about to hear before I actually tell them the message. Marketing works the same way. Before you actually make the program or product available, it's critical to tease your subscribers about it. For example, you can:

- ▶ Send your weekly newsletter and mention that the product is coming.
- ▶ Drip valuable content from the product that whets their appetite for more.
- ▶ Post the product cover (with the intriguing title) on your social media pages and then watch the comments come rolling in.
- ▶ Hold a 30 to 60 minute teleseminar giving slices of the product so that your listeners will want the entire pie.
- ▶ Send quotations and messages from the product to your social media sites.
- ▶ Send out short audio lessons that provide value and tease them to want more.

How are you teasing them before you tell them? If you really give it some thought, you can find endless ways to make them hungry for what's coming next. However, none of that will work unless you consistently treat them right while they're on your list. Below is a very specific game-changing surefire method for exceeding your subscribers' expectations, along with additional tools for turning them into loyal, die-hard followers.

The One Formula That Changed My Business and My Life

Everything I do with the internet is based on one Guerrilla Marketing formula. As a Certified Guerrilla Marketing Coach, I know that the number-one reason people will do business with you is confidence. They have confidence in you and confidence that they will get what they expect to receive from you.

The question becomes how do you get people to build their confidence in you? The Guerrilla Marketing answer is familiarity. Confidence comes from familiarity.

The next logical question is: How do you get people to become more familiar with you? The answer is through regular, ongoing contact. So let's take a look at this formula.

> Confidence comes from familiarity, which comes from regular,
> ongoing contact.

How Can You Gain Peoples' Confidence Online?

Knowing this formula sparked the following question I asked myself: "In what ways can I have regular ongoing contact online?" The original answer was through an online weekly newsletter. It made sense because most of the internet marketing gurus seemed to have one. I set out on my journey of having regular ongoing contact with the hopes that it would make people familiar with me, confident in me, and ready to eventually buy from me. I knew it would take patience in order to pay off.

Every week I put together valuable content and gave it away in the form of an email newsletter. It started getting traction and, after a few years, I got up to about 2,000 subscribers. That was a great first step to success online.

Wasted Content

Then I ran into my first real issue. I felt like I was running out of content. After all, I had been giving away everything I knew about speaking every week for a few years. However, what bothered me the most was a thought I kept having which went like this:

"The new people who opt-in to my newsletter are missing everything I posted before. That seems like such as waste of content. I know my subscribers can go back and look through the archives of my blog, but who really does that on a consistent basis? I need to find a way for my new subscribers to start from zero and see everything I posted before. That way I won't run out of content. Plus, they'll get more value by seeing not just what I have now but all of the absolute best posts I've done."

The Game-Changer that Leads to Die-Hard Loyal Followers

I was in Alex Mandossian's TeleSeminar Secrets class when I heard him mention a website offering 52 teleseminar tips. I visited it and was blown away because, once you subscribed, it automatically took you from Tip #1 all the way to Tip #52 in weekly installments. Alex mentioned that we can do the same for our industries. Hence, 52SpeakingTips.com was born.

I started the site in 2009 and rapidly went from 2,000 subscribers (a number I hovered around for a couple years) to more than 17,000 subscribers. I loved it because every single subscriber started from week 1 and had the opportunity to get all 52 lessons.

It was a game-changer. As a result, not only did my subscriber base grow significantly, but I began seeing sales come in every day and night without me doing anything extra. I got:

▸ More sales
▸ More speaking engagements
▸ A much larger and loyal following

Establishing my tips site is by far the best move I have ever made in business whether onstage, offstage, or online.

Your Turn for Profits

If you want a larger and loyal following that leads to profits, I strongly suggest that you set up your own 52SomethingTips.com site. Feel free to use mine as a model. If you don't want to do 52, just do 26 and make if a half-year course. Or do 13 and make it a quarter-year course. You can also send the lessons every few days instead of every week. Here are the keys to making this type of site work for your subscribers and for you.

Key #1: Give It Away for Free

I know there are people who say, "If I do all of this work to put together these lessons, shouldn't I get paid for it?" You will, just not immediately. Instead of getting a few orders now, you can get many regular ongoing orders later.

I've found that it's usually after about the seventh week (or seventh lesson) that my subscribers have gained enough confidence in me to start purchasing. Sometimes it's sooner, and sometimes it's later. The bottom line is it happens. People buy because they receive the regular, ongoing contact that breeds familiarity that leads to them placing confidence in me. When you give it away, you get a much larger pool of prospects and that pool IS your business.

Key #2: Make It Bite-Size

I learned a long time ago that time is not money, time is life. Time is of the essence for people nowadays, and many of them don't feel like they have a lot of extra time. Therefore, the key is to make your content practical, powerful, and bite-size. Make the content so motivating that your subscribers would be willing to pay for it even though they're getting it for free. Treat it like you're developing a paid product. It took me months to create my tips site, and it has been paying off for me for years. Don't hold back your great content because it will bring in greater rewards. Keep it short.

Key #3: Have a Strong Hook

Marketing online requires you to do what I call "Fight for free." This means even when you offer something for free, you have to fight to get people to sign up for it. Why? It's because there is so much available for free, and other marketers are giving you tremendous bonus material just to opt in to one of their free offers. You need to go big or go home.

For example, when I'm on stage, I say, "Raise your hand if, one year from now, you want to be at least three times better than the speaker you are today." Whether I'm speaking to speakers or leaders, almost all hands go up. Then I say, "Great, then for absolutely free, you can go to my site 52SpeakingTips.com and, every week for one year, you will receive an audio lesson. By the end of that year, you will be at least three times better."

What's the hook? It's "three times better."

To develop a strong hook, I suggest you adhere to the two following sales principles that helped me become the former Mid-Atlantic Three-Time Salesperson of the Year for Glencoe/McGraw-Hill.

Don't Sell the Product, Sell the Result

Online it's important to sell the result of what people will get if they opt in or purchase or take the next step you want them to take. For example, instead of focusing on the tips, the focus was on them becoming "three times better."

I see way too many websites offering "A Free 7-Part Newsletter." Where's the result? Nobody wakes up in the morning and says, "I can't wait to get on another newsletter list today." What they do say, however, is "I wish I could find a way to become a better presenter." Or they say, "I wish I could get more customers online." Or "I wish I could grow my list." Tap into their wish and show them how it can come true.

Put the Result Before the Resource (or Request)

How do I start talking about the tips from the stage (and online)? I say, "Raise your hand if, a year from now, you'd like to be at least three times better than the speaker you are today."

In other words, I mention the result (three times better) before I mention the resource. The key is to put the result before the resource.

If I did it the other way around, it might sound like this, "Raise your hand if you'd like to receive 52 emails from me." My audience would look for the nearest exit.

Key #4: Help Them Promote It

I'm not always the sharpest knife in the drawer, but one strategy I used with my tips site was a smart move.

As an online instructor with my 6- and 12-week courses, I've become aware of the power of accountability partners. The students in my courses always grab an accountability partner when the course begins, and many of them continue their accountability partnership long after the course ends. Why? It's because having someone to bounce ideas off and hold you accountable is priceless. It keeps your momentum strong as you go for your goals.

Seeing this, I came up with an idea for my tips site. Whenever someone opts-in and registers, they hear an audio from me strongly suggesting that they go through the program with at least one other person (an accountability partner). All they have to do is send the link to someone they know who can use it, and then they can go through the program at the same time because they'll receive the lessons on the same day.

To say this worked to grow my list is an understatement. I started seeing people sign up in droves. This is a fantastic win-win because I know they'll get more out of the year if they study it with someone, and I also win because it rapidly builds my list. It quickly grew my list from 2,000 to 4,000 to 8,000 to 16,000 and then some.

At the point your subscribers opt-in, suggest to them that they should share your link and grab an accountability partner with whom they can navigate your content. You'll see your list grow and grow and grow at blazing speeds, and your prospects and customers will get more out of your content because their partners will help them consume it.

Key #5: Don't Sell

Although I am big on giving my audience a next step when I'm onstage, I do not sell directly from any of the tips. Instead, every tip simply contains valuable content for them. Any sales-related emails they receive from me are separate from the tips site. This keeps the momentum going because they know every tip will be sales-free and will focus on making them a better speaker. This familiarity leads to confidence, which leads to them looking for other ways to invest in me. Several of them have expressed to me that "If I can get this great information for free, imagine what I can get if I actually buy something!"

Key #6: Automate (Set It and Forget It)

Let's face it. When you offer a regular online newsletter, can't it be difficult sometimes to get around to producing it each week? As a speaker who travels, I have fallen into times when I haven't been able to send a newsletter out for a few weeks straight. I either didn't have the energy or felt like I had enough time.

The solution is automation. My tips site is completely automated. In other words, I was able to "set it and forget it." I spent a few months writing, recording, and setting up the content and then I made it automatic using the shopping cart www.AutomateYourSpeaking.com. In a million years I would not try anything related to my tips site if it can't be automated.

As I write this, people are receiving my lessons around the globe. When I coach my son's basketball team later tonight, people will be receiving my lessons around the world. When I go to sleep tonight, people will be wide awake and focused on my lessons. Automation is the Eighth Wonder of the World!

Communities

In addition to having your own 52SomethingTips.com site that automatically feeds your list with great content each week, there are other ways to create loyal, die-hard followers. One of these ways involves creating communities.

Does the following scenario sound familiar to you at all?

You take a course, intend to act on what you learned, but then you don't get around to doing much with it? That's happened to me a few times. I now know that communities can help solve that problem because they are fantastic at helping you grow your momentum so that you feel unstoppable.

Trisha, one of our certified, world-class speaking coaches, called me one day and said, "Craig, do you mind if I set up a private Facebook group for the certified coaches?" At first I wasn't sure about the idea because I thought it would require more of my time, and one of my goals was to free up my time for myself and my family. Still, I said, "Go ahead," and I am immensely glad that she did.

Our private community on Facebook has:

▸ Created momentum for our members because they view what other coaches are doing and it fires them up especially since they see what is possible.

▸ Brought me loads of heartfelt results-based testimonials because the members share their successes in real-time.

▸ Made it much easier to engage our affiliates about new offers and ways they can make money from these offers. One way to establish a loyal following is by getting your affiliates paid!

▸ Helped us promote projects and offers. For example, we recently released the *World Class Speaking in Action* book, and our community promoted it. Within five hours, it reach number one in three categories on Amazon.com. That wouldn't have happened without the community. In fact, the community wrote the book!

▸ Solved problems for our members. They simply bring a business issue to the group and get fantastic feedback and advice from the other members.

▸ Let us keep our finger on the pulse of our loyal followers, which is important for us partially because it empowers us to know what to create next.

▸ Allowed us to give our members a heads-up about upcoming products and programs before we tell anyone else. Giving people this special treatment helps with loyalty.

▸ Turned our members into stars! Each time a member reports what he or she has done (great speech, awesome coaching session, etc.) the rest of the group congratulates them and they are stars for the day. This is healthy for their momentum, and it builds their connection with us.

One of the most surprising aspects of the community is that it doesn't take more of my time. In fact, I believe it frees up my time, because instead of the members always coming to me with questions, they bring them to the group. Sometimes I chime in. Sometimes I don't. The good news is I know they're being heard and helped.

Let Your Products Sell Your Products

Another way to have your loyal, die-hard followers stay ready for your next offer is to let your products sell your products.

Why do airlines have frequent flier plans and hotels have special club rewards programs? Because they work!

They promote loyalty at least to a certain degree. Having your own frequent buyer program will build loyal customers, too. It's important to reward those who have placed their confidence in you.

I remember reading statistics about how most marketers spend the majority of their time searching for new customers while the most successful marketers spend most of their energy and time focusing on the customers they already have. Why? It's much easier to sell to an existing customer than it is to get a new one. This goes back to confidence. They have confidence in you and so that barrier has already come down.

I strongly suggest you use the power of coupon codes to your advantage. For example, when someone buys one of my courses, he immediately gets an email giving him a coupon code for 50 percent off of another course. It's a time-limited offer. What often happens is this person goes through some or all of the first course and then purchases the next course at the discount. That next course then gives another 50 percent coupon code for another course, and many times that person will purchase that course, too. The key is to make it simple, easy, and attractive to invest in that next step. Reward your loyal customers with significant discounts.

Again, this should be completely automated, which is why I use my shopping cart software to manage the coupon codes.

Live on a Two-Way Online Street

Simply providing content is not enough to be hugely successful online these days. It's not just about content; it's about communication. People want to know the person behind the product. They want to hear from you and for you to hear from them. In other words, they want to have conversations with you.

When I arrived at this understanding, I made a few rules for myself that, yes, at times, I have broken but that I try to maintain.

1. Respond to every comment on each one of my blog entries.
2. Have conversations with friends and fans on Facebook.
3. Post personal as well as professional happenings in my business and life.
4. Like the posts of my prospects and customers, and show true interest in their endeavors.

When I'm speaking from the stage, I try to make it as much of a two-way street as possible. You can do the same whether you're onstage or online.

Make Them the Stars

Finally, one of the best ways to build a loyal following is to turn your prospects and customers into stars. You can do this by highlighting your followers.

For example, Will Reed, one of our Certified World Class Speaking Coaches, wrote a book called *World Class Speaking Japan*. I highlighted his success on my Facebook page along with the cover of his book, which reached the top of the charts in Japan. When you make one of your followers a star, others know that they, too, can shine. As a result, their future, along with yours, looks very bright.

The Magic Is in the Formula

Whether you're establishing communities, leveraging your list with a "tips" program, or having your products sell your products, it all comes down to understanding and following this failsafe, proven formula:

Confidence comes from familiarity, which comes from regular,
ongoing contact.

By spending time thinking about this formula, I'm sure you will find additional ways to put the formula into action. Test them and tweak them and see what happens. When you do, you might be surprised at the amazing results. Online marketing superstardom is right around the corner, and all you have to do is take your turn.

CHAPTER 25

Epilogue

WE LIVE in a world of ever-changing, exciting, and at times overwhelming technology.

With many changes occurring every month online, today's technology is seductive—and distracting. Who can resist a cool new video maker, plugins, or a social media site that promises to establish a plethora of fans at your fingertips?

To truly have a profitable business online, though, we can't be flying from one idea to the next. We must be grounded in solid principles of marketing and business development. With that in mind, here are three principles you should absolutely never forget.

1. You Are in the People Business

No matter what product or service you sell or what technologies you use to deliver them, you talk (and sell) to people. And people are unique. Each person has different desires, ways of communicating and perceiving information. One size does not fit all.

As a practicing psychotherapist for nearly 20 years, I learned the best ways to engage a person are to:

1. Listen with empathy and reflect back what you hear.
2. Sell the result of your product or service in words they understand.
3. Build the human bond by remembering personal details and by being consistent, caring, and professional.

2. Every Contact Is Marketing

In the Guerrilla Marketing Coach Certification Program, we focus on "small details" because they are timeless and effective. Consider this:

You spend a pile of money on online advertising, yet when they come to your site they find a broken link, typo, confusing navigation, or unclear benefits. Perhaps when they call you, they are greeted with a frustrated tone of voice or no return call at all. Imagine how this will affect your bottom line.

Realize that if you pay attention to details, it will be easier to nurture a prospect into one who refers you to others and is a continuing customer than to constantly find new leads.

3. Stay Focused and Take Consistent Action

The path to true online success demands that you focus, prioritize and take action . . . one step at a time. Simple but not easy.

To help you stay focused, we have provided you with many tools you can read and download at www.MasteringOnlineMarketing.com. We encourage you to use them on a consistent basis.

As you read and reread the wisdom of the 24 Online Marketing Superstars in this collection, I hope you not only become inspired and energized. I hope you also become organized, strategic, and action-focused in your thinking.

If you follow this advice in combination with the other tips and strategies outlined in this book, you can reach your goals and create the life you truly desire.

—Mitch Meyerson

Index